9-26-16

Teresa,

Boozehound!

Breaking a 30-Year Obsession

by

Blessings!

Eric T. Houghton

Cover Art—Eric T. Houghton Admission Photo
to Carrier Clinic April 12, 2010

My Green Publisher
P.O. Box 702 Richland, MI 49083
e-mail:mygreenpublisher@gmail.com

To my wonderful wife, Carol.
You extended your hand one last time, and I took it.
I will love you always

Prologue: The End

"I, who had thought so well of myself and my abilities, of my capacity to surmount obstacles, was cornered at last. Now I was to plunge into the dark, joining that endless procession of sots who had gone on before. I thought of my poor wife. There had been much happiness after all. What would I not give to make amends? But that was over now.

No words can tell of the loneliness and despair I found in that bitter morass of self-pity. Quicksand stretched around me in all directions. I had met my match. I had been overwhelmed. Alcohol was my master."
—*Bill's Story, Page 8, Alcoholics Anonymous*

It was Friday, April 9, 2010. Only a few minutes after 7:00 PM, I had just finished teaching my last piano student at the community music school in Princeton, New Jersey where I had been working with the young and old for close to 26 years.

In one respect, this Friday evening was no different than the hundreds that came before it. Before heading home after work, I was going directly to my favorite watering hole in town for a few drinks. That's where the similarity ended. Over the last few years, especially where alcohol was concerned, my life had taken a dramatic turn. What used to be a few Friday night drinks *at* the bar was now drinking on the way *to* the bar, on the way home *from* the bar, and drinks long *after* the bar had closed. Lately, there were drinks all the time, or the insatiable desire—the obsession—to get them. On top of that there was the drug use—lots of it.

Of course, Carol, my wife of 21 years, didn't know anything about the extent of the drinking, let alone all the drugs. After years of continual lies and concealment, I finally admitted to her the other day that I had been drinking "a little." She had to laugh at that one. She knows well that I haven't been able to limit myself to "a little" since I was in high school. Hell, it was like being "a little" pregnant.

Home was different now, too. Since late January, home had been "HQ," a tidy ranch in Morrisville, Pennsylvania, owned by George, a friend who had kindly taken me in because Carol had kicked me out of my own house in Ewing, New Jersey. Carol, disgusted with my bad behavior and extremely unhappy with the marriage, had told me to go live with him for a month or so, and then "we'd see how things go." That was nearly three months ago, and "things" had definitely *not* gone well. Since that time, as a direct result of all the drinking and drugging, my behavior toward Carol had only gotten worse; and—booze or no booze—she didn't want this raving, ranting *asshole* back in her house.

My life was rapidly spiraling out of control. I was now taking this time away from Carol to, well—destroy myself.

Before stopping at the Ivy Inn up the street, I got into my Honda and reached for a CD case. The Honda was a 2002 Accord with 125,000 miles. Like me, it was recently battered and beaten, but still running. It had interior stains and cigarette burns, numerous dents and dings to the body; but, it was a faithful booze-mobile—perhaps my last—and we had logged many a drunken mile together.

I hadn't had a drink in nearly eight hours, so jittery as I was, I spilled a little coke-shake cutting out a fat line. *Damn! There's probably a couple grams on the floor of this car,* I thought. I grabbed the straw tucked away with the money in my wallet. *That would be quite a feat,* I considered, *explaining a straw in my wallet.* I sighed heavily.

Seconds after snorting, my stomach performed its nightly wrenching ritual. I gagged and fought to hold down the contents. *Something is definitely wrong down there,* I said to myself. I succeeded in not vomiting, but knew that the next round of turbulence would come as soon as I took that first drink of the night.

I quickly opened the cooler and grabbed a ready-mixed Smirnoff. The flavored water and vodka was a roughly half-and-half mixture, and I took a long pull. My gut heaved, and I gagged again, but it held. I took another drink, and there was less unrest this time. *It's getting better,* I thought.

I lit a smoke, put my mobile-bar in gear, and traveled the quarter mile to my long-time hangout on Nassau Street. I parked in the back. *Time for another.* Out came the CD case, chop-chop-chop, then it was up the nose again. My stomach twitched, started, and then went silent. *Ah, that's it,* I thought—on my way already.

After three quick double-vodkas, courtesy of my old friend and mixer, Scotty Muncy, I was walking back to the car. *Why was he looking at me like that?* I pondered. *And why does he want to talk with me this weekend? That was strange. Carol's got something in the works, I know it. She has to be onto this Xanax business from India. How in the hell those Indians ever got my cell-phone number, I'll never know. And, what about all that fucking money? Jesus, when Carol finally discovers the extent of what I've bilked from the home-equity line for booze, coke and Xanax, I'm through.*

I shelved that thought. It was now dark outside. *More safety in the dark,* I thought, smiling slightly. I looked around. Another round? Why not? I had at least two more fatties left in this little baggy before returning to HQ. I poured, chopped, grabbed the straw and snorted. I put the straw, tied-up baggy and credit card back in my wallet. *What if Carol ever found that straw?* I wondered again. *How could I ever explain that one away?*

Oh, who gives a shit, anyway? Another voice hissed in my head. This was my alcoholic voice. This part of me was now calling the shots more and more in my life. *You worry too much. That bitch, Carol, will be history soon. That's right, I said it! Face reality! You'd be better off without her. Text Trevor; maybe he can meet you back at HQ with another bag of blow.*

On the trip back to Morrisville, I finished my first vodka and opened another. I lit another smoke. I had sent Trevor a text saying I'd be at HQ by 8:30. He responded that he was good-to-go with more coke and would be arriving shortly thereafter. Andy, my other "booze brother" living with George, had called and asked if I could pick up another handle of Smirnoff. *Shit! I bought yesterday's handle, didn't I?* I thought. I was pissed. *No,* I recalled, shaking my head in disgust. *That was the day before. Oh, well.* Also, both he and George needed smokes. I'll stop up here in Hopewell for everything.

I took a drag, flicked hot ashes out the cracked window, and then drank some more. Suddenly, red and blue flashing lights appeared in the mirror. My heart jumped, and my stomach leaped. *I didn't do anything wrong—nothing!* I knew. I pulled over, and the cruiser came right up behind me and stopped. I was still holding the lit cigarette.

He came up alongside the passenger window. I made a quick inventory of the interior, making sure nothing illicit was visible. The wallet was sitting on the passenger seat, no cocaine shake or pellets were evident, and my half-pint of Smirnoff was neatly tucked away, as usual, in the sleeve behind the passenger seat. The plastic "water" bottle was at least half-full and sitting in the cup-holder. I pushed the button rolling down the window. He bent down, shone his flashlight in my eyes and said, "Good evening, sir, New Jersey State Police. How are you tonight?"

"Good," I managed, trying to breath, and squinting through the blinding light.

"License, registration and proof of insurance, please," trooper ordered me politely.

I pulled my license from the wallet, and reached over to the glove compartment. In seconds, I handed the three items over to him.

While glancing at the paperwork, the trooper said, "The reason I pulled you over tonight was that I observed you throwing your cigarette out the window back there."

What did he say? I thought. I looked at my left hand. It was holding the lit butt out the open window. I struggled for a second or two to give him an adequate response. I didn't want to be smart and piss him off, that was for sure. He was still looking at my information when I managed, "But, um, sir?" I held it out for him to see. He looked. "I have it right here." My hand was shaking a bit, so I quickly put it back out the window.

He made a tiny cough, and still regarding my paperwork, said, "Any warrants or anything on you, sir?" He seemed to ignore the alleged butt-throwing issue.

"No, sir," I told him truthfully.

He handed me back the three items. "Okay, then. Be careful. Have a good night."

He turned and walked back to his cruiser. Within seconds, he was gone. The whole episode took about two minutes.

I sat there in stunned amazement. *What in the hell just happened?* He obviously thought I had thrown my cigarette out the window, but it was only a fiery ash. He never even mentioned the drink, but he certainly saw it. Of course, he didn't know what was in it. To him, it *was* just a water bottle.

A bead of sweat rolled down my forehead. Sitting there in my Honda, on the outskirts of Hopewell Borough, I downed the entire drink. I gasped. I had dodged yet another bullet. Did this make four or five times over the course of my drinking career that fortune had shined on me in regards to run-ins with the law? With only a tiny bit of investigation, this guy could have easily become "trooper of the month," and I probably would be in jail. I had an open container present, I'm definitely borderline over-the-limit, and that little bit of coke in my pocket—he would have loved to find that!

I thanked God for sparing me yet again. I knew that it must have been Will and Bill, my two guardian angels. When I was very small, my mother had asked God to provide me with an angel for protection. I presume that God, all knowing that he is, saw the troubles ahead for me and then "informed" my mother that two angels, not one, would now be looking after me. Mom gave them the names "Will" and "Bill;" and I have no doubt that these days they are with me 24/7. *How else could I still be alive and free from the law?*

The next morning, Saturday, April 10, 2010, I rose in agony. It was nothing new. Last night with Trevor had been yet another major drug and booze event, as they go by. George and Andy had turned in early—about 2:00—but Trevor and I kept at it for a couple more hours. It wasn't quite a "triathlon" event—20 drinks, lines and smokes—but it was damned close.

Thank God for the two Xanax I took around 4:00. At least I was able to get a couple hours sleep. But now, I had to go teach all day, and then play both masses up at my church in Elizabeth. I decided to call my last few students and cancel. This would allow me extra drinking time before the services.

I stood in front of the mirror in the bathroom at around 8:00 that morning and took stock of myself. My stock had crashed. I was now at least 40 pounds overweight. I stopped weighing myself months ago, for fear of the shock. My graying hair was receding, but badly in need of a trim. As I frowned in the mirror, taking in my wild hair and blood-shot eyes, I remember thinking that I looked a bit like Beethoven in that classic portrait hanging in my teaching studio in Princeton.

As I patted and stroked my distended belly, I wondered if his liver had swollen as much as mine by the time he was my age. Of course, he had been drinking his beer and wine out of lead goblets all those years, and I read somewhere that it was more that heavy metal than the booze that finally killed his liver. As for me, it was all booze, and I'd never make it to 57, as the great master did. Shit, I wasn't going to make it to 48 at the rate I was going. And that was less than 6 months away!

My face was red and grotesquely puffy. Joe Frazier looked better after the *Thrilla in Manila*, for Christ's sake! I was shaky, exhausted and looking like hell, but I had to get going. I took a long shower, changed, and went downstairs.

George was sitting at his counter with a cup of coffee when I walked into the kitchen. I immediately went for my 32 ounce plastic cup, and filled it with ice. I grabbed the half-empty Smirnoff and shakily poured a large amount into the cup.

I looked over at George. He was frowning at me and shaking his head slowly. "I can't believe you can do that," he said simply.

Reaching for the jug of iced-tea in the fridge, I shrugged and considered what my friend had just said. George was no slouch in the drinking department. He hit the bottle extremely hard and often. I liked being around George and Andy because they were like me. They partied hard, just like me, and they didn't judge. How could they? But, it occurred to me at this moment that I had graduated to another level where drink was concerned. George no longer drank like me. At this moment I realized that no one I now knew drank like me.

I said to George, "I can't believe it either, but I have no choice." I looked at him. "Something's gonna happen to me, I know it. But, until then, I have to keep drinking."

Later, after somehow making it through my morning lessons in Princeton, and cancelling my final three afternoon sessions for the third time this year, I stopped at my favorite liquor store in Plainsboro on my way up to Elizabeth. Hadji, one of many store clerks in the area that I knew by name, greeted me with a warm smile and a pint. "How many minis today, Eric?" he asked me, gesturing behind him.

I looked up at the dozens of flavored airplane bottles all lined up in neat rows. "Give me three apple and three vanilla, and another half-pint of the regular" I said. I also ordered a pack of Marlboro Lights and Hadji bagged the entire purchase. I gave him my credit card, and was surprised when he told me that the card was rejected. *The Xanax purchase from India*, I immediately thought. This time, Rose, the supercilious drug-dealer from India, wanted a money order for the goods, and I knew that Carol had gotten a call from MasterCard inquiring about the odd transaction. *They were issuing us new cards—* that was it. This one was simply cancelled until the new one arrived.

The voice broke in. *I think Carol shut you down. I think that ungrateful nag finally found out about everything. Try the ATM.* I walked over to the money machine and was able to get $200 without a problem. *No, it was just that particular card that was deemed useless*, I reasoned. I needed the cash anyway. Now, I could pay off Trevor, and still have enough for another gram later that night.

There was still plenty of money in my checking account, too. Andy, my house-mate, had loaned me some money. He had written me a $1000 check a few days ago, and I had deposited it. However, at the time Andy was worried, I re-membered. When he made out the check, his hand was shaking badly. He had been concerned it wouldn't withstand the scrutiny of the bank examiners. Recently, they had rejected his checks three other times, I remembered.

I took a leisurely route north to Elizabeth, avoiding the turnpike altogether. By the time I got there, I was well-tuned. I drank two of the minis playing the first mass, and two more during the second. I remember little of that mass, but I do recall nearly falling off the organ bench after the final hymn ended.

I made it back to HQ exhausted and drunk at about 7:30, but when Trevor and his powder arrived shortly thereafter, I quickly rallied. The night was another carbon-copy of the one before, and, aside from a call from Carol reminding me of a bowling date with Natalie, my nine-year-old, the following afternoon at 2:00, nothing out of the ordinary occurred. Late that night, I popped two more Xanax and snorted couple big lines of Oxycodone courtesy of Joe, another friend who had stopped by HQ. This allowed me a few hours of sleep before getting up to prepare for my Sunday services.

I was still drunk when my cell-phone alarm went off at 7:00. *What else is new?* I thought. I showered and got myself ready for church. I wobbled downstairs and made another strong drink for the ride up. Sitting in my Honda, I took a drink. My stomach revolted and heaved. I opened the door and stuck my head out. My stomach contents—liquidly green and yellow—emptied on the gravel below. *At least there's no blood*, the voice said. *You feel awful now, I know, but you'll be fine once you get that first one down.*

Having finished my roadie and the remaining two minis on the way up, I felt marginally better by the time I arrived in

Elizabeth; but I decided to tell the secretary that I was coming down with something and leave after the first of two services. Although I hadn't been at the top of my game lately, and had missed more than a few masses, I had been music director for close to 25 years, and everybody at church seemed to like me well enough. Missing this one mass wouldn't be a big deal. Lately, I had been missing all kinds of things, I knew. I had missed business appointments, dates with my three kids, lessons, masses—anything that interfered with my appointment with the next drink. I never missed one of those.

I still had a half-pint left in the car, and that would keep me going until the liquor stores opened up at noon. I went directly to my house in Ewing. Carol and the kids were at her church, I knew, and I had a pressing issue to deal with. A few days before, I had read in the *Trenton Times* another article about the spiraling property taxes in New Jersey. I was outraged, and wanted to write a scathing letter to the editor addressing the issue.

After all, wasn't it the state's inability in dealing with out-of-control spending that was causing much of *my* current financial hardship? I had to dip time and again into our home-equity line just to pay the quarterly property tax bill, for God's sake. If something wasn't done, and fast, we'd be in foreclosure before long. My forceful letter would show those assholes in Trenton, that's for sure!

As I drunkenly typed out my letter, I thought about my wife. Carol didn't see things the way that I did regarding taxes and bills. She was concerned about the taxes, too, but she believed that we were making quite enough money to cover the increases, and then some. Carol always talked about coming up with a clear, household budget, and then trying to stay within that budget. *What nonsense!* The voice hissed again in my head. *How could she possibly understand? She never understood anything! She doesn't pay the bills. She doesn't know the extent of all those taxes and credit card bills. She's just after you, that's all!*

I had just sent my "masterpiece" off into cyberspace when Carol and the kids walked through the door. It was only just noon, and I was sure that she wouldn't be home until 1:00, as was typical on Sundays. I was just about to leave, and this was not good. I didn't want to see her. Being almost constantly drunk, I had been doing my best to avoid her lately.

I turned to look at her. Saying she was surprised to me was an understatement. "What are you doing here?" She asked. "You're not supposed to be here until 2:00."

I stood up and greeted Matt and Natalie. Sensing trouble between their parents *again*, they both quickly disappeared. "I, uh, left church early," I stammered. "I'm not feeling well." The morning drinks were starting to wear thin, but I was in the midst of a three-day bender and certainly must have looked affright. I glanced at the clock and suddenly felt an intense desire to go see Hank behind the counter of the West Trenton Liquor Store. "I was just leaving," I said, facing Carol.

Carol, done up beautifully in her Sunday finest, instantly knew that I was drunk and gave me that look. It was the look of total disgust that I had been seeing more and more lately. Her pretty, brown eyes were bearing into me. "Will you be back at 2:00?" She asked me.

"No. I have things to do" I said, blood quickly bubbling into my brain. I started for the door.

"Yeah, whatever," Carol said with utter disgust in her voice. She started away from me.

"*Yeah, whatever,*" I replied, mocking her voice malevolently.

She turned on me, "Eric, you need help. You're drunk now! Look at yourself! *You are killing yourself!*"

"I am not drunk!" I lied, adding, "*You're* the one that needs fucking help!" I was nearing the front door when I heard the next words.

"I know about the drugs," she said matter-of-factly. "Holly found the Xanax in your glove compartment last weekend when you went down to see her."

I stopped and turned to face her. *So, she does know,* the voice whispered. I was paralyzed with terror. *Your sister ratted you out,* said the voice. I could now see anger in those brown eyes now to go along with the disgust. I said nothing. I opened the front door and moved unsteadily toward the car.

She continued after me, but I had had enough. She said, "Eric, you are in no shape to drive! Where are you going?"

I ignored her, got in my car and slammed the door shut. I backed out of the driveway and gunned it down the street. In the rearview mirror, I could still see Carol standing there—shoulders slumped, head bowed—in the driveway as I sped away.

Within minutes my cell rang. It was Carol, I saw. I let it ring. While at the liquor store, it went off again. This time I noticed it was Scott Muncy, and I took it. "Stop by for a drink," he said. "We can have a talk." I told him I'd be right over.

At this point fear was what gripped me most. I was fearful of what I knew had to be done, and petrified by the mere thought. My secret life had been found out, and I now knew that I had to get help. My drinking had to end, yet I had no idea how I could ever *not* drink. My mind was racing in a hundred different directions as I pulled into Scott's driveway a few minutes later. Scott was waiting for me on his front porch. I asked him to make me a stiff vodka, and he told to me go around to his back deck and wait for him.

I had known Scott for years, since he had come of age and started bartending at the Ivy in Princeton. He looked up to me as a kind of big brother, and I had scooped him up at many a party and taken him home when he was inebriated. I hated to see people like Scott at parties or in bars, stumbling around, babbling incoherently because they couldn't hold their liquor. I could always handle mine, and I could never understand why people allowed themselves to get to that point.

For close to 30 years I had handled my liquor, but now, as Scott came out on his deck holding my freshly made drink, I knew that the end had finally come. All my lying and deceit had come to the fore, and I was finished. Booze had finally, inexorably—resoundingly—kicked my ass, and it was time to throw in the towel. But not quite yet.

As I sipped the vodka and lamented my miserable existence, Scott made a good sounding-board. After listening for a while, Scott suggested that I go to rehab. "We were going to confront you about all that today at 2:00. That was Carol's plan," he told me. I winced at the thought of this "intervention," but resolved myself further as to what I now needed to do.

Scott told me that he would drive me to Carrier Clinic or Princeton House tomorrow morning if I wanted. My family and my life hung in the balance, he said, and I needed to get help. Carrier would give me the help I needed. They would ease me off the booze, and all would be well. Like many bartenders, Scott knew how to listen, and when to give sound advice.

I listened intently to everything my friend was telling me. Then I said, "There's more, Scottay. There's been a lot of cocaine lately—a lot! What the hell do I tell Carol about that?"

"Just tell her now," he told me, unfazed. I'm pretty certain Scott knew about the coke anyway. "It's better to get it all out in the open now. I'm sure she's shocked by all this news, so a little more shock won't kill her. Just be honest."

I put my head in my hands. "I've been living a lie for so long, I can't even remember the last time I was honest about anything," I said.

"It might not be too late, Eric," Scott told me, putting his arm on my shoulder. "Just do it. You have to. Now go get some sleep. You look like shit, man."

Tired as I was, sleep was not an option. It was an early spring afternoon, and the weather was gorgeous, so I decided to take a long, circuitous route back to HQ. Restocked with plenty of vodka and mixers, within an hour I was slowly winding along some desolate stretch of road in rural Mercer County. Carol kept trying to reach me on my cell, but I didn't answer. I needed to think—and drink. After a few, I found a third or fourth wind, and the alcoholic voices started their howling chorus in my head.

So, Carol knows about it all. You knew it was going to happen sooner or later. I told you to plan your next move, and now you can without that nagging bitch hounding you relentlessly. After all, there are many other women out there waiting for a guy like you. The children, that's a tough one, I know, but...

"Stop!" I yelled aloud. I pulled the car over to the shoulder. "No! I won't listen to your bullshit anymore! I need help!"

The voice went silent for a moment, but soon returned. This time it was the alcoholic's close companion, fear that spoke to me. *But how can you stop drinking? This is all you've known for 30 years, for Christ's sake, and you think you can just stop? Remember the photo that guy showed you at that AA meeting you went to. He was lying in a hospital bed tied to a ventilator, nearly dead of DTs. Remember that? You'll suffer miserably coming off the sauce.*

And then, what happens if you do survive? Your friend Tom Patterson's father-in-law had to quit, remember? He sat in his chair, every night until the day he died making notches every half-hour, marking another miserable span of time he had to endure without his friend. Is this what you want? You'll be forever going to all those AA meetings, listening to all those losers cry and moan about their wretched existence.

In my mind's eye, I could see my tombstone. Without drink, my death may well be put off by 20 or 30 years, but at what cost? The inscription would read: *Eric T. Houghton 1962-? Gave up drinking, and he lived miserably sober for the rest of his days.*

I started down the deserted road again. I drank and drank. I was going to drink like there was no tomorrow, which was true enough. I had to numb the voices and mask the mounting fear with alcohol. I sighed and voiced a small prayer. "Please help me, Lord," I said. "Please give me the strength to do this thing."

Early in the evening I finally pulled into George's driveway and reached for my cell. I knew it was time to return

Carol's repeated calls. I had somehow taken a break long enough from the drinks to gather my wits and face the inevitable.

When she answered I told her that I was ready to go to rehab in the morning. I was able to follow Scott's advice and admit everything—including the cocaine use. Scott was right. Although she was shocked and horrified by the news, it somehow made me feel good to be honest for a change. When Carol asked me how long I had been drinking, I simply told her that I never really quit. I told her that eighteen months ago when I was found out down at the shore, I had promised to quit, but I never really did. "I tried to improve my behavior, but I could not even do that for long," I told her.

"I know about all the money you stole from us, Eric," she told me matter-of-factly. "I'm shutting down the credit cards in the morning."

"I understand, Carol." Sitting there in my Honda, I could feel the tears welling up in my eyes.

"Eric," she continued, "I don't know what the future will hold for our marriage, but I am reaching out my hand to you right now. If you get help, and get the treatment you need, there may still be a chance."

My gut was wrenching now. I blubbered, "I am going to get help, Carol. I promise."

"You know, you really need to go right now, Eric," she said.

"No," I replied quickly, wiping the tears from my eyes. I did not want to face that yet. I had one more, good drunk left in me. "I'll be there first thing in the morning."

"Come at 8:00, then," she said, not pressing the issue. "I'll drive you to rehab."

I could tell after I hung up that the marriage might well be over, but I knew that my life would soon be over if I didn't make this move. I composed myself as best I could, stepped out of the car, and gingerly made my way inside HQ. I steeled myself for what I hoped and prayed would be my last night of drinking. Tomorrow would be the end, but *that* was tomorrow. I had one more night ahead of me.

I tried texting him a few times early that night, but Trevor was nowhere to be found. Running on fumes as I was, I could have used a cocaine boost, but it was not to be. George, Andy and I went at the bottle heavy, and by midnight, I was a sulking, pitiful mess. It was "poor me, poor me—I'll just pour myself another," well into the wee hours.

At some point, I threw up my hands in disgust. Andy kept trying to tell me that I was just in a bad rut, and that if I could only slow down a little bit—control the booze more—all would be well. He sounded a lot like my troubling inner voice, and I couldn't take it anymore. "I can't control it!" I boomed. "I can't fucking control it! Do you know how many times I've tried to control this fucking thing?" I held up the Smirnoff. "It's fucking impossible! I NEED HELP!"

Drunk as he was, Andy kept plodding forward with his twisted logic, repeating himself over and over. George got pissed at him and wobbled off to bed. I left the counter and gingerly made my way outside. "Where are you going?" Andy asked me, his head bobbing and dipping.

"I'll be right back," I said, nearly falling out the front door.

I came back in with all the Xanax from my glove compartment and threw them down on the kitchen counter. "Wow!" said Andy in amazement.

"They're yours," I said, gesturing at the 15 or so plastic packets containing the goods. "Take 'em! I'm through with the shit. And furthermore," I boomed, slurring loudly enough that the entire neighborhood might hear, "Fuck that dizzy Indian bitch, Rose, too! She's the one that fucked this entire situation up. *Hi, Eric, this is pharmacy. This is your pharmacy, Eric*," I mimicked her high-pitched, Indian accent. "What a fucking joke! Money orders my ass! She ruined me! Even my sister is against me—the turn-coat! What a world! What a fucking world!" I held out my empty glass to Andy. "Oh well, fill me up again, my brother. Hic!"

We were both nearly passed out at the kitchen counter when Joe, our Oxycodone friend of the night before showed up at about 4:00 AM. After snorting a few big lines, and popping a Xanax or two, the rest of that early morning was one big, hazy, rubber-legged blur.

I do remember taking a shower and packing some items in my gym-bag as the sun rose. And I vaguely recall Andy pleading with me to stay and get some sleep, but I wanted none of that. I had to get home and get two of my kids off to school. After all, it was Monday and that was my job, right? I'd drive Matt to the high school, and then I'd get little Natalie on the bus. After that, I would get a ride to Carrier Clinic and start drying out or die—one of the two. I had a plan and I was sticking to it, by God!

I got in my Honda—cocktail in cup-holder, of course— and started home. As I crossed the Delaware into New Jersey, I found that I was having some difficulty keeping my eyes open. My head kept dropping, and I had to keep slapping my face to stay conscious.

It was still a bit too early to be arriving home, so I slowly drove around my neighborhood, killing time. I was on Lochatong, a side street across the main road from my house. I was trying mightily to keep my eyes open when—BAM!

Was I dead? I opened my eyes. No. There was smoke, or dust, or something. My airbag had deployed. I looked around. On my left, not 20 feet away, was a lady walking her dog. *Oh my God*, I thought. *I could have killed her.* I looked forward. I had struck a telephone pole, and smoke or steam was coming from the engine hood.

Snap out of it! It was a different voice in my head. *Do you want to go to jail? The cops are coming. Get your ass to the gas station up the street right now!* I was now clear-headed. For the next 15 minutes, I would be miraculously sober. It had to be Will and Bill, my two guardian angels. They were saving my ass once again.

I backed up, turned around and drove the quarter mile to the service station that was only a block from my home. I got out, popped three pieces of gum in my mouth and inspected the damage. I had struck the pole with my license plate, and the entire front end of the Honda was now U-shaped. The radiator was leaking, and the car was surely totaled. *How ironic*, I thought. *My last booze-mobile is dead on the day of my last drunk.*

I went about collecting my gym-bag and my shoulder brief case. Just then, three patrol cars came pulling into the station, coming to a stop directly behind my gravely wounded vehicle. *Oh, Lord*, I thought, breathing hard. *Will I be five-for-five in avoiding the law? Please help me.*

The lead officer jumped out and approached. "Are you the driver here?" He asked me.

I stood bolt upright and looked at him directly in the eyes. "Yes, sir," I said firmly.

"Let me see your license. What happened?" The other two officers were milling about my Honda.

I gave him my license. "I was coming home to take my kids to school. I was tired and nodded off over there on Lochatong. I hit a pole. Luckily, I wasn't hurt. I'll pay for any damage done to the pole, but I was going really slowly. I don't think you'll find any damage," I told him. I was amazed at myself. I actually sounded believable.

"Have you had anything to drink today, sir?" He asked me.

"No, sir," I lied, hopefully for the last time. "I just fell asleep for a second. I haven't been getting enough sleep."

He looked at the license, and then me, and then the car. "Okay," he said, handing me back the license. "Good luck to ya."

He motioned to the other officers standing around. They all got back in their cruisers and drove away. They tore down the road, late for a staff-meeting at Dunkin Donuts, I guessed.

I was dumbfounded. I felt a little light-headed and leaned against my useless car. I took a few deep breaths. I closed my eyes and opened them again. *What is that?* I was looking straight ahead at a shiny, red car in the corner of the station's parking lot. It had a "for sale" sign on the passenger window. I walked up to the window. *Low mileage? Seven grand? This would be an ideal replacement car for my Honda*, I thought. Deranged as I was, I was ready at this moment to call the phone number listed and make an offer. Buoyed by the thought, I picked up my gym-bag and brief case and wobbled for home.

"Where is the Honda?" Carol asked me when I walked through the front door. Delayed by the incident, Carol was already getting ready to take Matthew to school. Thankfully, Natalie had spent the night at a friend's house.

"Well, I had a small problem up the street," I mumbled evasively. "It's at the gas station, kind of, well, banged up. Honey, you should see the car that's for sale up there. It looks great. It's red and…"

"Don't move!" she said, cutting me off. She ordered Matt in the car as I stood there. She gave me that look again: *You drunken bastard*! She had obviously seen something in me that the police had missed. They both hurried out the door.

Now I was pissed. *I can't even drive my son to school!* I dropped my bag and made a bee-line for the brandy. I had received a bottle of Greek brandy from a student as a Christmas present a few months ago, and I quickly opened it and poured a few fingers into a glass. I downed it in one gulp. *Don't take any shit from that bitch now*, the voice boomed in my head. *You're going to rehab. I don't know why, but you're going. Doesn't she know how hard this is for you? Now, don't you have something else to do?*

I poured another healthy dose and drained it. *The car!* I thought. *I'll go check out that car for sale.* I went out and started the mini-van. It was our third vehicle, and wasn't being used much now that Katie, our 18-year-old, was away attending Princeton University. I backed it out of the driveway and barreled up the street to the gas station. Those last two brandies really had me spinning now, and everything that happened from here on out is a foggy blur.

At some point my cell rang. "Where are you?" Carol demanded.

"I'm up the street looking at that car I tried telling you about. I'm getting the phone number. It's a beauty! Why didn't you let me finish what...?" She hung up. *What is the matter with her?* I was extremely confused. Within a minute or two, Carol and an attendant at the gas station were yanking the keys out of my hands, and I was back at my house.

Carol was now on the phone—or was it me? Something about Princeton House was being discussed. "I'm not going to Princeton House!" I boomed. "My grandmother went to Carrier Clinic, and I'm going to fucking Carrier Clinic!" There was more confusion.

At some point, I vaguely remember Scott standing between Carol and me. I was hurling choice obscenities her way. I didn't want anything at all to do with her. Stoked by the brandy, I heard myself scream to Scott, "Get my wife out of here! Get my fucking wife out of here!"

She left, thank God. I went to the kitchen and poured another brandy. Scott followed me, took the bottle, and I never saw it again.

The next thing I knew I was in the ER at Princeton Medical Center. I later found out that I had to be tested at an ER or by a doctor in order to get clearance for admission to Carrier Clinic. Scott had left me for the time being, this I remember; and when I was tested and cleared, I decided to go out for a walk.

Wandering down Witherspoon Street toward Nassau, I was perturbed that the sidewalk kept moving on me. Not only would it shift left and right without notice, but it also was swaying up and down. I felt as if I were on the deck of a ship in rough seas. Pain-in-the-ass pedestrians kept bumping into me, and I finally had to claw along the wrought-iron fence guarding Princeton Cemetery for stability.

Thankfully, one of my favorite liquor stores in Princeton just happened to be right up the street, so, when I finally reached its door, I straightened up and went inside. I bought a pint of Smirnoff and two Diet Peach Snapple's. I found a secluded spot and mixed two terrific drinks. I had just finished the first one when my cell rang. "Where the fuck are you?" It was Scott.

"I'm in Princeton, dummy!" I retorted indignantly. "Didn't you leave me here? *Why* did you leave me here?"

"I told you I'd be back, and not to move. Where *exactly* are you?"

Soon we were traveling along toward Carrier Clinic about 10 miles away. I was sipping my "Snapple," making call after call on my phone. I had to inform all my private students that I would not be coming this week. Much later, after the student's parents listened to some of those choice messages, I would be amazed to discover that I had any private students left at all.

In the parking lot at the venerable Carrier Clinic, 10 miles away in Belle Mead, I finished my last drink. "That's it, Scottay! Das Ende!" I told him, throwing the bottle in the grass, as he guided me toward the front entrance.

"I hope to God it is," Scott mumbled.

Scott stayed with me as I was being processed for admission. I'm uncertain of the time of day, but I believe it was early afternoon by now. At some point I asked a person if I could go out for a smoke. They said "no problem," and I did so. I stepped outside and walked a few paces to the grassy area in the middle of the circular drive.

I found a shady spot next to a tree and lit up. Inhaling, I leaned back against the tree. It wasn't there. For the briefest moment, it felt as if I were in space. I went crashing backwards, ass over tea-cups. My head and upper-back hit first, striking the nearby pavement with a loud "thunk."

Onlookers were horrified and cried out. People came running from all directions. I thought I heard a distant siren blaring. I sat up on the curb and took it all in. I grabbed my fallen Phillies cap and put it back in place. My smoking butt was at my feet, so I stuck it back in my mouth and continued puffing.

I couldn't understand why all these people were huddled around me. I felt no pain at all. Of course, I had enough drugs and alcohol in me to numb a moose, so that wasn't surprising. An official looking guy helped me up and guided me slowly back toward the admissions building. "We have to get you checked out at the ER," he told me.

"No, please," I said. "I'm fine, really. Nothing's wrong with me."

"No," The man replied firmly. "You hit your head, and we have to get you checked out."

For the next 15 minutes, I begged and pleaded with them to just let me be. They would hear none of it. When the paramedics arrived, I started yelling and carrying on. I did not want to go back to another ER. Scott, my faithful keeper, tried to calm me, and insisted everything would be okay. "Just do what they tell you, Eric," I remember him saying. I continued to protest.

The police arrived. The fall had sobered me up a bit, and the last thing I wanted was to languish in another ER for what I knew would be hours. I refused to get up from a chair, and an officer came over and rudely hauled me up. "Come on, let's go!" he ordered me. They had dealt with enough surly drunks and addicts checking in at Carrier to know how to handle the likes of me. I submitted.

Flanked on either side by the officers, I reluctantly walked toward the waiting ambulance. Just outside the entrance doors, I held up my Diet Coke bottle and asked one of the cops, "Can I take this with me?" He made a grunting sound and smacked it smartly out of my hands. "I guess that's a no, then," I said. I was tied down to the gurney and taken to Somerset Hospital.

This was my bottom. For the next five hours, I lay immobilized on the gurney, waiting for a CT-scan. Several attendants took turns sitting next to me the entire, agonizing time. I was alone, afraid and hopeless. The alcohol was starting to wear off, and I started to shake uncontrollably. Years before I had endured debilitating panic attacks, but they were nothing compared to this. A feeling of total desolation enveloped me.

The worst part was my inability to move. I kept asking the person staying with me if I could just get up and walk around a little. They kept refusing. "You may have a head injury. Just try to relax." I could not. A cold sweat poured off of me. It was absolute torture. At some point, I began sobbing. I was pitiable wreck. For me, I knew this had to be "the valley of the shadow."

Toward the end, the fear and alcoholic voices were hissing loudly in my head. *So, this is what you get when you don't listen to me. Right now, you could've been sitting back at HQ enjoying a drink and a line, but—no! You had to endure two accidents, two run-ins with the law and two trips to the ER all because you knew better. You listened to that nagging wife of yours, and this is what you get. Well, now you know what it feels like. Now you know what happens to people who think they know better.*

You know, you may not survive this ordeal, my friend. The DT's are not pleasant, I can assure you. That heart of yours may just stop—all because you didn't listen to me. I've seen it over and over, people just like you.

Of course, if you do survive, when you get out, I'll still be there to help you. If you get through this, I'll be waiting to...

"STOP IT!" I screamed. "GET OUT OF MY HEAD!" I looked from side to side. It seemed as if every eye in the ER was on me. The woman sitting next to me asked me if I was okay. I nodded and took a few deep breaths. The breathing helped relax me a little. And then, from somewhere far away, another faint voice calmed me even more.

I'm here, it said. *I will help you through this. Just ask me, and all will be well. Just ask me.*

"Lord, please help me."

I closed my eyes and faded off.

It was close to midnight when the ambulance finally returned me to Carrier. The CT-scan taken at the hospital revealed nothing. Completely exhausted as I was, I remember little of the remaining admission processing. There were interviews, paperwork, a photo and a blood-test, but I remember none of that.

At around 2:00, they scooped me up off the floor of the deserted admission office and guided me across the parking lot to Blake Hall. Safely inside Blake, I vaguely recall a tall, thin young man named Matt searching through all my belongings.

There was my gym-bag of clothes, and a plastic bag filled with cigarettes and phone-cards, courtesy of my friend, Scott Muncy.

After he was through inspecting my belongings, Matt guided me down a long, darkened hallway. He opened a door for me and pointed to an empty bed in the corner. I walked by two occupied beds, dropped the bags on the floor and crumpled in a heap on the bed.

Matt closed the door. I pulled a blanket up over my shivering body. Before all went dark, a final spasm of fear struck me. *Would I wake up alive in this place, or dead— somewhere else?*

Chapter One

"And acceptance is the answer to all my problems today... Until I could accept my alcoholism, I could not stay sober; unless I accept life completely on life's terms, I cannot be happy. I need to concentrate not so much on what needs to be changed in the world as on what needs to be changed in me and my attitudes."
—Page 417, *Alcoholics Anonymous*

"What the hell is that lump of shit?" I hear this faintly from my bed in the corner of my room in Carrier Clinic. The voice is low, almost a whisper; then comes a reply.

"I think they brought him in after midnight," reports the second voice quietly.

The deep, raspy first voice goes again. "That fat fuck kept me up all night with that snoring. Jesus! I've never heard anything make noises like that. If he does that again tonight, I swear to God he's dead! DEAD!" I open one eye just in time to see two figures leaving the doorway.

I hear their footsteps retreating down the hall, but the voice imitating Robert De Niro's Capone character in *The*

Untouchables only gets louder: "He's DEAD! I want him DEAD! His family...DEAD!" They both laugh.

It's Tuesday, April 13, 2010, and I'm surprised to find that I am not dead. I certainly should be, but I suppose one has to be alive to feel this bad. I sit up and rub my eyes. My mouth is dry, every muscle in my body seems to ache and my head is pounding. I feel like I'm burning all over, and I can't stop trembling. The burning and muscle aches are fresh to me, but the pounding head and shaking are nothing new. For months now, every single morning has greeted me similarly. But this last weekend, oh my God, what happened? I try to think.

"VITALS!" a voice shouts at me from the door. It's a nurse, I suppose. I gaze up at her. She's young, about 25, I think, with long light-brown hair and an attractive face. She looks at me and frowns. "Get that dopey look off your face, get off the bed and get down there for vitals—now!" she orders me. Oh God, this is no drill. I start to get up. "And put some pants on!" she says, and then grunts, "You'll scare the other patients." She disappears from the open door.

I do as told, and make it out into the busy, long hallway. It's barely 7 am and already lots of people are shuffling about. Some are older, many are younger, but they all seem to look like I feel: awful. Before I even make it to the line of people waiting for their vitals to be taken, another nurse sticks her head out of a window and calls to me. "Eric H?" I nod. "Go directly to the doctor's office."

"Can I go to the bathroom first?"

"Right there," she points to a door, "then down to the end to see Dr. Shariff, pronto."

I push open the door to the can and head for a stall. Two guys are standing at the twin sinks to my right as I pass. One of them is shaving and the other, a bulky, half-naked brute is combing his hair. Shit! That guy looks just like Elvis.

"You the asshole that was snoring in our room?" the familiar raspy voice asks loudly, as I empty my bursting bladder.

"Yeah, I'm the asshole. Sorry about that" I say. When I finish up, I walk to the sink and wash. He stands back and looks me over.

"Jesus!" the Elvis guy says in wonder, "I thought I looked bad when I came in here. Wow! Are you red! Check this guy out, Ebby. He was that lump of shit in our room!" The guy shaving next to him, a lean, good looking fellow of about 35, glances at me through the mirror, smiles and nods.

"I'm Mike Cass," says Elvis, holding out his hand. I shake it shakily. "Welcome to the funny-farm."

"Eric Houghton," I reply.

He grunts and returns to the mirror. He continues combing his long, dyed-black hair. He's digging at it with gusto; he just can't seem to flatten out. Mike is about 5-10, 50ish, very dark—probably Italian—and about 30 pounds overweight. He definitely favors "The King" in his later years.

"Are you in here because of drink like me?" I venture.

"Nah, I'm not a boozehound," he laughs. "Xanax! That shit kicked my fucking ass."

I nod. "Yeah, did some of that towards the end, too," I say. "God, I need something. I feel like my whole body's gonna explode."

"Nurse Ratchitt will hook you up after vitals." Mike Cass tells me, now using a healthy dose of hairspray. "You'll be good as gold in a couple days, Buddy Boy, if someone doesn't knock you off because of that snoring." Mike Cass points an elbow at Ebby. "He was pissed!"

"Sounded like a dying buffalo," Ebby interjects with a chuckle.

I look at both of them and shrug. "I probably should be dead."

Mike gives me a kindly grin. "Ahh, you'll make it, Buddy Boy."

"I gotta go see the doctor." I tell them simply, and start for the door.

"Good luck, Header Boy. See ya after," says Mike Cass, still teasing his recalcitrant dyed and sprayed hair.

"Header Boy? What's that?" I pause and ask, puzzled.

"Thanks for taking that header yesterday out in the parking lot." He tells me with a laugh. "You broke up all those God-damned meetings. You're a big hit, Kid!"

"I'm lucky I didn't break my head." I say, rubbing the back of it and my aching neck. "See ya."

"Just knock off the snoring, and we'll get along just fine," says, Mike Cass as I exit. Two steps down the hall, I hear his raised voice again. "Or else, YOU'RE OUT, TOM!"

I force a smile. That was Michael Corleone dissing Tom Hagan in *The Godfather.* If I survive these first couple days of detox, I get the impression the remainder of my stay at Carrier will be filled with classic movie clichés.

Who I assume is Dr. Shariff greets me at her office door less than a minute later. She's a gorgeous woman, possibly 30, of Middle-Eastern—probably Indian—descent. She has big, brown eyes; and her long, jet-black hair blends well with attractive grey pants suit. She sits me down on the exam table. God, I feel terrible.

"How are you?" She asks sincerely. "I'm Mona Shariff."

"Not good," is all I can muster, hanging my head.

"Well, that doesn't surprise me," says Dr. Shariff. She's obviously an American, as she has no accent whatsoever. "Headache? You had a bad fall, yes?"

"I did—and yes." I respond. "But the worst part was lying in that ER tied to a gurney for all those hours. My head does hurt, but all of me hurts."

Dr. Shariff is expressionless, and studies what must be my chart. She changes the subject. "Your numbers are in from last night's blood test, and frankly, I might need to send you back to the ER."

"Oh, God! Please, no!" I cry out. "Anything but that!"

My outburst doesn't faze her. I'm sure she's seen it all, and heard it all in here. She glances again at the gathered papers and slowly shakes her head. "I can't remember the last time I saw liver enzymes this high: 1354! That's almost 15 times normal levels."

I realize that maybe I did show her something new. But that's not a good thing. I suddenly get the feeling that I really could be dying.

"Let me look you over," Dr. Shariff says. "Take off your shirt and lie down."

I gingerly do as I'm told. The table is cold and I start shivering.

She presses and prods on my distended belly. I've certainly been aware in the past year or so of a gradual increase in the size of my midsection, but I passed it off as simple weight gain. The truth, I knew in my heart, was the swelling of my liver. Hell, I've been testing high on enzymes for 20 years, and just drank my way right through it. I certainly wasn't going to stop drinking, for goodness sake. I'd just slow down as I got older, like my dad. Yeah, that's what I'd do. What bullshit! For 20 years I promised myself that I'd slow down, and for 20 years I continued to drink more.

"Any pain here?" she queries, breaking my reverie.

"No. Maybe a little discomfort, but it doesn't hurt."

She presses in a few more spots and asks the same question. It really doesn't hurt. Dr. Shariff then listens to my heart, takes my pulse and blood pressure, and then looks for a long minute into my eyes. She takes out a pen and looks at the chart again.

"No jaundice," says the doctor, making a few notes. "That's a mild miracle." She directs her big, brown eyes at me. For the first time, a glimmer of a smile appears. This relaxes me slightly. "Sit up, Eric, and put your shirt on," she says. "We'll take another blood test tomorrow and see if there's any improvement."

"So, no ER?" I ask cautiously.

"No, not right now; but you're not out of the woods by any means, Eric." There's nothing even close to a smile on her face now as she continues. "You may have permanent damage, and there's a possibility of liver failure. And your pressure is 170 over 110—dangerously high. You're very lucky to be alive. How much were you drinking on a daily basis?"

I've dodged this question for years, but I think the time is right to come clean. The "few drinks before dinner" line just won't cut it anymore.

"I drink all the time," I hear myself say, head bowed. "I drink about eight to ten in morning, and then maybe a bit more than that after work." I take a deep breath and sigh. "I've been drinking at least a quart a day for the last couple years, I guess. But I've been drinking heavily since before you were born, probably."

Dr. Shariff looks at me and shakes her head. Her expression is hard to read—inscrutable. What she says next, however, is *not* inscrutable. "Eric, you have to accept the fact that if you want to live, you can never drink again. Your liver is a ticking time bomb and when it blows, you will die—understand?"

I nod my head. *I can never drink again—ever? How am I ever going to do that?*

Dr. Shariff continues. "If it's not your liver, then it will be a heart-attack or stroke. Your blood-pressure is through the roof. Or, perhaps you may live only to lose your mind to wet-brain. The potential outcomes are all bad—if you continue drinking."

She pauses to let the words sink in. I look up and sigh. I honestly can't believe that I *am* still alive. I've been putting so much shit into my body—alcohol *and* drugs—for so long, it's a miracle that I am still here.

The doctor continues. "We can get your BP under control, and your liver *may* regain full function, but believe me, if you drink, the progression of this disease will cause it to become cirrhotic—if it's not already. *And*, it will fail—and soon. *You* are an alcoholic, and you can never drink again. Do you accept this?"

I look up at this beautiful young doctor who I know is absolutely telling me the truth. I've answered similar questions many times by other doctors, and more frequently from my wife and close family members, but always fought off what I knew I should say with the incessant lies or qualifications. This time, my answer is for real—I hope and pray. "Yes, I do."

Chapter Two

From an actual AA meeting...

Leader: "Yes!"

AA: "I'm Carmine, alcoholic."

Group: "Carmine!"

Carmine: "Yeah, nothin' was gonna stop me from getting a drink. Nothin'! I needed to drive, and so I did. I had this old, beat-up station wagon that was completely falling apart. It still ran, though, except in forward. (laughter) That's right! That piece of shit ran fine—backwards. Well, I wasn't about to walk that mile to the liquor store; so for a while I drove that baby backwards through Trenton, to and from the store just to get my booze! Can you imagine the sight of an old station wagon barreling backwards down the streets of Trenton? (more laughter). The cops got me, though. That was my fourth and last DWI, and thank God it finally led me into these rooms. That's all I got."

Group: "Thanks for sharing!"

Lone voice: "Keep coming back!"

From early childhood, the thread of alcohol and the beginnings of a lifelong obsession was spun. I remember my dad sitting in his lounger in the corner of our spacious living room in our Jersey shore home at Harvey Cedars. This was where he'd relax every day after his school teaching duties were done with the afternoon Philadelphia Bulletin and a beer.

This was when I often made my move. Being six or seven, I loved playing the part of a clever family dog, sneaking up on his master, sniffing out a treat. Hugging the wall, I'd crawl silently around the big dining room table unseen. I had to be extra stealthy navigating the big rocker in my path. Even if I bumped it slightly, its movement would surely give me away. My last hurdle was the folded table used for big holiday dinners. The collapsed ends created a tunnel of sorts, and when I would emerge out the far end, Dad was there. Whether he was or not, he always acted surprised, and after a hug and some talk about the day's events, I usually got my reward: That sip of cold, bubbly stuff that warmed my entire body.

I really had a wonderful childhood. I was the youngest of four, and peace, love and general happiness ruled most days at the Houghton house. I was a good boy, listened to my mother and father, got good grades and did my chores gladly. None of us kids liked to go to church much, but Mom always insisted and we went. God was never far from Mom's lips, and we all believed and prayed.

Mom, like so many others of the time, was a stay-at-homer, as Dad's teaching salary kept plenty of food on the table and decent clothes on our backs. Also, like so many others, they both drank. But aside from Dad's isolated outbursts and occasional overindulgence, a potential problem never materialized.

Indeed, for many years, I had no glaring problem with alcohol. However, by the time I started drinking on a regular basis, right up until I landed in Carrier, I always tended to imbibe too heavily. I could stop and check myself, and this was a tremendous source of pride for me throughout my early career, but right from the get go, my drinking could never have been characterized as "moderate." Simply put, Dad could stop when dinner arrived. I couldn't.

Growing up in a summer resort town meant that for three -quarters of the year, nothing much was going on. The summer population of Harvey Cedars swelled to over 10,000, but the year-around residents barely numbered 200. This fact helped me to develop from an early age into somewhat of a loner; thus beginning a lifelong tendency to be out and about by myself.

Mom and Dad called my early excursions "mystery walks," but there was really no mystery about them. I was simply out playing war games, exploring and wandering around the shore community enjoying time alone. I'm certain this loner mentality—this comfortability with me—has plenty of plusses and minuses, but when combined with the disease of alcoholism it can certainly become a devastating duo. Indeed, most of my drinking during the last 10 years or more of my career had been with no one but me. After the disease took hold at that indeterminate point, there was always that intense self-will and self-seeking—the thought, desire and the eventual obsessing about the next drink.

For over 30 years, this self-centeredness took root and grew in all facets of my life; and I would comfortably sneak away into the corners of my world. Just like my earliest alcohol recollections sneaking up on my father, throughout my entire life, I'd sneak away to get, or to plan to get, and then to administer—that next buzz. George Thorogood's *I Drink Alone* spoke to me.

Around the time of my first drunk in the summer of 1975, something profound happened and changed my life forever: I took a piano lesson. Mom had been prodding me for a couple years to start taking lessons, because it seemed every time I walked by the family upright in the living room I felt a pull to sit down and bang out something or other. And often when I did, both my parents seemed to hear something in the banging that wasn't too awful. Being the good son, I finally gave in and dropped my hockey stick and basketball and acceded to their wishes. The results were instantaneous. Within a few short months I was playing pieces that many of my present day students take years of lessons to conquer. There was a family genome bouncing around from somewhere in the past, and I had it.

After only two years of formal lessons, I had gone through two teachers, and now every week travelled 45 minutes up to Toms River to study with Elsie Fischer, the most widely regarded teacher in the area. Elsie quickly enabled my budding talent to blossom, and I took off. Making up for my late start, she pushed me into every talent show, competition and showcase she could find. Our efforts paid off. For two years, I was practicing three hours a day after school, and working on six or seven pieces at a time—excelling at all of them. I won many of the local and even state-wide events, and by the time I was 17, was preparing to audition at a few of the finest music schools in the country. The fact that I was totally at ease with myself was a perfect match with my talent, as I thrived in the private nature of solo piano work.

The sensation I had become around high school and with my friends, the exceptional grades I was bringing home, and my solid work around the house all stoked a formidable ego. Especially where music was concerned, I was the king of my little world, and I reveled in it. More and more, my hard work and success were rewarded on the weekends with a cold six-pack. When I was 15 or 16, it was my older brothers who were my party helpers: buying the beer and helping me drink it. After my best friend, Scott Seward got his driver's license; much of the partying was with him, and we didn't miss many opportunities to tune it up.

In the beginning of my senior year in 1979, I received my license, and my alcohol use was becoming almost daily. But there were never any problems. I kept the drinking in a small compartment nicely separated from all the other aspects of my life. Then and for years to come, I prided myself on total control where drinking was concerned.

I was already seeing friends and others at parties falling all over the place, getting into drunken brawls, or heaving their guts up. It was disgusting, these people who didn't know how to drink properly. I could drink properly, and proceeded to do so with abandon. Right up until the end for me, nearly dead from a failing liver, I was always appalled by people who just couldn't handle their booze. Send them all off to some sanitarium, and leave me alone to drink in peace, I often thought.

It was at this point in my life where the most important chapter in my world of drinking began to emerge: drinking and driving. For the next 30 years, almost without pause, I drank and I drove thousands of times. It was the perfect way to hide my big secret. What could be better for a man who feels completely at ease with himself, knows how to handle booze and a vehicle, and is hell bent on catching that buzz?

Indeed, throughout my undergraduate years at a music school in Princeton, the two years I spent getting my Masters in New York City, and far into my married years, I honed my prodigious skills at getting what I needed from booze from behind the wheel of a car. There were no adverse consequences. There were many close calls with the law to be sure, and, in the end, all my superb skills at concealment would be discovered; but it wasn't as a result of any motor vehicle incident. It was inevitably my behavior following a drinking binge that got me into trouble. And nine times out of ten, this bad behavior followed a drinking binge in my car. I partied everywhere to be sure, but, through the years, it would be inside my many vehicles where I would consume the lion's share of my booze.

Chapter Three

"The alcoholic is like a tornado roaring his way through the lives of others. Hearts are broken. Sweet relationships are dead. Affections have been uprooted. Selfish and inconsiderate habits have kept the home in turmoil."
— Page 82, *Alcoholics Anonymous*

I shuffle my way out of Dr. Shariff's office feeling completely numb. The physical pain throughout my body and tremendous anxiety caused by the beginnings of alcohol withdrawal are all there, but mentally, I feel a strange, calming sensation taking shape. It's almost as though I've just been through something that has taken away a small piece of the confusion and chaos in my life. I admitted something, and I really believe that for the first time in my life that I meant it. Now, I feel a small sense of freedom, and a tiny bit of strength. That strength tells me to get to the nurse's station before the skin shakes from my body.

I turn the corner and there he is again. Mike Cass is in front of the station arguing with the same nurse who told me to go see the doctor. I walk up and stand just behind him as he rants. Mike is now attired in full blue denim, and his dyed, jet-black hair is set just so. It seems that he wants something.

"But why can't I have it? I don't want to have to bother you every time I want a splash." He proclaims, both hands pressing on either side of the window to the station.

The nurse, a 50ish, attractive blond with glasses hanging off the end of her nose, is unmoved. I see her nametag says "Sharon," and when Sharon's gravelly voice emerges, all the unfortunates around us can hear it.

"I keep telling you, Mike, it's got *alcohol* in it!" She almost screams the word alcohol. "Get those dirty paws off my station and get to breakfast! You, Eric!" she shoots me a quick glance. "How are you, dear?"

I open my mouth but she continues. "Yeah, not so good, huh? Get in line over there for vitals and then come back," she says quickly, pointing down the hall toward our rooms where about a dozen people are waiting in a line. I begin to move, but stop, wanting to hear how the Mike Cass confrontation resolves.

Mike looks at me and winks. There's a mischievous spark in his eyes. Then he turns to face Sharon again. I assume this is whom he was referring to as "Nurse Ratchitt" before. "But I'm not *here* because of booze," he moans, now standing a bit further away from the window and a frowning Sharon. "*I'm here because of Xanax!*" He emphasizes every word with that pure north Jersey accent. "Come on!" pleads Mike, "I'm not gonna drink my God-damned Aqua Velva, for Christ's sake!" He looks pleased with himself, as if the argument is settled.

Nurse Sharon's response is immediate. "No, but your *roommate* might!" At the word "roommate" she points directly at me. I cringe and probably turn an even brighter shade of crimson.

Mike Cass laughs a big laugh and starts walking away. He pats me on the back and tells me he's going for breakfast. "But not you, Buddy Boy!" he tells me, over his shoulder. "You're stuck here in Blake for two days. Bon appetite!" and he's gone through the double doors and outside.

I'm still feeling rather numb as Sharon speaks again to me. There is a compassionate tone in her voice. "I've seen people drink worse than Aqua Velva. Can you imagine drinking shoe polish?"

"Oh my God," I manage, a sudden shiver enveloping me.

Sharon shoos me away with a hand. "Come on—vitals—move. Then come see me," she says kindly. I can tell she's got a heart of gold—but don't mess with her.

I make my way to the end of the line for people waiting to get their vitals read. About halfway down that line there's a person slumped in a chair. It's a woman, I think. I know I must look pretty bad, but this poor soul is a special case. She's white as a ghost, her hair is a tangled, matted mess and she's wrapped up in a tattered blanket or comforter. The person behind her in line, a tall, clean-shaven, dark-featured man taps her when the line moves. She gives a pained expression when he does so, struggles mightily to her feet, then plops into the next chair. I get the feeling as soon as she sees the nurse for her meds, it will be straight back to bed with her, if she lives that long.

At the end of the line, I greet Ebby, who's smiling broadly at me. He's a fine looking guy, well built and lean. He's dressed in jeans and tee-shirt, and looks like he should be out working on some roof or something. I shake his offered hand.

"Didn't have a chance to formally say hello before; how you making out? Eric, right?" He asks me.

"Yes, and you're Ebby?" He nods. "Well, I'm alive." I say, trying to smile. "The doctor says I'm lucky to be here. My liver is in bad shape."

"I avoided that problem," says Ebby. "But, the cops and my wife gave me enough reasons to be here." His smile fades. "Got my fifth DWI and she threw me out. I think we're through," he says matter-of-factly. "Are you married?"

I can't relate to the DWIs, because somehow, someway I never got one. But the wife stuff? Oh yeah. There were all those lies about the drinking; the theft of thousands to feed my habits; and the terrible way I treated her—actually blaming her for all the problems that brought me here. What a complete asshole I've been. I shudder at the thought of my three children enduring all those drunken tirades aimed at Carol. I take a deep breath and look away. "Yeah, I'm married. Things are bad right now—really bad."

I change the subject. I don't want to go anywhere near my marriage right about now. "You got five DWIs? God, when can you get your license back?" The line moves, and we each take a chair.

"Around 2024, I think," replies Ebby. "I'll be 54." He pauses and looks at the floor. I guess he's closer to 40, but he certainly doesn't look it. "What a mess." The smile is now long gone.

A short, thickly built guy slowly approaches and sticks out his hand. "Hi, I'm Henry," he says in a deep monotone as I stand and shake it. Henry's got a round face and short-cropped, graying hair. His movements are slow and robotic, and his eyes have a fixed gaze about them. "Thanks for helping us out yesterday," says Henry, trying to crack a smile.

"Yeah, what happened anyway?" Ebby asks earnestly. "You fell out in the parking lot, and we got to miss the last 15 minutes of our group. It was great."

I endure another sudden shiver and sit back down. My stomach is queasy and all I want to do is get whatever Sharon will give me to help ease my pain. I take a deep breath and answer Ebby's question. "I was still all twisted up when I was checking in," I tell them. A few others, I notice, are eavesdropping with intense interest. "I can't remember big chunks of it, but at one point I asked if I could go out for a smoke, and they said sure. Well, I went up next to that big tree out there and lit up. I leaned against the tree, but missed, and took that header."

"Missed the tree," Henry says, airily. "I hate that. Wow, missed the tree." His face is serene, but kind of confused. He continues, "Everyone went running when the siren went off. 'Man down! Man down!' The voice over the loudspeaker said." He manages a curious grin. Ebby and a few of the others around are chuckling, so I do too.

"Well, I hit my head, so they made me go to the ER. They *made* me!" I emphasize. "Cops and all! And I sat there for six hours tied to a gurney. I could only get up to take a leak. It was horrible. I finally got a CT-scan and it showed nothing," they all laugh again, "I was a mess when I finally got here sometime after midnight, I think."

"Wow!" says Henry again, and then in one motion he slowly turns and shuffles away. When he's out of earshot, I turn to Ebby. "What's Henry's deal?"

"He's here for booze I think, but he's got other issues—anger and the like. I hear him screaming at his wife on the phone." Ebby shakes his head. "It ain't pretty. I can't imagine how bad it would be if he were drunk."

I nod my head. I can relate—big time!

Ebby continues, "They got him on some heavy-duty meds."

"My wife," I respond vacantly, holding my head in my hands, "and…my mother!" I sit bolt upright. "Oh Shit! It's my mother's birthday! It is the 13th, isn't it?"

"Yup," replies Ebby, as we shift another chair closer to the young girl checking vitals. "Well," he continues with that broad grin back in place, "if you stay clean, you'll never have a problem remembering your sobriety date."

"That's for sure." I notice the girl who looks like death getting her readings done, and whisper to Ebby. "What about that sad sack?"

"That's Eva," he tells me, leaning in. "Heroin—bad! She's been puking ever since they brought her in two nights ago. Her roommate's ready to commit suicide, or murder, I think."

I follow Henry's lead and simply say "Wow!"

"How long have you been here anyway?" I ask him.

"Over two weeks. I'm staying 28 days—on the state's nickel, of course."

"Our tax dollars at work," I mumble.

Ebby chuckles again. "Yeah! What insurance do you have?"

"My work through the Archdiocese in Newark," I reply. Eva slowly shuffles by it the general direction of our rooms, and Ebby takes the vitals chair.

"Archdiocese, huh? Well, they might pay for five days, but don't bet on it," he tells me. "They might pray for you alright, but the bastards will fight to pay one penny more than they have to, believe me. They'll try to get you kicked out as soon as you stop shaking. It's all about the insurance companies." He laughs and greets the attractive brunette taking vitals.

I hold out my hands. Jesus, I've never shaken like this. And the worst part is I feel like it's coming from the inside out. Every inch of me seems to be vibrating. I'm a wreck.

Ebby stands up. I ask him if he can show me around later, and he says sure.

"Just relax today." He tells me. "You don't have to go to meetings if you're not up to it. You can't go to the cafeteria until tomorrow at dinner, I think, but just take it easy. I'll talk to you in a bit."

I say goodbye as the girl, Carley I see on her nametag, does her job on me. Despite my awful state, I do feel very fortunate to have Ebby and that nut, Mike Cass as roommates. I shudder again thinking how it would be to have someone like Eva.

After she's finished taking my temperature, blood pressure and pulse, Carey hands me the paper with my numbers on them; and tells me to go to the nurse's station.

Once there, I hand the paper to nurse Sharon. She puts it aside and picks up another sheet with my name on it. She looks into my eyes. "No jaundice, that's good, but you're red as a rhubarb!" She frowns and makes a couple notes. "Are you seeing anything like visions or having hallucinations? Hearing any voices, or anything like that?"

"No, not any of that," I respond, and she ticks off a couple of boxes.

"Zero being nothing, and ten being unbearable, how bad is your nausea?"

I think. "Three or so, at the moment," I say, "but I haven't eaten since sometime yesterday. I've had terrible heartburn the last six months or so."

"Yeah, well your stomach probably doesn't have much of a lining left after all you've put it through," Sharon states flatly, then adds as a matter of fact, "Some guy had an esophageal hemorrhage right over there a few months ago." She points down the hall toward the lounge. "There was blood every-where! He's lucky to be alive"

I give her a pained look, and grab my head again. She continues with the quiz.

"How bad does your head hurt?"

"Eight, no, maybe seven," I respond. "It's not worse than my general pain."

She nods and ticks off another box. "Now, because of your fall yesterday," Sharon tells me, without missing a beat, "make sure to tell us if you get dizzy or anything like that, okay"

"I understand," I say and continue, "and for dizziness, if it's on there, zero."

"Oh, it is! Ha!" she gives a brief laugh and marks the box.

"Nervous, agitated? Hold out your hands," she commands and I obey. "Holy cow! Is that how you feel all over?"

"Exactly," I say. "It's like I'm plugged into a socket! Nine or ten, I guess"

"You're body is just now starting to detoxify, Eric," she tells me. "You may not know this, but alcohol is the only drug that can actually kill you in withdrawal." She sees my body slump and pleading eyes, and then continues. "Delirium Tremens, DT's, sometimes provoke seizures that can stop the heart, you know. Not to mention what booze does to the liver and other organs. I saw your liver numbers." She shakes her head. "You're a lucky man. You don't have jaundice and your brain still seems to be functioning."

"Barely," I interrupt.

"But you can never drink again. You know that, right?" I nod. "What about your family?" She asks me.

"A wife and three kids," I tell Sharon, trying to absorb all the things she's told me.

"Well, we're going to fix you up so you can get back to them," she assures me brightly. "I'll be right back." She disappears behind a rear door in the nurse's station.

I don't know if I'll be going back home to my family. Those three months I've been living across the river in Morrisville have only made matters worse at home. There's no way I can stay sober and go back to George's, I realize. But how can I return home after all these recent events? I feel almost despairing standing there waiting for Sharon. Oh God, how could she ever allow me back home? Without knowing it, tears come to my eyes, and I begin to lose it.

Sharon returns with two small plastic cups and sees me, head down on the counter at the window, shaking uncontrollably and crying.

"Okay, Eric, settle down." She puts down the cups and starts stroking my back. "Here you go." She hands me a box of tissues and I grab about ten, and start blowing and wiping.

"Here, you need to take these." I look up and she's holding a cup with five pills in it.

"Thank God," I blubber, and try to stand up straight again.

She then explains what each one is: "Here are two vitamin pills, a mega and a B-12," she tells me. "This one is Lisinopril for your high blood pressure. We'll probably need to up that dosage as your numbers are sky-high." I'm gaining a bit of control again as I listen to her calmly explain the pills.

"Here's a Prilosec for your heartburn, and the last is Librium to ease you out of detox."

"Will it calm me down?" I ask imploringly.

"Without a doubt," Sharon assures me. "You'll feel better in 30 minutes. You'll take two of these a day for the next three days until all that toxic crap is out of your body."

I take a deep breath, and then take the cup and pop the pills in my mouth. She gives me the other cup with water in it, and I down everything.

"Now," she fixes the glasses back in place on her nose and points toward the lounge, "go get some breakfast in the lounge down there, and try to relax. You okay?"

"I feel a little better," I respond, but the thoughts of Carol and the kids come back and start to overwhelm me again. "I just don't know if I'll be able to get my family back again," I blurt out.

"Listen!" she tells me harshly. "You need to get well. That's all you need right now. Don't worry about any of that now. You got it? Just concentrate on rest and healing, okay?"

I smile, nod and thank her, then head for the lounge. She's absolutely right. I have to start recovering before I can even begin to attempt anything else. As hard as I try, however, I simply cannot stop thinking about Carol.

Chapter Four

"Though there is no way of proving it, we believe that early in our careers most of us could have stopped drinking. But the difficulty is that few alcoholics have enough desire to stop while there is yet time."
—-Page 32, *Alcoholics Anonymous*

Not surprisingly, the pub at Williams School of Music was my frequent haunt. It was there that I met Carol in the fall of 1984. I had recently graduated from the school with a bachelor's degree in Piano Performance, and was taking a year off to make some money teaching at the Music School, and study more intensely with my current teacher, a professor at the college, Harold Zabrack.

Carol, a native of St. Louis, had just transferred from St. Louis University, and was now technically a sophomore heading towards a Church Music degree. Although we are almost exactly the same age—Carol August 24th, 1962, me September 19th—she was now a year behind me. For three years she had been spinning her wheels out at "SLU," and thought a small school away from home with a more focused curriculum would be the kick in the butt she needed.

That first night drinking beer with her in the pub is memorable to me for one reason: Carol was testing a unique and utterly useless plan to quit smoking. To be sure, I remember being attracted to this shapely brunette from the heartland. She had a terrific sense of humor, witty charm, and a sincere and warm smile. On top of that, she came from a well-to-do family and was highly intelligent. But, how on earth could it be possible to quit smoking holding an unlit cigarette in your hand while everyone around you is puffing away? It would be the equivalent of me, at this tee-totaling point in my life, going into a crowded bar and sitting in front of a Jack-on-the-rocks for two hours and not drinking it. With either tactic, failure must be the result. A hokey maxim I hear frequently these days, referring to ways to avoid relapse, says simply, "If you sit in a barber's chair long enough, you're bound to get a haircut." And so it was that within days of her valiant but not-too-realistic attempts at quitting smoking, Carol relapsed, and was exhaling smoke rings with gusto.

Carol and I hit it off great and were dating almost immediately, but there was a problem. Although I was free from physical attachments at the time, I was still tangled up emotionally from a relationship that had ended a few months earlier. I was still in the mental grips of my first love, Susan Parker.

Susan arrived at Williams two years earlier in the fall of 1982. This southern beauty from the mountains of Virginia could have easily played Scarlett O'Hara in a remake of *Gone With the Wind*. Tall and elegant, with a long and full head of luxurious, auburn hair, Susan's smile and southern gentility had captured my imagination almost from the start. She was a Voice Performance major, and possessed a massive, coloratura soprano voice that could rattle the window panes if she let it loose.

She soon discovered that I was one of best pianists on campus, and asked me to be her accompanist. Not too long after I accepted, I was accompanying her everywhere. Actually, many people accompanied Susan, as she more or less commanded a cadre of friends and acquaintances. Wherever she went around the tiny campus, a retinue of admirers followed in her wake, and I was one of them. Susan's true love was beauty pageants, and she had big dreams in this regard; but for now, I was overjoyed to be a special member of her entourage. Indeed, we had become lovers, and for Christmas break she invited me down to her home in Covington.

I had never seen such a beautiful part of the country as I did in those Allegheny Mountains. Situated in the spine of the Appalachians near the West Virginia border, Covington, as small mill town with about 10,000 residents, sits lazily amid the spectacular countryside.

Susan's parents were all south. Her mom, Patsy, proper and polite, and once a striking beauty in her own right, treated me royally. Orion, her dad, was short and stocky with the thickest, deep southern drawl I'd ever heard. He was a larger-than-life character and I loved him right from the start. He liked nothing more than needling and berating me incessantly when I acted like an idiot—which was often. "God-damn!" he loved to say with that drawl of his, "I don't know *how* you Yankees ever won that war!" "O-E," as he was known, took me around to his special haunts, introducing me to friends and things this Jersey Boy had never seen before. However, it was on my first hunting trip with O-E, during that Christmas break, that he altered the way I lived my life.

Apart from the occasional wine that I drank with meals, up until that point in my life, I was strictly a beer drinker. O-E changed that forever. That day during the holiday break, he took me high up into one of the nearby mountains, hunting for deer. We saw a few in the three or four hours we spent standing around in the frozen woods, but we never got off a shot. With the sun retreating, and our feet and hands numb, we walked the half mile or so back to where he parked his truck. The vehicle was sitting on a dirt road, adjacent to a large cow pasture that rose in all directions high up the now cloud-shrouded peaks.

We reached the truck, and he pulled a bottle and a couple Styrofoam coffee cups from the glove. "Come with me, boy!" he ordered me, and I followed him a short distance to a small stream coming straight down the mountain. It had started to snow. Once there, Orion leaned over and partially filled both cups with the fresh, cold spring water. "Now, take this cup." He handed it to me solemnly, like a communion. "I'm gonna show you how to drink bourbon, boy." I don't believe I said a word. He then poured two healthy doses of the rust-colored liquid from the bottle into each container. "Cheers!" he said, and we touched cups and drank.

The combination of all the elements present was almost magical: The cold, the snow and the season; the absolute beauty of the mountains, and that fresh, clean, icy-cold water. Of course, what really made it magical was that warm, smooth Virginia Gentleman bourbon. *Ah!* It tasted *so* good. The only thing better than that first drink up there in that surreal place, was the next one—and the next one.

We saved a stiff drink for the ride home, and began crawling up the dirt path toward the main road. We slowed almost to a stop when we noticed a dog ahead of us in the headlights. He was taking his time, simply walking up the same path we were on. He was a short, bourbon-colored hound-mix himself, with long, floppy ears, and the headlights of the truck shown directly on his rear-end. His tail stood straight up and wagged, revealing his prominent exit hole. The hound's pace was tectonic, and he refused get out of our way, but we didn't give a lick. We just inched along, sipping our booze, mere feet behind him. After a while O-E spoke up, his words even slower and thicker than usual.

"You know what that is, Boy?" He gestured to the dog.

"No, what?" I said, just smiling and taking another sip.

"That there is a one-eyed dog, walkin' backwards."

Never before or since, have I laughed so hard. Bourbon, and lots of it, would be by my side for the next 20 years.

Susan never finished her degree program at Williams. Her long-term plan didn't include boring music classes and those never-ending choir rehearsals. She had bigger, more pressing fish to fry. She knew she had one chance in her life to achieve stardom. She was going to take that million-dollar smile and that booming soprano voice then enter and win the Miss America Pageant. God love her, she nearly succeeded!

In May of 1984, she won her local Allegheny Highlands pageant, and the following month, I was there with most of her family when she captured the Miss Virginia crown in Roanoke. The writing was on the wall for me, it seemed, when at the reception following the event; I had to wait two hours in a receiving line to get a peck on the cheek. Throughout the summer, while she prepared for her big moment in Atlantic City, she rarely returned any of my repeated calls. When she did, it was always a rushed conversation, and then a vague promise to get together "later."

Susan's 15 minutes of fame ended when she didn't crack the top ten in the Miss America Pageant, but I was there again to root her on. I'm sure I knew we were finished when I didn't get to see her at all following that event, and in the weeks to come, Susan never officially severed our relationship. She preferred what I considered to be the torture method of "death by a thousand cuts"—a slow and unresolved end of a love affair. I was in the midst of this mental and emotional limbo when I met Carol at Williams.

Carol, throughout that entire school year, knew what I going through, and waited for me to snap out of the "Susan Syndrome," if you will. I slowly emerged from my funk, and began to feel a close bond with her—to a point. Almost daily, after her classes and my teaching at the college were done for the day, we'd hang out with friends at the Pub, or any number of local Princeton bars. If I had the money, I'd opt for the Jack or Jim, but usually had to settle for draught beer—and lots of it. Carol, then and now, prefers beer or wine—and one or two.

Carol thought she understood me, and loved me, and wanted to give me the space I needed. She was very patient with me, but I took advantage of her trusting nature and good heart. When I found out in the spring of '85 that I was heading to the Manhattan School of Music for a Master's Degree in Performance, I more or less made it clear that a commitment wasn't a good idea; but I didn't close any doors either. I was going to be living in the big city, and I certainly wanted to taste and see what that was all about. Perhaps I could still be with Carol, but, perhaps not.

Like Susan did to me, only worse, I led Carol along, not being honest about my feelings—and intentions. When I met Nancy Kissel that summer down in Harvey Cedars, where I was living at home digging clams commercially to make money, and partying up a storm every weekend with my new "friend," I didn't bother to tell Carol. After all, she knew that I didn't want anything serious, and I was simply looking out for myself. It was all about me. As usual, I was completely self-absorbed, and Carol's feelings simply didn't concern me.

I was still seeing her well into the fall semester, when she finally discovered the truth about my two-timing relationship with this older woman who lived on the Upper East Side of Manhattan *and* held a high position in the fashion industry there. I thought Carol was out of my life forever that day when she slammed the car door shut, just after I broke off yet another date with her in order to meet Nancy at Gleason's Bar on 75th and York. That very day, it *had* to be over when she screamed at me through the open window of my Toyota: "Have fun with Nancy! I never want to see you again!" Fate would not have it be so.

For the next year and a half, with Carol safely stowed away in the back of my mind, I lived the high life in the Big Apple with Nancy, and studied music and practiced my piano with diligence. I arrived at the Manhattan school with my ego in full bloom. I had been the "big fish" at Williams and had my sights set on a performing career. Even my wonderful teacher at Williams, Harold Zabrack, a man who knew a lot about what it takes to become a performing artist, told me that if I worked hard enough, and had a few breaks along the way, it could be possible for me achieve this lofty goal.

The problem for me, however, quickly became apparent when I noticed all the young and fanatical Asian and Russian pianistic studs practicing six, eight hours a day at my new school. I soon discovered that the discipline required to keep pace with these automatons was beyond me if I didn't abandon every other aspect of my life. It wasn't going to happen. I simply liked "other aspects" of life too much: primarily drinking.

The type of practicing required would interfere with my daily dose of cocktails. Even then, I wouldn't allow such things to stand between me and my bottle. In the years to come, it would only get worse.

I had already begun teaching, and seemed quite adept at it, so the adjustment in my mind to a long, happy life in music as educator first, and performer second was not a hard pill to swallow. I proceeded to work hard at school, but also set aside plenty of time to enjoy my life in the big city.

Nine years my elder and conveniently flush with cash, Nancy was a tall, elegant brunette. She possessed a ready-made smile and a bubbly personality, but, in relatively short order it became clear that it was her money and status that attracted me, not nearly so much anything physical or emotional. Of course, I kept those thoughts to myself. I would never risk her financial support of my ever increasing Jack Daniels consumption.

Night after night, we went out on the town and she invariably picked up the hefty bar-tabs. I began to notice that my drinking wasn't exactly "normal," and Nancy was no slouch either. She could easily make it through a bottle of wine in one sitting—and on a daily basis. Sure, I understood that it's not exactly normal to have six or seven cocktails before dinner, and then just keep plowing right on through to bedtime, but hey, I was in New York and I was 22. After all, we did hang out with many who drank just like us. It was the 80's, for God's sake, and I was a gifted musician, and, yes, I'll take another Jack! And what's that, cocaine and weed? Sure, I'll take some of that, too.

As noted, my head was unusually enlarged at that time, so, in the end, despite the almost daily hangovers, I realized that I could easily maintain the drinking routine I was in and set boundaries. I could control it, and did to a point. As was my custom during my undergrad years, I rarely took a drink before all my work was done; and I tried to never miss a class or lesson. This well-structured plan to compartmentalize my drinking served me well, and it kept the progression of full-blown alcoholism at bay for many years to come.

Toward the end of my graduate studies, a nagging problem began to surface. Nancy and I became restless about the nature and future of our relationship. Unfortunately, we had differing opinions about what direction it should take. While she was hinting about for a ring, I was eager to sever our 18 month party session. I was nearing the end of my two-year term in New York, and Nancy's services, having run their course, were no longer required. I wasn't looking forward to the nasty business of the breakup. She would immediately see the awful way that I had used her and my extreme selfishness in the relationship. I knew that the end would be bitter indeed, but also I knew that it had to end.

To make matters even worse, the more I considered the problem with Nancy, the more I felt a pull back toward Carol. Although I hadn't spoken with her for well over a year, by the beginning of 1987, with the thought of moving back to the Princeton area in the spring looking like a reality, my thoughts kept returning to that mid-western girl with the witty charm and shapely beauty. But, had she moved on and written me out of her life? I had to find out.

I composed a long letter to Carol in January, honestly admitting my faults in the past and my hopes and dreams for us in the future, and then sent it to off to Williams on a Wednesday or Thursday. Every Saturday, since I began my studies in New York, I had commuted to Williams and taught a full day at the school. That, along with my new church job, playing the organ and singing at a Catholic church in Elizabeth on the weekends, was helpful to defray Nancy's support of my expensive lifestyle.

This particular Saturday, I was safely tucked away in one of the teaching studios at Williams when the knock came at the door. It was Carol. She looked beautiful as ever, with her shoulder-length hair, tight-fitting jeans and warm smile all in attendance. She never mentioned the letter, but only seemed interested in how I was doing and other mundane issues of the day. She told me that she would be graduating in May, as I would be from Manhattan, and that maybe we might get together for a drink sometime. There was nothing more to it than that. I told her that I was sorry for the way I behaved in the past, but I didn't push the idea of a get-together. She obviously had been thinking about me, and that fact buoyed me greatly; but she gave no hint about receiving my long letter outlining my intentions and apologies. What would be her reaction when that arrived?

The next week, when she appeared beaming with my letter in her hand, the coincidence of the week before wasn't lost on either of us. It's been my experience that nothing important happens by chance, and this certainly was the case with Carol. With big changes on the horizon for both of us, we had been thinking about each other at the same point in our lives. This was too much for me, and when I asked her if she wanted to go out that night, she eagerly accepted.

Within weeks, I was doing to Nancy what I had done to Carol when I first went off to New York, but this time I sucked it up and came clean. On a cold night in late January I took a few shots of courage and simply told Nancy that I wanted to break off our relationship. She simply threw a drink in my face; called me a user, an ungrateful asshole and dozens of other things that I deserved, and ended it all by physically throwing me out of her apartment. I was free, and I actually felt good about being honest for a change. By March, I was commuting almost daily from my Brooklyn apartment to Princeton.

Carol, for some reason, was giving me another chance. She didn't exactly wait for me, and had had a few minor flings in the interim, but, just the same, I felt blessed that she was taking me back. I soon fell madly in love with her, and we partied out for the remainder of the school year. That summer, I visited her home and family in St. Louis and proposed. She accepted, and I was the happiest man in the world. We were married in October 1988, and many contented years seemed ahead for the three of us: Carol, Eric and Jack, of course. Indeed, it was a happy and loving marriage for many years, until three finally became a crowd.

Chapter Five

"We admitted we were powerless over alcohol—that our lives had become unmanageable."
—Step 1, Page 59, Alcoholics Anonymous

After leaving Nurse Sharon, I walk gingerly the ten steps or so into the common lounge of Blake Hall. Upon entering, I see a pathetic looking upright piano standing against a far wall. Its wood veneer is chipped and peeling away and many of its plastic key-coverings are missing, exposing the wood underneath. I'm sure it hasn't been tuned since some time in the last century. I think it must resemble me in a strange way, and I make an attempt at a smile. Although I haven't had much time to practice lately—drinking and drugging for more than three months almost without pause—I think if I survive this detox, I might sit down and entertain the "troops."

As I make my way for the cold cereal boxes, I walk past a couple young guys playing ping-pong. These young bucks are all wound up, laughing and shouting insults—four-letter words flying as fast as the little white ball. A few people are sitting around the scattered tables and chairs, eating and talking; and I notice Henry and some other guy in the far end of the lounge watching the wall-mounted flat-screen TV. I grab a box of Rice Krispies, a plastic bowl and spoon, and a small container of milk from the fridge and sit down at an unoccupied table.

I hear him before I see him. "Bobby, Bobby, that language! What would your momma say if she heard you saying such things?" Mike Cass ambles into the lounge with a tall, lean young man of about 25 following close behind. The tall guy's forehead has a big bandage on it.

Bobby is laughing. "Yeah, like somebody gives a fuck what I say around here." His brown hair is close-cropped and his cut-off tee reveals numerous tattoos. Mike sees me sitting and they both approach.

"Rice Krispies, Header boy?" he asks jauntily, and pats me on the back. "May we join you? Or are you busy? This is Bobby Brooklyn." Mike Cass heads for the cereal boxes himself. I shake Bobby's hand and introduce myself. Bobby takes a seat with a cup of coffee he brought back from the cafeteria. Mike soon returns with a bowl and spoon, three boxes of Cheerios, a cinnamon bagel with cream cheese and three containers of chocolate milk.

"Didn't you just get back from breakfast?" I ask.

"Yeah, so?" Mike smiles. "I gotta bulk up!" He gives his ample midsection a couple swift pats. It looks to me like he's bulked enough. "I can eat 50 eggs!" Mike says. Or, rather, *Cool Hand Luke*.

"Jesus! You just had nearly a dozen, about 10 sausages and six pieces of toast!" Bobby Brooklyn says, with that unmistakable accent.

Mike Cass just shrugs and rips open a cereal box and fills his bowl. "I just can't stop eating. How are you feeling, Buddy Boy?"

"Shaky as hell," I tell him. "Nurse Ratchitt gave me some Librium. I'll let you know in a little while."

"Six-pack in a pill, oh yeah!" he laughs. "Tomorrow you'll feel better. Just make it through today." He starts shoveling it in.

"Mike tells me you're the nut who took that fall yesterday," Bobby says. He's holding an open notepad. On the page is some wild-looking multi-colored pencil art—very intricate caricature stuff.

"Yeah, that's what they tell me," I say, and then add, pointing to the open page, "Nice stuff there."

"Bobby here is probably the best artist in Brooklyn," Mike interjects, his mouth already stuffed. "Too bad he's a boozehound just like you."

Bobby shoots Mike a look. "It's just a hobby," Bobby shrugs. "I'm really a union man like Mike here. But, after my accident," he points to his bandage, "my boss told me if I don't get help, I'm out. So, I've been here three days like Mike, and I got about five to go. They're gonna send me to a rehab in Florida, I hear." He looks at me and shakes his head. "God, I think I looked worse than you when I arrived."

"And that's pretty bad," says Mike with a laugh.

"What happened to your head," I ask. Bobby frowns and stares at his coffee.

"Tell him, Bobby," Mike says, and then adds, "He's a pipefitter like me, only my local is in Manheim where I'm from, just 20 miles north of here."

"Okay," goes Bobby. "Well, of course the guys and me were out for an extended lunch hour, as usual. God, we got fuckin' ripped, *all* the time! So, after 'lunch' the boss, who wasn't with us of course, asks me to use the sawzall to remove some old fittings. I started in and somehow the saw hit something and flew back and clipped me. There was blood everywhere. I ended up getting 55 stitches."

Mike picks up the story. "Yeah, but before that, can you believe even before the EMTs arrive, the boss has some guy come around with a breathalyzer? He's lying there bleeding all over the place, and they check and see if he was drinking. Un-fucking-believable!"

I shake my head. "What did you blow?"

".18. He could've fired me on the spot, but he gave me a break. He said 'get clean or get lost.' So, I better get my act together. This shit has been going on too long." Bobby lowers his head and takes a drink. "Too long," he repeats softly. Bobby's a good looking kid; obviously talented and has a great job. He looks up. "For the last two years, my life has been out of control. I have a beautiful wife and a baby, and here I am." I know *exactly* what he's talking about.

"I'm going out for a smoke," Bobby says, standing up.

"We'll join you in a few, after my snack," replies Mike, still stuffing his face. He looks at me. "You smoke, Buddy Boy?"

"Oh yeah," I say eagerly, getting up and throwing my garbage in the can. "I'm ready for one." Mike's now tackling the third box of Cheerios. I suddenly feel a little queasy and sit back down. I just want a smoke and then a long nap.

"What do you do for a living, Eric?" Mike asks me. For the first time since I met him, this cartoonish character is using my real name.

"I'm a piano teacher, mostly," I reply.

"A piano teacher? God, what next?" Mike laughs again, only louder. His entire body shudders as he roars, but his black hair remains unmoved, courtesy of the spray he used earlier. "You can play us a tune later." He motions to the pathetic-looking upright against the far wall.

I smile. "Not today." I hold out my hands. They're still vibrating uncontrollably.

"Yeah, not today, *she said*," he giggles, and continues his attack on his 'snack.'

"I haven't sat down and played in months," I say somberly. "I've had absolutely no interest in it."

"Yeah, well you've been busy doing 'other' things," says Mike Cass knowingly. Indeed I have.

After a pause, I ask Mike, "How did you get ripped up on Xanax?" I can see his face contort when I say the word "Xanax." It's like I touched a nerve.

"Jesus Christ!" he cries, milk and Cheerio bits dribbling from his mouth. "I thought I could go 15 minutes without thinking about that shit." He wipes his mouth, and then takes another huge bite of cereal. "My eye," he points up to his left eye.

"Your eye? What happened?" I ask, puzzled. Just then, Henry appears out of nowhere. He's standing right next to our table.

"This is a classic!" states Henry flatly. His eyes are wide and his big gut is pushing his tight-fitting tee-shirt out. He has that same, unreadable expression pinned to his face. He's no doubt familiar with the story.

Mike looks up. "Henry! How's Henry? You know Henry, Buddy Boy?"

I nod. "Yeah, we met a little while ago."

Mike continues, "I know it's hilarious, Henry, so here goes. Okay, my cousin invented this new kind of dog leash, and I was trying it out on my dog. It was just like that other kind, you know, where the dog can go out 20 or 30 feet and then you can rein it in?" I nod. He pauses and puts the last quarter of the bagel in his mouth, then gulps down a generous portion of chocolate milk. After swallowing, he then sits bolt upright, braces himself, and lets loose a lengthy, sonorous belch.

"Gesuntheit!" Henry says airily.

"Anyway," continues Mike, "the latching part of my cousin's leash was what was different, and he kept tinkering with it, and I would keep trying it out. But this time, for some reason, it just snapped off from the collar. It just broke off, and the latch came flying back and hit me right on the eyeball. God, the pain was unbelievable. After all this time, it's still just a blur when I cover my good eye." He puts his hand over his left eye and looks around the room.

I just shake my head.

Mike continues. "For the last six months, I've tried everything: specialists, laser-surgery, even acupuncture, and nothing's helped. Nothing helped but Xanax." A faint smile appears on his face at the mention of the word. He obviously has mixed emotions regarding the drug. "It just made everything numb, and I could even work—for a while."

"You had to keep increasing the dosage, right?" Henry asks, still hovering next to us.

"Did I ever!" Mike continues, as the smile disappears. "In the end, I couldn't get out of bed. Try doing 25 of those suckers a day. Jesus, my 83 year-old mother kept saying, 'what the matter, Mikey, what the matter?' I couldn't tell her the truth. I finally just told her that I was depressed, and that I needed help. It totally kicked my ass, and I just hope I can stay away from it. It helps my eye, but it ruins everything else." Mike takes another drink of chocolate milk and sighs heavily. "I still have two prescriptions waiting for me at home. I really don't know if I'll be able to…" he trails off in mid-sentence and shakes his head. "It's so fucking weird."

There's a loud whoop from the ping-pong table behind us, and a ball bounces underneath our table. One of the young, muscled fellows quickly comes over, bends down at our feet and grabs it. "Excuse me, guys," says the highly energized young man, as he jumps up and returns to the game.

"That Jason" whispers Mike, "but we call him 'Mr. T.' He's a nice enough guy, but he never shuts up at group. And he's always after the young honeys."

Henry leans over and adds dryly, "any question about anything, and he knows the answer: women, drugs, recovery, rehab centers, you name it. He's been there and done that. He thinks he should be running the place."

"Why do you call him Mr. T.?" I ask quietly, glancing over my shoulder. "After all, he's not black."

"Because he's *loaded* with testosterone," says Mike. "He's got more than all of us put together—hence Mr. T. Just like most of the younger ones here, he's in for Heroin and other assorted drugs.

"Speaking of which, group starts in 10 minutes," Henry says, and he turns and starts shuffling toward the door.

"We'll see you there, Henry," Mike says, addressing Henry's retreating back. Henry doesn't acknowledge. "He's an odd bird," Mike says, shaking his head. "Oh well, here, help me clean this mess up, and we'll go have a quick smoke. Are you going to group? You don't have to on your first day, you know."

"No, I think I'll rest for a few hours," I say, rubbing my aching head. "Isn't there an AA meeting tonight?" I ask.

"Yeah, I go to NA in the other lounge. Those meetings are mandatory, but resting now is a good idea," Mike says. "You do look at little better, but that ain't saying much."

I look at Mike. "I just thank God I got you and Ebby for roommates. Somebody's watching over me. I actually think I might make it."

He smiles. "Yeah, we'll make it, Buddy Boy." But then he sighs again and makes a grumbling noise. He suddenly looks troubled, and blurts out, "that damn Xanax—Jesus! I just don't know if I'm capable of laying off of it. Look at me! I'm a nervous wreck just thinking about it. Why did you have to remind me of it?" He looks pissed. I open my mouth to reply, but he cuts me off. "Forget it! You'll find out right away in the AA meeting tonight that step number one, just admitting that you're licked by this disease—that your life is unmanageable— this is *so* important. But how do we live day to day without it? That's the question, but what's the answer?"

"I guess we're gonna find out," I say, without having the foggiest notion myself. "Right now, I'm just thankful to be alive."

Mike Cass smiles again, but then narrows his eyes. He points his finger at me menacingly. "Well, that could all end real fast if you don't do something about that snoring. You'll be fucking DEAD!" He screams the word "dead," al la De Niro again. "You're family—DEAD!"

We start gathering up the empty bo when I hear my name shouted from the do and see Ebby entering the lounge. He see "Phone call for you on the other side of th ...., Ebby points down the hall. "Thanks Ebby. See ya pal," I say to Mike, as I make my way unsteadily for the phone.

"Hello?"

"Eric? It's Scottie, how the hell are you doing, man?"

"Scottay, my savior, how the hell did you get this number?"

"They gave it me before I left yesterday. How are you?"

"Terrible, but I'm alive. They gave me Librium and it's already helping, but I'm shaking all over. I'll never be able to thank you enough for what you did yesterday."

"Never mind that shit, just get yourself clean. God, you were a complete mess yesterday. Do you remember?"

"Bits and pieces. I remember cursing out Carol before you took me to the Princeton ER. God, have you talked with her? I was *such* an asshole."

"Three times already this morning, and yes, you were. She's glad you're where you need to be, but I wouldn't advise calling her for a couple days. Eric, I really don't know if she's going to take you back. She's beyond pissed-off, that's for sure. Did you get the stuff I left for you?"

"Oh yeah, Scott, thank you so much for the smokes and the calling cards. I'll pay you back."

"Forget it. How's your head? Man, you fell hard. I saw the whole thing."

"I think it's my back more than my head, but I need to rest more than anything. I think I'll be okay."

"Eric, I gotta run, but please let me know if you need anything else. Do you have enough to wear and all?"

"Yeah, I somehow managed to pack a few shirts and a couple pairs of jeans, and my toilet shit. I'll let you know, but I think I'm good. Did I call anybody on the way up here? I can't remember."

"You called all your private students, I think. I'll be surprised if you have any of them left after they listen to your drunken messages. You were bad, man."

"Oh, my God."

"Eric, let me tell you something. I don't know if you'll ever get back home with Carol, but I know one thing, if you don't stop drinking, they'll be no chance at all. And what about work? These last few weeks, I can't believe how bad you've been. Shit, you drank all that brandy at your house yesterday before I took it away from you. Dude, you were completely out of it."

"I guess I wanted to out with a bang. I'm sorry for putting you in the middle of all this. I guess I had to sink this low, Scott, and now, like you told me, I have to get honest. Anyway, the doctor here says my liver was about to explode. She almost sent me back to the ER!"

"Jesus! How bad was it?"

"The numbers set some kind of record around here, I think, and that's saying something. They're like 15 times higher than normal. So, let's put it this way, if I don't quit drinking, I won't have to worry about Carol, the kids, work—anything, because I'll be dead. They're taking more blood tomorrow, so hopefully the numbers will start coming down. I could have permanent damage, we'll just have to wait and see."

"All right, man. You're definitely in the right place. Take care and get well."

"Scott, I mean it, thank you for everything. So, you don't think I should call Carol?"

"Not today. Let her cool down a bit. I'll tell her you're doing well as can be expected. Wait until tomorrow. Get some rest and take care."

"Bye."

I walk down the hall to my room, trying to absorb the conversation with Scottay. I've known Scott Muncy for years. Lately, he's been about as close a friend as I've had, and he's been an eyewitness to my swift decline. At least three times in the past two weeks he's tried to talk some sense into me, but I've just blown him off and isolated even more. I realize that my world and my relationships have been shrinking to the point where I find myself right now: all alone in a rehab center.

I'm almost to my room at the far-end of the long hallway, when Eva comes barreling out of a doorway on my right. She still looks like death: hair all askew, face ashen, and both her hands covering her mouth. I watch as she bounces off the side wall a few times, and then lurches for the bathroom door about 30 feet away. As soon as she disappears inside it, I hear her lose her breakfast. She didn't quite make it to the toilet. I find my room, walk inside and close the door.

I lie down on my bed and close my eyes. The words of Nurse Sharon and Doctor Shariff fill my head. I'm exactly where I need to be right now, and I need to get myself together. I need to get this shit out of my system and get sober. I'm alive, and I want to live, but now I want to live an honest life. For the first time in many years, I want to be honest with myself and to others. But how can I accomplish these monu-

mental tasks when all I've known for all these years is drinking, and then all the lies that inevitably follow? I need to pray.

I say a quick prayer of thanks, and then ask for help. I ask
God to forgive me, and to give me the strength I'll need to
carry on, whatever happens. I ask Him to show me the way to
somehow live without drinking. "Help me, Lord. Please help
me, Lord." A small sense of peace washes over me, and I drift
off to sleep.

Chapter Six

"...He enjoys drinking. It stirs his imagination. His friends feel closer over a highball. Perhaps you enjoy drinking with him yourself when he doesn't go too far. You have passed happy evenings together chatting and drinking together before your fire. Perhaps you both like parties which would be dull without liquor...Some, but not all of us, think it has its advantages when reasonably used."

— Page 110, *Alcoholics Anonymous*

For the first year of our marriage, Carol and I lived in an apartment in Plainsboro, New Jersey, just outside of Princeton; and we settled into a comfortable life together as newlyweds. Carol, after graduating from Williams in 1987 with a degree in Church Music, held down a position as manager of a book store in Princeton, and also played the organ and directed the choir on Sundays at a church in Morristown, in the northern part of the state. Within a few years, after we moved to our first home in Ewing, just outside of Trenton, she found a part-time position with wonderful benefits as an Assistant Librarian at Firestone Library on the campus of Princeton University. She now works full-time at Princeton, and presently leads the music program at another church in Ewing.

My working career has not veered noticeably for over 25 years. I started teaching piano at the Williams School of Music just after graduating in 1984, and have been on the Artist Faculty ever since. Also, I've held the same position as Music Director at a Catholic church in Elizabeth, New Jersey since the summer of 1985. I've also taught privately on Mondays and Tuesdays, going to people's homes, since our days in Plainsboro.

Just like so many others, I've always craved consistency and routine in my life, and my daily work regimen then and now exemplifies this. During the week, Carol would leave for her "real" job, first at the book-store and then at Princeton, and I would get to work around the house doing the daily chores of food shopping, laundry, simple cleaning tasks, etc. As usual, I enjoyed the quietude of being by myself, and after doing the chores, often practiced piano or composed music during the day. Ever since running across those pianistic monsters at the Manhattan School, I had come to terms with the fact that a performing career was out of the question, but that was okay. Until his death in 1995, I studied with my wonderful mentor, Harold Zabrack at Williams, and gave many solo recitals throughout the region. Within a few years, I also discovered my abilities as a composer were respectable too, and many rewarding concerts featuring my own works would soon be performed.

It was a simple American Dream, but it was ours. We worked hard, made decent money, and by 1989, with the help of our parents, we were able to purchase a small rancher in Ewing Township. By the time baby Katie arrived in May of 1991, we couldn't have been happier. Sure, there were the occasional marital spats, and we often complained that what we were doing was beneath us. As with most people, the money never seemed to go far enough, and we almost never agreed politically. But, I think we both felt that our lives were full, and now we were building a family together. On top of that, Carol and I were happy people and in love. Although our work schedules often kept us apart—she would often be arriving home from work when I'd be leaving—we worked it out and tried to spend as much quality time together as possible. We had much in common: music, sports, and we both loved to have a good time, whether by ourselves or with others out at dinner or a party. She gave me the space I needed, and I tried to be a good, loving husband. I just wanted to please my wife.

I couldn't get over the fact that she had given me another chance after the way I treated her with Nancy. She forgave me for the lies and deceit of the past, and I promised never to go there again. I was determined to be honest—at least in most areas—with her and myself about my feelings, and I was fortunate enough to get her back. I made Carol a promise to be faithful to her, and that is a promise I'm proud to say I kept.

But, faithfulness is not the same as honesty. The honesty part, unfortunately, proved to be a much tougher nut to crack. Indeed, from the beginning of our marriage, being honest with Carol and, more importantly, with myself, was not something I could come to grips with. When it came to the question of alcohol, and tempering its use, my answer could never be a definitive "no."

There were events that occurred within the first few years of our marriage that were troubling. There were drunken rages scattered among the many blissful days. There were brushes with the law from which I always seemed to escape from. These close calls would usually center on my near-pathological desire to drink and drive. More and more, as my obsession with alcohol slowly escalated over the years, I found myself escaping to my vehicle, and driving with plenty to drink. It started almost from the first day that I received my license, when I was cruising the lone thoroughfare on Long Beach Island with beer in hand; and it slowly progressed over the next 30 years to the absolute insanity that it became at the end.

Looking back, the first incident seemed innocent enough at the time, but it easily could have landed me my first DWI. It was Christmas Eve 1989, and I had just finished my evening service at my church in Elizabeth. After a few pops at a local gin mill in the working-man section of the Port where my church is located, I grabbed a six-pack and headed west to Morristown where I would catch some of Carol's midnight service.

I had pretty solid directions, but when I arrived in Morristown, I couldn't locate the entrance to the church parking lot. One thing that definitely strikes fear into the heart of any serious drinking driver is being in a place where you don't have good knowledge of the ground; and this certainly was the case here. Late at night, especially on a holiday, one wrong turn or mile over the limit will often lead to the terror of flashing lights in the rearview.

What got me into trouble on this occasion was turning into what I thought was the church's parking lot, but what turned out to be its front lawn. I immediately saw my error and began to back out onto the street when the lights came on. In what seemed 10 seconds, three Morristown cops were right on top of me. I quickly popped a stick of gum, made an attempt at stuffing the empties under the seat and stepped out of the car.

I could hear the music coming from the candlelit church mere yards away as the first flashlight-bearing officer approached. I told him truthfully that my wife was playing for the service, and that I simply made a wrong turn because I had never been there before. I was also truthful when he asked if I had been drinking, but not so truthful when he asked how much. He then shined the light into the car, and for some unbelievable reason didn't notice the empty cans sticking out from under the seat. Hell, they were obvious to me standing right next to him.

Having dodged that bullet, he had me recite the alphabet, touch my nose and walk a straight line—all of which I miraculously performed without a hitch. More than likely, a breathalyzer test would've condemned me, but the kind-hearted officer didn't see fit to give me one. He told me I might have to pay for any damage to the lawn, but other than that, simply wished me a Merry Christmas, and let my shaking and tattered psyche go.

The delay forced me to miss all but the end of Carol's service, and afterward I did tell her about the mishap, neglecting, of course, to mention anything about alcohol. She and other choir members related to me the magical nature all those flashing lights appearing through the stained glass just at the time of Christ's annual birth.

The next major alcohol-related incident occurred a few years later in the fall of 1992 after we had moved to our first home in Ewing. It surely would have caused much more dire consequences had I not summoned a least a bit of honesty afterward.

Sundays in the fall—indeed throughout most of the year—I liked to go to my main hangout in Princeton in the late afternoon and drink with the guys. I didn't work a ton of hours during the week, but it was seven days a week: six for teaching, and four church services on weekends. Sunday afternoon was basically my weekend, and Carol, even well after all three of our children were born, would gladly grant me these few precious hours to go out and cavort with my friends at the Ivy Inn.

This Sunday was no different than many before and after. I left the house in mid-afternoon, and made a bee-line for the liquor store. After all, I couldn't possibly be expected to make the 30-minute drive to and fro without a few "road-sodas." On this day I think I bought a half pint of Jack, and I mixed that with the ice-water in the quart-sized container that I brought from home. At the Ivy, I had more than a few Jack and waters with my buddies, and I left for home in fine feather at about six or seven.

To save a few minutes, I took the busy stretch of Nassau Street in downtown Princeton leading south. Just before or after one of the main intersections on that road, a car travelling directly in front of me, for no apparent reason, decided to make a sudden stop. My stop, unfortunately, wasn't quite so sudden, and it took the rear-end of that vehicle to actually bring mine a complete halt.

It wasn't a violent collision, but I certainly hit him hard enough for both of us to know it. I cursed the idiot as he pulled ahead of me slightly and then signaled me to pull over behind him. My drink, still at least a third full for the ride home, was still safely between my legs when I pulled to the curb. I put it on the floor then stepped out to survey the damage. I didn't notice any dents on either vehicle, but wanted to make sure he and the woman with him were okay before I made my move. I asked him if they were unhurt, and he responded that they were. I told him that I needed to get my insurance information in the car, and I returned to my vehicle.

My number one fear—and it was a real one—was that at any moment a Princeton cop would be coming along. The cops in that town are notorious for sniffing out boozehounds behind the wheel, and I could not afford to even risk an interaction with one after 8 or 10 stiff drinks—not to mention the big drink now sitting on the floor-boards. Even if one didn't just happen by on this busy Sunday evening in the busiest part of Princeton, I was pretty sure that this moron would call one in order to get a police report. I just couldn't risk it. I had to get my ass out of there.

The moment I climbed back into my car, I looked ahead and then to the right, and saw my escape: a narrow side street that I knew well. In an instant I shifted into drive and bolted. Just before I made the quick right onto Bank Street, I glanced in my rearview and saw the couple staring intently at the rear of my car. Within a block or two I threw my drink out the window, took some deep breaths and thought I began to sober up quickly.

Luckily, I made it out of Princeton unscathed, but when I rolled into my driveway in Ewing I had the distinct feeling that

I hadn't heard the last of the incident. Selfishly, I needed to tell Carol about it. I may have been identified, and it would not go over well at all if she found out about it from the police. I walked through the door as Carol was preparing dinner. Baby Katie, just one-year-old, was joyously bouncing about in her jump-seat when I spilled the beans.

I told Carol that I had made a big mistake leaving the scene, and that I had simply panicked—both of which were the truth. When she asked me how many drinks I had had at the Ivy, I was less than honest when I replied "three or four." She shook her head, told me it was a serious wake-up call, and hopefully I had learned a lesson. "You just can't go out and drink that much, then drive" she told me emphatically. "It's just stupid!" She was right. I nodded with contrition, and told her I would try to do better. That's when the phone rang.

It was the Princeton police. They had received a call about a hit and run, and had a partial tag number. He recited the license plate number, and it was close indeed—one letter off. He asked if that tag number matched ours. "That's not our license number," I answered truthfully, not telling him how very close the couple had come to a match. He then asked me if Carol Houghton had been in Princeton that day. Luckily, again, I didn't have to lie here. The car was registered in Carol's name, and that's why they asked the question. I told the man that she had been here in Ewing the entire day. He said that they would be investigating further, and that they might be calling back. I was puzzled that the couple didn't tell the police that it was a man who was involved, not a woman, but I would have been a complete fool to broach that subject. I hung up and breathed a huge sigh of relief. We never heard another word.

Boozehound!

It was indeed a wake-up call, and I had learned a few valuable lessons. Although in the short run I was more careful about drinking to excess when out and about, that eventually picked up steam again, so nothing was really learned there. I did discover that self-serving honesty can be quite helpful. I was buoyed with the knowledge that honesty, especially when trying to cover my ass, can be a sound policy. But, what I really took from the incident was that I needed to redouble my focus and concentration when driving and drinking. I also discovered the importance of never again taking Nassau Street when leaving the Ivy. These last two commitments served me well, and I adhered successfully to both for many years.

After this particular event, and more so, the gradually increasing number of nasty temper flare-ups that started to occur, Carol would sit me down and discuss my ever-increasing intake of alcohol. I would always nod, and say "yes." I agreed that I had been at fault at the time, and I was truly sorry for what I said and how I acted. I said "yes, I would cut down," and "yes, it would be better." And there would be long periods of relative peace and harmony.

We both, especially in the early years of marriage, loved to go out and have a good time with ourselves and friends. She usually drank moderately, but occasionally overindulged herself, and once in a while found herself praying to the "porcelain god" or spending the night with her head between her knees. It was no big deal. When I would blow up for some ridiculous, alcohol-induced reason, I would later apologize, and we would move on. We didn't have a perfect marriage, but we loved one another, and she was very patient with me.

But because I loved to drink so much, inevitably, deep inside of me, many times without me even realizing it, the honest answer to Carol's concerns over my drinking always turned out to be a resounding "no." And, as typically occurs, over the course of time, one lie or dishonest action would invariably compound into many more.

I never thought about it in such a way at the time, but my ordered and regimented life had gradually evolved into three distinct areas. Each area was well-defined, and rarely did one interfere or threaten another—at least at the beginning. These were, and are, the three "compartments" of my life, and many people, I'm certain, have their lives arranged similarly.

The first compartment would be family life. Back then it was Carol, eventually our three children, and of course our parents and brothers and sisters. The family was always first and foremost. The second area was work, and all the things that go into the process of providing for my family, keeping the home in order, paying bills, etc. Lastly, leisure time, friends, sporting events and personal time is what made up the final third compartment of my life.

I believed in God, and he was always out there for me, overseeing from afar the entire production. It was in the third and final compartment of my life that alcohol started to take control, and would eventually run riot over the other two, while God stood by—allowing me to run my show.

Chapter Seven

From an actual AA meeting...

Leader: "Yes, Harry!"

Member: "Harry, alcoholic!"

Group: "Hi Harry!"

Harry: "Toward the end of my drinking, my entire world began to shrink. At the very end, it seemed it was just me in the bar, and my drink. But even then, when the place was crowded and everyone was whooping it up on a Friday, I found that I was all alone. I was completely isolated and lonely. My drinking buddies didn't drink like me. Nobody drank like me. It became a non-stop, around-the-clock binge.

"When I finally surrendered, confronted my disease, got help and made it into these rooms, I discovered something amazing: I found a bunch of people who took the loneliness and isolation away. I found God—a Group Of Drunks. I finally found a bunch of people who drank just like I drank. And the miracle was this: we were all living sober. That's all I got."

Group: "Thanks for sharing, Harry."

My first bewildering day at Carrier Clinic proceeds in due course. I wake up after a nearly three-hour nap on my stiff, plastic-coated mattress drenched with sweat from the effects of withdrawal, but soon discover that I'm actually feeling a bit better. My first thought upon opening my eyes is the same, insane one I've had for months: Where can I get a drink? That ridiculous notion instantly vanishes when I realize where I am, and why I'm here. I grimly recall my recent discussion with Dr. Shariff, and I sit up and take note of my surroundings.

The room is set up just like a dorm, with my bed lying against the far wall, and Mike's against the opposite wall arranged the same way, abutting the lone window. There are two dressers and small desks at the foot of each of our beds, and Ebby's bed lies perpendicular to ours, just to the right of the door as you enter. Ebby is sitting up writing when I look at my watch. It reads 11:45.

He smiles and tells me again that I sounded like a wounded buffalo, and that it might be a good idea to get a nasal strip from the evening nurse later. "I know Mike and I snore just as bad," he tells me. "Mike's harmless enough, but don't give him a reason to go postal. He's nutty enough as it is."

I nod in agreement, and wipe my face dry with a washcloth sitting on the small, bedside table. "I've used those strips at home in the past," I tell him. "They definitely help, but Carol still booted me out of bed many times because of all the racket I make. I don't know what makes the snoring worse, the booze, the weight gain or the coke."

"All three I think," he replies.

"How are you feeling?" he asks me. "You still don't look too good, but did the sleep help at all?"

"I think I'll make it," I say, standing up. "It's probably the best rest I've had in three days."

"You'll get plenty of that, don't worry. You'll be much better tomorrow. Take another nap later," he tells me, knowingly. I plan on it.

I ask Ebby what he's doing, and he tells me that he's working on a fourth step inventory list that he will be presenting to the group in a few days. He explains to me what a fourth step is, as I haven't a clue. A couple years back I went to a bunch of AA meetings, when, after being caught in yet another lie, I had promised Carol to quit the drink once and for all. I was only pretending, though, and usually drank before and after each meeting. I then proceeded to diabolically re-double my efforts at deceit and dishonesty, all the while sporadically attending meetings. I obviously took little away from my first go-round with the program, and Ebby gives me a quick overview of the all-important fourth step.

"I'm writing down a thorough list of all my resentments, fears, sex-issues—basically a complete inventory of my life. The biggest problem is me, of course. They tell me it has to be complete and fearless. In the 'Big Book,' that's this one here"— he holds up his copy of *Alcoholics Anonymous* "—it talks about resentment being the number one offender. It's about getting to the heart of why we drink.

"Steps four and five go together," he continues. "Step five is simply admitting these things to another person. I'm not looking forward to that, I can tell you, especially in front of you knuckleheads. It has to be done, though. They say it can be a freeing experience, and is vital for staying sober. I *have* to do it. I *have* to do something and get off this never-ending merry-go-round." He emphasizes the word "have," and stares down at his notebook.

Vitals are taken again at noon, and my blood-pressure is still sky-high. I again present the sheet with my readings to Nurse Sharon, and she dismisses me without any further medication. Most everyone is heading over to the cafeteria for lunch, and I go outside for a smoke, then go in and eat a sandwich in the lounge. After about half an hour, Ebby, Mike Cass, and many of the other 30 "inmates" return from lunch. As promised, Ebby gives me a tour of Blake Hall. Having been here for two weeks already, he's able to explain to me all the little ins and outs that will help me during my stay.

We start in the lounge, and he explains how to order my meals for these first two days of "captivity." Nurse Sharon has informed me again that I'm not to leave Blake, except to smoke out back in the designated area, or to walk around the spacious grounds surrounding the hall. Ebby tells me I need to check off items on a meals list he shows me. "Check off what you want for dinner tonight, and put it in this box." He points to a box on the wall above the microwave. I take a minute and do so. "Then, after dinner tonight do the same thing for tomorrow's breakfast and lunch. You got it?"

"I got it."

We walk out into the hall. He shows me the two phones, and explains the procedure of signing up for five-minute blocks in the evening when everybody wants to use them. "Have you tried your mom yet?" he asks me. "It's her birthday, right?"

"Oh, God, you're right," I say, startled. "No, I need to do that."

"Well, make sure you do it when group's not in session," he tells me. "The nurses turn them off during group time. You also can't go outside for any reason during group time, so if you want to smoke or walk, it has to be during breaks like now."

"I got it."

We then walk past the nurse's station, and he points out the two big bins standing in the hallway leading to the rooms. "This first one has clean towels. Grab two or three when going in there for a shower." He points to the bathroom door next to us. "Then, when you're done, throw them in the other bin, okay?"

"I think I can handle that," I say.

A tall, dark, well-dressed man of about 50 shuffles up to us. His eyes are fixed like Henry's, I realize, as he sticks out his hand.

"I'm Stanley," he says to me in a low monotone. His lips barely move when he speaks, and I notice he's trembling all over as I take his hand. His tremors, I see, are more of a slow-motion, exaggerated variety, unlike my speedier gyrations.

"Eric. Nice to meet you," I say. I remember this is the guy who was helping Eva in the vitals line earlier.

He looks at Ebby. "Did you hear they took Eva out on an ambulance while we were in group, Ebby?"

Ebby nods. "Yeah, I was there. Everybody saw it. I hope she's alright."

"It has to be dehydration," Stanley says flatly. "She just keeps throwing up. It's unbelievable. She'll be back soon, I hope." He starts to shuffle away. "See you in group. Nice to meet you, Eric."

"You, too," I say.

After Stanley disappears into the group lounge across from the nurse's station, Ebby leans over. "Stanley's got MS really bad. He's on about eight different meds."

"He's in here for MS?" I ask, confused.

"No, he's here for smoking crack day and night. He found *that* medication helped his MS symptoms—to a point."

"Until the crack got the best of him?" I ask.

"You got it," Ebby replies. "And now he's trying to shake that, while also trying to get his MS meds straightened out. They got every variety of fuck-up in here, I'll tell you."

Next, Ebby takes me into the bathroom. "This is important," he tells me. "Always wear something on your feet when you go in here. Don't come in here barefoot. You'll get Athlete's Foot faster than anything if you do." He looks at me. "I've heard of one guy who actually died from it."

"You gotta be kidding me," I respond incredulously. "From Athlete's Foot? How can that happen?"

"I don't know how it happened," he tells me, "but it was a real shame. That was one fun guy."

"Now I've heard everything," I say, still shocked.

He looks at me and smiles. "He was a real Fun Guy. Get it—*Fun Guy*?"

I burst out laughing. "My nine-year-old will like that one." I walk over to the urinal, and he follows me and stands at the second.

"Oh, you'll love this," he tells me, a huge smile now on his handsome face.

"What?" I say, still giggling from the cheap humor.

We finish peeing and flush. "Stand back," he commands me, "and wait." I do as he tells me. He starts counting off. "One, two, three…" Suddenly, from inside the wall behind the urinals comes a deep, loud, metallic belch that lasts about two seconds. It sounds ominous indeed.

"What the hell is that?" I say with wonder.

"I have no idea," Ebby says, "but the Carrier plumbers have been by three times since I've been here, and it's still making that noise. I think it's gonna blow one of these days."

I laugh again. "I can see the headlines now: *'Two Drunks Drown in Carrier Bathroom Mishap.'*" We both laugh.

Ebby explains a few other important things to me as we walk back to the main lounge. "Get a Styrofoam egg-crate for your mattress from either Carley or someone else. That will help. Those mattresses are the worst," he tells me. I can agree with that assessment.

"The washer and dryer are over there, near the Doctor's office." He points to a door. "Just make sure you change the lint filter after drying, or else Maxine will bite your head off."

"Who's that?" I ask. We're now in the lounge, and many people are talking and milling about.

"She's that skinny, black lady over there with her friend, Kara Alcoholic." I look where Ebby is pointing and see two women, one black and one white, sitting at a table next to the far windows.

"Kara Alcoholic?" I ask, puzzled. "Please don't tell me 'Alcoholic' is her real name."

He chuckles. "No, it's not, but Mike calls her that. You'll know why after you've been around her for a while. Maxine's in charge of the laundry room, and she's tough. Everyone has little jobs around here," he tells me. "You'll have one soon enough, I'm sure." Ebby glances down at his watch. "Well, that's about it. Any questions?" he asks me. I tell him I can't think of any, but I'm sure I will soon.

"I've got to go talk to someone," he tells me. "What are you going to do now?" he asks me. "You're basically free until tonight's AA meeting at 8."

"I've gotta take a shower." I tell him. "I've still got yester-day's filth on me."

"Good idea. See you later."

Just before 8 that evening, I get my vitals checked for the fourth time today, and bring my sheet over to the nurse's station. Stanley is the only person in front of me at the counter. He's about two inches taller than me—about 6-3—and is holding a cup halfway-full with pills. A large, round-faced woman inside the station is explaining each one to Stanley. After a few minutes, he downs the contents and slowly steps aside. I move toward the woman and hand her my sheet. This person is obviously the night nurse. She's well-dressed, powerfully perfumed and adorned with a wide variety of gaudy jewelry: hooped earrings; glittering, emerald-studded necklace; half-a-dozen rings—all with large, replica stones, I assume.

"Eric, how are you, dear?" She asks me kindly, studying my sheet. I read her name-tag.

"I'm a little better, Donna."

"How's your head and neck from the fall yesterday?"

"I have some neck pain, but not too bad," I offer. "That Librium helped my shaking, I can tell you, but it's wearing off. You can put me down for a 7 on the agitated box."

"Hold out your hands, dear," she commands me gently. "Yes, I'd call that a 7. Don't worry; I'll give you another one of those. Have you had any nausea, hallucinations, headache, anything like that?"

"No, nothing like that. Just tired and shaky," I say.

"We need to up your dosage of Lisinopril," Nurse Donna tells me. "Your blood pressure is still way too high. You'll see the doctor about that. Did you get some rest today?"

"Yes, some. I didn't do much of anything."

"Good. You should take a sleeping pill later. Come see me before bed," she tells me. "I'll go get you your Librium." She suddenly looks up over my shoulder, and her demeanor instantly turns sour. "Not you again; what do you want this time, King?" Her tone is now rough and sarcastic.

I glance back and see Mike Cass standing just behind me. He's wearing a pained expression. I smile as I notice that his hair hasn't changed a lick in over 12 hours. It's still pinned to exact spot.

"Jesus, I can't breathe!" he gasps. Then, with an exaggerated snort, he pleads, "Can't you give me just a little more nose spray?"

"You just had some!" Donna yells at him. "I told you, no more tonight! Don't look at me like that. Please, just go to your meeting."

"Ah, come on!" he cries. "First, I can't see, now I can't breathe? I told you that spray bottle you gave me was defective. Please, Donna, just a couple more shots?"

Donna doesn't reply, but simply gives him a "get-lost" gesture. She then turns and heads back to rear of the office where the drugs are kept out of sight.

Mike leans over and whispers in my ear. "That bitch is on the list."

I continue smiling, trying to consider all the people, myself included, who must be a part of Mike's ever-expanding "hit list."

"Tomorrow, we'll get her," Mike continues quietly, glancing about for eavesdroppers. "I have a plan, Buddy Boy. You stick with me."

"I don't have anything else to do," I say, turning to see Nurse Donna returning. He pats me on the back, shoots Donna a strange look, then turns and walks toward the group lounge where the nightly NA meeting is about to begin.

"What a character," Nurse Donna says to me, handing me my anxiety relief, then shaking her head, "and a big pain-in-the-ass!"

"He's exactly what I need in here, I think."

Donna frowns. "Take this and get to your meeting," she orders me.

I do as commanded.

I walk into the main lounge room, known simply as Darcy. I learned earlier from Ebby that Joe Darcy was a patient at Carrier a few years back, and had died from alcoholism. In his will he left a small amount of money earmarked for Blake. Aside from a few upgrades in the Darcy Room itself, Joe's small bequeathing allowed for a small, stone-enclosed garden out back near the smoking area.

About 20 chairs are now arranged in a straight line at the far end of Darcy, past the ping-pong table. There's a lone man sitting in one of the few chairs sitting opposite the straight line, against the wall. I take a seat next to Ebby, and we're joined by about a dozen others from the floor. I see Henry sitting about six chairs down on our right, staring blankly down at his open, black and white composition book. Bobby, directly to his right, is madly sketching something in his well-used notebook. I make a mental note to get myself one of those pads. I need to start writing some of this stuff down.

I see Maxine and a few other women talking on our left. The lady whom Ebby pointed out to me earlier as Kara Alcoholic walks up and introduces herself.

"You must be the new guy on the block. I'm Kara, alcoholic," she says, smiling.

I stand and offer my hand. "Eric Houghton," I reply, then add hesitantly, "I guess I'm an alcoholic, too."

"Well," Kara says without missing a beat, "I suppose we wouldn't be here if we didn't have a problem, right? I just keep repeating it out loud all the time, and maybe, just maybe—this being my third visit here—it might sink into my thick skull that I *am* an alcoholic, and once and for all, get off my ass and finally *do* something about it. You know what I mean?"

She said the words so fast, I didn't have time to absorb them all, but I nod vigorously anyway. Kara, about 50, is big-haired, heavily made-up and has thick-rimmed, designer glasses. As with most of us, she appears quite weathered as a result of her way of life. Before she can offer another rapid-fire word-burst, the guy sitting in front of us starts talking and Kara smiles at me again and takes her seat.

"This is a meeting of Alcoholics Anonymous," the man announces solemnly. "My name is Frank, and I am an alcoholic."

"Hi Frank," the group responds lethargically. Frank is an intensely serious looking fellow of about 55. He's very lean, and sports a thick, salt-and-pepper mustache. I notice he's wearing a navy-blue PAL tee-shirt, and a matching baseball cap.

"It's the tradition of most AA meetings to begin with the Serenity Prayer, so please join me." I have but a vague recollection of the simple prayer, and as the recitation proceeds, the words seem to slip off my tongue without registering in my brain.

At its conclusion, Frank looks up and eyes each of us slowly. He says nothing at first, but glares dolefully down the line, one person at a time. "I hope you're in pain," he finally states, with sincerity, and then he looks us all over some more. "I hope you feel as bad as I did when I sat in one of those chairs a little over five years ago. That's right, I was sitting exactly where you are, and I was in pain. My wife had left me, my life's work as a police officer was coming to an end, because they were putting me on permanent disability. My entire life was spinning out of control. I was losing everything because of this disease. The only thing left to lose was life itself. But that was coming soon. My entire world was reduced to finding the next drink. Everything important in my life was either going or already gone, and, you know what, all I wanted to do was find the next drink. I was sick and in pain—lots of it. Sound familiar?"

A few of us nod. I completely identify with what Frank is saying. He spends the next 40 minutes giving riveting personal testimony of the ravages of this disease. He tells us how he nearly killed people while he was drunk on the job, behind the wheel of his speeding cruiser; and what a miracle it was that the police department allowed him to leave the force on a disability rather than being fired out-right. I identify even closer when he tells us in detail the pain of having to leave his wife of 30 years, after all the lies and deceit finally caught up with him. He tells us of all the broken promises to his wife, to his family and to everyone else. He explains that he made countless good-faith efforts to stop drinking. But, he found, as almost all recovering alcoholics eventually do, that he was completely powerless over the disease, and that he had to get honest and to ask for help. He finally came to believe, in his darkest hour, that the program of Alcoholics Anonymous was the only thing that could help. It was his last refuge. He ends his talk with an incredible anecdote.

"This place is called the Darcy Room," he says, looking around. His grim expression still fixed in place. "Joe Darcy was here when I was here." Frank now looks straight ahead. I can see his eyes moistening. "Joe Darcy was a great guy. We were friends, and we had a lot of laughs here. But, Joe Darcy was in a lot of pain—and he couldn't deal with it." His tears are flowing now. I find it difficult to look at him. "He couldn't face life without the booze, and Joe Darcy froze to death in an abandoned vehicle in New Brunswick. They found an empty bottle of cheap bourbon on the passenger seat next to him. That was his only companion at the end. That's what his life had become, and there it ended." A few soft moans and quiet gasps are heard, as Frank pauses to wipe his eyes.

Again, he looks slowly down the row of current unfortunates. "I hope you're in a lot of pain," he tells us again. "But, more importantly, I hope you remember the pain when you're feeling better, and deal with it positively. Joe didn't do that. Most of you will leave here and get well—at least for a time. But, some of you will think that you're cured, and that you can return to the life you had, and all will be well. Don't fall into this trap. Joe Darcy did. Alcoholism is a fatal, progressive disease. This will be told to you a hundred times in here over the course of your stay. And, believe me, *this* is the *truth*! Remember the pain that brought you here!"

He lets these words settle in for a few, powerful seconds before he begins again. His tone now is softer—almost kind.

"You never have to feel this way again, you know. Get out of here, and go to a meeting. Find yourself a sponsor, and make 90 meetings in 90 days. Start working this simple program, find your higher power, and then you'll be able to live again—really live! I didn't think I could live without booze, but, amazingly, I found it better than I could have possibly imagined. You can, too, and you'll be amazed before you're halfway through. Thank you."

The dozen of us erupt in loud applause. Frank still doesn't even come close to cracking a smile. He looks at his watch. "We still have about ten minutes, if anyone has any questions," he says.

Kara's hand shoots up, and she begins even before he has time to call on her. "Kara, alcoholic," she says, and then continues breathlessly, even while others are saying "Hi, Kara."

"I'm practicing. I have to keep reminding myself that I am an alcoholic. Thank you so much for that inspirational message. I just want to say a few things. My husband basically made me come to Carrier, but he was right. I definitely was drinking too much, and it became a daily, almost hourly trip to the liquor cabinet. I even stopped walking my four dogs, and they'd keep looking at me with this weird expression. It's kind of hard to explain. They were just, kind of like, bewildered that I was just sitting there drinking. The Jack Russell—Joey is his name—he knew more than any of the others that something was wrong. Every time I'd make a drink, he'd bark and bark, kind of crazy-like. I don't know why he acted this way, but it had to be …"

I glance over at Henry. He's sporting the most pained and confused look on his pudgy face. He's just staring at Kara with his mouth agape, and his eyes seem to be asking, *What the hell is that crazy lady going on about?*

I'm trying desperately to stifle a laugh, when Bobby sighs heavily and buries his head in his hands. I feel Ebby leaning in close to me.

"See what I mean? That's Kara *Alcoholic*," he whispers. I laugh out loud, but Kara just keeps rambling.

"…I definitely want to stop drinking. This is my third time here. Third time! I have to start going to more meetings. It seems like it is the only real way to stop, and I can see that it really helped you. Thank you."

Frank manages a brief smile and joins a few of the others in a desultory "thanks for sharing."

"Time for one more," Frank states, and calls on a large, bald fellow seated on this side of Henry. "Yes!"

"Hi, my name is Sal."

"Hi, Sal," we respond.

Ebby leans over and quickly whispers, "This guy doesn't think he has a problem—total denial."

"Yeah, thanks for sharing," says Sal, rather bored-like. "I have a problem with this 90 in 90 business. I work for a living, and I'm extremely busy. How can I possibly be expected to traipse all over the place finding meetings day and night?"

"You're in trouble," says Henry to Sal, loud enough for all to hear. Henry's eyes are wide and he's now wearing an evil grin. I laugh again, and Sal looks puzzled.

Frank is not amused. "Listen," he says loudly, pointing his finger at Sal. "Did you have time to drink every day?"

Sal shrinks in his chair a bit, and shrugs. "Yeah, I guess so."

"Yeah, and it was probably for a hell-of-a-lot longer than an hour, too, right?"

Sal nods his head.

"So, if you had time to drink, you have time to get your sorry ass to a meeting. It might save your life."

Sal shows a small smirk and lowers his head. He's gonna be a hard case.

We all join in *The Lord's Prayer* at the end of the meeting, and afterward, I walk up to Frank and shake his hand. "Thank you so much for that message," I say, and mean it. "I could relate with *so* much of what you said. This is my first day here, and I need some serious help."

"Well," responds Frank, "You're in the right place. Get yourself clean—you look like you've been through the ringer—and get out, and get to a meeting—lots of 'em. Remember, you never have to feel this way again."

At about 11:45 that night, I get my vitals taken for the last time, get my sleeping pill and nose-strip from Nurse Donna and head for my room. I smile and realize that this will be my first sober night sleep in years. I pass Henry on the phone and wave as I go by. He doesn't acknowledge, but seems to stare right through me. It must be his wife on the line, and I can tell the conversation is not going well. "I told you not to do that," I hear him say forcefully, but in a restrained voice. "Why did you *do* that? Jesus Christ, I asked you over and over *not* to fucking *do* that." The further I get from Henry, the louder his voice gets. By the time I get to my room, he's almost screaming.

I get to my room, and proceed to my bed after closing the door. I move the new notebook from the bed to the table next to it. I've already made some notes in what will become my journal. I stretch out on my bed and pull up the covers. Ebby is already under his, but Mike Cass is not. Within ten minutes, he's been back and forth from the room to the nurse's station and bathroom a half-a-dozen times at least. I've never seen anyone so disorganized about going to bed.

"Isn't he here yet?" Ebby asks sleepily.

"Nope," I say, trying to pump up my three pathetic pillows. "This time, he was in the bathroom trying to get the correct temperature for his bridge to soak. How did he lose his front teeth, anyway?"

"Don't ask him about it now, *please*, but I think it has something to do with water balloons."

I laugh out loud. "I'll ask him tomorrow."

"Open the pod-bay doors, HAL!" says Dave, I mean Mike Cass, in a deep, mechanical voice.

"I'm sorry, Dave," I say calmly, trying to replicate HAL's performance in the Kubrick classic. "I can't do that."

The door opens and Mike turns on the light. Ebby and I both moan, and Mike laughs hysterically.

"Are you *finally* going to bed?" Ebby asks him. "Enough is enough."

"Stop busting my balls," Mike snaps, but not unkindly. Mike seems completely incapable of being anything other than happy-go-lucky. "It's a complicated process. Look at me! I'm still a nervous, fucking wreck because of the Xanax. I'm walking into walls, for Christ's sake! My eye's killing me, I can't breathe and my teeth need to be soaked. And, that bitch, Donna won't give me a decent snort of that nose-shit. *Plus*, she keeps *screaming* at me about going to the bathroom in my wife beater. 'Put on a sleeved shirt! Put on a sleeved shirt!' SHE'S DEAD!"

The laughter surely must be heard in our neighboring rooms.

"By the way, are you all set for tomorrow, Buddy Boy?" he asks me.

"Yes, yes," I say, still laughing. "You told me three times."

"Good!" says Mike. "We'll get her! And that other bitch, Sharon. Oh, yes. I have bigger plans, too. We need to take over that entire, fucking nurse's station. We'll get to that stash in the back, and then—party time!"

I get a vision of the wild scene in *Cuckoo's Nest,* when the inmates take over, and laugh so hard that I have to wipe away tears.

Eventually, we calm down, and Mike finally crawls into bed. Ebby asks me if I was able to get a hold of my mom. "No," I reply. "Three times I called, and no answer. I left a message. She's knows where I am."

"How about your wife?" Mike asks. "I know she wanted you to call and tell her a bed-time story."

"Very funny," I say. "I'm calling home in the morning. We'll see how it goes."

"I think you're out, Tom!" says Mike with a yawn.

I think about what he just said. The harsh reality is that I may well be out. I hope and pray that I can get back into my home, but I also know that I have another blood test tomorrow, and if my liver doesn't improve, I could be out for good. I again offer up a silent prayer.

Mike and I talk for a while. Ebby's breathing becomes more regular as he slips away. The conversation settles in on our mutual love of movies, certain characters, and, of course, memorable lines. As our yawns become more frequent, Mike offers up a *Dirty Harry* quote or two, and I respond in kind.

This continues until Mike finally drifts off. My mind, however, continues to race.

I keep coming back to the haunted main character in Clint Eastwood's *The Outlaw, José Wales.* As my incredible first day of sobriety comes to a close, a line keeps replaying in my head:"Dyin' ain't much of a livin,' boy!"

My old life has to be over. It *has* to be.

Chapter Eight

"Your husband may be only a heavy drinker. His drinking may be constant or it may be heavy only on certain occasions. Perhaps he spends too much money for liquor. It may be slowing him up mentally or physically, but he does not see it. Sometimes he is a source of embarrassment to you and his friends. He is positive he can handle his liquor, that it does him no harm. He would probably be insulted if he were called an alcoholic. This world is full of people like him. Some will moderate or stop altogether, and some will not. Of those who keep on, a good number will become true alcoholics after a while."
—Page 109, Alcoholics Anonymous

I take a tremendous amount of pride in my children. All three: Kathryn, Matthew, and Natalie, are quite simply the light of my life. Happily, because of our unorthodox work schedule—Carol, for years was a part-time librarian at Princeton, and I was a late afternoon and evening piano teacher—

our children never had to be shuttled away to daycare. It was, or so we thought, an ideal parental situation.

Every work-day, until Carol arrived home around two, I was there for them. For the first few years of all their lives, I was there for the daily meals, diaper-changing and doctor visits. I took them shopping, played games with them and drove them back and forth to pre-k music classes and pre-school. When I had to travel to Elizabeth to play funerals at my church, the babies came along. They were a top priority in my compartmentalized world, and I did everything I possibly could to proudly earn the title of "part-time stay-at-home-dad."

Carol, of course, took on much of the heavy lifting with the wild, exasperating, evening hours, but I came in handy once in a while around bed-time, too. In total, I can't look back at those years and feel anything other than a deeply fulfilling sense of accomplishment. It was a job well-done.

With each one in their turn, I worked out a daily routine. In the mornings, there was usually a long walk, or, later on with Matt and Natalie, a bike-ride. First with Katie, and then with baby Matt, I loved to go for long walks with them around our old, closely-packed residential neighborhood. When we moved to our present, more rural location in 1997, I met a new friend while pushing two-year-old Matt up a steep in-cline.

One fine day, Tom Patterson, a retired and disheveled-looking Ewing High School teacher, was biking in the hilly, more upscale Ewing neighborhood where he resided. He stopped and immediately asked little Matthew if his daddy had a bicycle. Frowning, Matt-Matt shook his head, as did I. Soon, with the gauntlet thrown down, I procured the necessary equipment, and we joined Tom for almost daily, grueling workouts on the hills. In addition, for the next seven years, I often joined my new, older friend and his wife, Cindy during the evenings after work. Usually at their home, or sometimes out, Tom and I would share stories, problems, concerns and lots of laughs. We also shared hundreds, if not thousands of cocktails.

Tom Patterson, as I would soon discover, was an intriguing figure. 60 in 1997, Mr. P., as he was fondly known by legions of former students and athletes alike, was chronically overweight, sported a weathered, puppy-dog face and a wild shock of graying hair. Obsessively frugal, Tom rarely had his unruly mane cut at all, and when he did, it was invariably done by a non-professional—himself or Cindy. This was painfully obvious to anyone.

Tom's calming demeanor and incredibly varied interests attracted me instantly. He was an avid Red Sox fan, and had grown up idolizing Ted Williams. He loved to read philosophy, and was actually in the process of writing a pseudo-existential tome himself, eventually self-published as "The God I Know." He was politically savvy, and, although we rarely agreed on anything in that area, the debate and full exchange of ideas always was a great pleasure. His opinions were honest and simple, composed and measured, and his life's experiences were vast and offered freely. I was happy to listen, and fortunate to accept much of what he had to offer.

Tom Patterson was fanatical about physical exercise, and methodically tracked the number of hills he rode every day. His home lay at the bottom of one of the four "Patterson Hills," as I called them, and he made it an absolute necessity to make 125 loops—or 500 total hills—each and every month. If he fell short of his monthly goal for any reason at all, the next month he would have to make amends and catch up.

Every day spent with Tom was a new and unique one. However, I believe the principle reason I liked to hang around Mr. P. so much was the astounding organization and clock-like precision his drinking took on. He never imbibed before a set hour, which would vary depending on the day, and on whatever he and Cindy had planned. At a certain ordained point, however, he would commence drinking. It might be beer or wine, and eventually it became vodka; but, whatever the drink of choice, he drank it like a parched sailor—*and* for a prolonged period. Then, at some indeterminate point, he would simply stop. That was that.

It was amazing to me that even after over 40 years of daily over-imbibing, he had this drinking business completely under control. He was a model of consistency, and it seemed he had the unique ability to exert his will over the amount of his drinking. He rarely got sloppy, and never—unlike myself—got nasty and behaved like an idiot. I wanted to be just like him, and tried desperately to find that elusive middle-ground every boozehound longs for, but seldom attains: enough but not too much. Indeed, for a time he did help me sustain a level of stability with my drinking.

Largely because of drink, we both had the same problem with our weight. Because of Tom's inclination to consume a minimum of 12-15 adult beverages per day, he was constantly fighting an uphill climb in this regard. The hour or two of intense physical exercise required to bike 20-plus hills per day certainly helped, but was never enough. He knew that exercise alone couldn't stem the tide, and so he endeavored to try a multitude of weight-loss methods to reduce his robust, 240-pound frame to his self-proclaimed fighting weight of 190. Since every variety of diet Tom considered had to include alcoholic calories, the task was daunting indeed. He finally settled on a "modified Atkins" method, banning all pasta, potatoes, bread, junk food or candy. He was making glacially-slow progress with this method when I started riding the hills with him.

I certainly identified with his "battle of the bulge," as I had been trying for years to reduce the onslaught of my own weight-gain with a daily exercise regimen. I was also taking in too many booze calories, though, and my regular diet, although well-balanced, was far from perfect. I always tended to overeat and wasn't averse to the late-night, alcohol-induced pig-outs, as well. Hence, over the years, my 6-1 frame was similarly gathering more and more bulk. After only a few weeks of riding hills with Tom, however, the increase abruptly stopped at approximately 225. And then, when I finally followed Tom's advice and started laying off the carbs—booze exempted, of course—I really started to see results. By mid-1998, I was tipping the scales at a mean and lean 205, and because of the unforgiving hills, was probably in the best shape of my life.

And so it was, that for a few years, with the help of my sage-like drinking buddy and mentor, I was able to acquire a bit more control in a couple important areas of my life. In addition, work and life at home continued to move along in their ordered, properly structured compartments. I had two beautiful children, and, Carol and I were actively considering a third. In that regard, Tom had actually helped to advance my part of the decision-making by suggesting that I consider filling up the now-empty child seat on the bike. Eventually it worked, and after much thoughtful and somewhat agonizing deliberation between Carol and me—and a little over six years after the birth of our only son—Natalie Ruth arrived on October 4th, 2000 and blessed the Houghton household further.

Since my mornings with Katie and Matt were at an end, now it was time for me to enjoy that same quality time with Natalie. So, once again, after Carol returned to work, I revisited my role as "Mr. Mom," and all seemed well in the world. Despite the stabilizing impact Mr. P. had on my life, however, there were some 80-proof storm clouds looming on the horizon.

Years earlier, around the time of Katie's arrival in May of 1991, I became aware of the physical problems that can occur as a result of excess drinking. The first symptom, acute but frightening, could be dealt with fairly easily. But the second, following a doctor's visit and a subsequent blood test, would prove to be the classic, chronic nemesis that afflicts many heavy drinkers. The weight-gain problem, arrested for a few years around the turn of the century, would eventually return with a vengeance. But, it would be behavioral problems at home, directly and incontrovertibly linked to alcohol that would turn out to be the deciding factor in my decision to give abstinence a try.

My work-week has always been unconventional. Ever since I began teaching at the Williams School of Music in 1984, I worked on Saturdays, and I suffered through many long mornings right from the get go. If I didn't want to pay a heavy price, my weekend drinking would need to be held in check. This, of course, was easier said than done.

Starting when I lived in New York City for two years, chugging Jack Daniels by the bucket-full, I usually commuted to Princeton on Saturdays, and taught my piano students straight through from 9-4. I then drove to Elizabeth, played the evening vigil mass at my church, and finally limped back to the city where the Saturday night's festivities would typically instigate a rough, Sunday morning three-mass schedule of playing, singing and directing the church choir.

I was young and fit, and simply endured the hangover misery. Many folks I knew seemed to do it, and live, so that would be my fate, as well. There were times when the drinking could be tempered and managed—sometimes. Indeed, especially after marrying Carol and moving to Ewing, I was often able to keep the drinking somewhat under control. If I could keep the night's tally under ten, I figured, and get to bed at a reasonable hour, the morning teaching or playing wouldn't be so bad at all. Eight or ten drinks in a night, however, may seem reasonable to a well-seasoned drunk; but it is still far too many to be considered anything close to temperate—not to mention anathema to a normal drinker like my wife.

My first panic-attack struck me without warning just before the 8:00 am mass started in early 1991. For no apparent reason, my heart started to race, my palms began to sweat and I couldn't breathe properly. The inescapable thought of me keeling over right there on the organ bench in the choir loft was palpable. I tried to start the opening hymn, but my hands were trembling uncontrollably and my vocal-cords had become semi-paralyzed. It was a terrifying experience, and I left the church almost immediately after telling the pastor that I wasn't feeling well.

I saw my doctor the following week and told him of my symptoms. He checked me over and asked me some questions. The results of the EKG he gave me seemed normal, although my blood pressure was borderline-high. I told him, somewhat truthfully, about my drinking habits, and he sternly ordered me to cut back, noting that the panic attack was probably an isolated incident, but alcohol was likely the main contributing factor. He also told me that I should try to lose 10-20 pounds, and then he ordered a blood test.

He called me with the results of the test and informed me that my liver enzymes were elevated. He called attention to the potential seriousness of the issue, but also told me that the liver is an extremely durable organ, and can take a lot of punishment without exhibiting any outward side-effects. He told me to exercise more and to "stop drinking alcohol on a regular basis."

Aside from exercising more, I took the rest of my doctor's advice and twisted his prescription to suit myself. He said that the liver was "an extremely durable organ," and that it "can take a lot of punishment" and still function. Damn! I was only 28, and surely *my* durable liver had just begun to take a bit of punishment. I could certainly get another 100,000 miles out of it, for goodness sake. I definitely wasn't going to stop drinking, but the *regular basis part* I could possibly consider. One thing was for sure, the next time I took a blood test I would stop drinking on a regular basis for at least a few days. *That* was reasonable.

I experienced a few more panic attacks of varying severity in the months (and even years) ahead, but never one as virulent as that massive, first one. For some bizarre reason, they seemed to occur just prior to my performance of the opening hymn at church. I was able to identify a possible trigger: In my mind, I always put an immense amount of pressure on myself by thinking the congregation was depending solely on me. I saw myself dying right there on the spot, leaving all in attendance disheartened by the absence of music. After a silent procession of priests, I could envision them all looking back and up toward the organ. The parishioners would not see me sitting there as usual, but see only two stiff legs pointing heavenward. It was weird.

Exercise, I soon discovered, was the key to avoiding the acute panic-attack symptoms before they cropped up. Every Sunday, no matter how bad the hangover, I forced myself to work-out intensely before the mass began. Sometimes I'd rise early and go for a jog, or simply run the basement steps for five minutes. Other times, I'd get to church early and run up and down the 26 steps leading to the choir loft eight or ten times. As long as I was able to break a sweat, and tap into a few, calming endorphins, I found that I was able to manage my anxiety.

As our family started to grow, I figured it might be a good idea to buy some life insurance. Anyone will tell you it's a prudent and responsible thing to do. But, for me, I thought, this was especially sound thinking. After all, from time to time, I was nearly dropping dead at church; and my liver was already showing signs of wear and tear. So, after Katie was born, I applied for a policy, and they asked me to take a blood test.

I employed the advice of my doctor and stopped drinking on a regular basis for a week. When I was cleared for the insurance, it was the green light my ever-sickening mind needed: *Well, this liver of mine is indeed durable! After I punish it for a prolonged period, all I need do is stop for a bit. I'll simply let it catch its breath. No problem.*

Every time I needed a blood test in the years ahead, I employed this method of deception. Toward the end, however, I found that the "regular basis" thing had to be extended for longer and longer periods of time; and even then, the mounting wreckage to my liver couldn't be cleared away so easily.

I certainly informed Carol of the panic attacks, but never breathed a word about the enzyme business. This would not go over well in my self-seeking, self-centered world where relative peace and stability relied heavily on a level of covertness. When Tom Patterson arrived on the scene, however, I found that I had a true confidant.

As mentioned, Tom's unique insight had a grounding and somewhat pacifying influence on me. But my behavior with Carol continued to be a problem. He counseled me on how I might successfully deal with her, and avoid the pit-falls that sparked my more frequent outbursts. He told me to avoid at all costs engaging her in conversations about politics. "Just change the subject, or leave the room," he implored me. Because I had such a short fuse, especially when drinking, he advised me to "not let yourself be drawn into subjects that get you riled up." He urged me to "focus on the kids, and other areas where you agree, but try not to say things that get her going." He knew that when I was drinking, I usually took the bait and the battles commenced. I took much of his thoughtful advice to heart, and things really were better at home for quite some time. During 2003 and into 2004, however, things started to go downhill in a hurry.

In late 2002, Tom had a couple nasty spills on his bike, and came to the conclusion that the hills were getting a bit too dangerous. He was now getting older, and decided that walking would now be his principle source of daily exercise. I continued to ride with baby Natalie, but, without Tom to coax me up and down those blasted hills, the outings started to become less frequent and more leisurely in nature.

The success I enjoyed with Tom's Atkins mock-off diet was now gone. I just couldn't continue avoiding all those foods that I loved so much. And so, with the intense workouts and the structured diet out of the picture, the weight-gain slowly commenced. My alcohol consumption, relatively stable for a few years, began an almost imperceptible increase as well and contributed to the weight-gain. By early 2004, I had replaced all the pounds shed during my diet and hill days, and had actually gone beyond the 225 peak by quite a few pounds. I now was exhibiting the classic "dunlop." The first time I had heard this amusing term was by O.E. Parker in the Virginia mountains all those years before. He possessed a healthy dunlop himself, and explained its meaning to me in his colorful, back-woods twang: "That's when your belly *done-lops* over your belt-buckle."

I discussed the nagging weight and booze problems with Tom over and over again—usually while relaxing at his home over drinks, of course. We had both made the switch to vodka by then. We discovered that the clear liquid seemed a bit easier on our systems, and, more importantly for me, it was much easier to conceal because of its bland odor. Vodka does smell of alcohol, of course, but it doesn't have the reek that bourbon or wine have. I found that one stick of gum, or a breath-mint would do the trick—and I employed this cloaking tactic to great success right up until the final day of my "illustrious" career.

Regarding my daily drinking, Tom told me again and again to temper my intake, and to never imbibe before the day's work was done. Then, "go home, have a drink or two with Carol, discuss things you agree on, eat dinner and then call it a day." I listened and followed his thoughtful suggestions to the best of my ability, but I could never sustain my success for long.

I noticed that when arguments began at home, it was usually just before or after dinner. Now, I can look back and understand why. Food, for a person like me with alcoholic tendencies, is always a problem. A big meal tends to rob the drinker of his edge—or buzz, if you will. In the consciousness of a boozehound like me, dinner time is not something pleasant or welcome, but sadly puts an end to our daily jag. A happy-go-lucky drinker friend of mine put it best with his oxymoronic admonition to "never eat on an empty stomach."

With Carol around meal time, it might only take a sideways look or a few innocuous words to set me off. I would interpret the look or the words as some sort of slight, or, more frequently, a blow to my fragile ego. And then, once I would start to lose control, I was rarely able to recover my senses. I'd rage about how I never felt appreciated by her, or Carol's failure to simply accept who I was.

Whatever the cause—and that list ran the gamut—the reaction was an over-reaction on my part, and the words I chose were often hateful and expletive-laced. Carol, never a wall-flower, generally gave as good as she got; and, after hearing a dose of my ridiculous bull-shit, gave me plenty. It was never pretty. Sadly, and terribly troubling, the children had to endure these awful tirades. Filled with remorse on the mornings after, I begged forgiveness. However, my frequent apologies were starting to wear thin, and Carol was growing weary.

Even more ominously, by 2004 the drinking had started to creep dangerously into a few mornings. I still didn't imbibe on work days, but on more than one occasion, when the opportunity presented itself, I did take a drink. This really pushed me into an honest appraisal of where my drinking was going, and what it was doing to me. The alcohol was causing problems and I had to do something about it.

Around this time, "tomorrow" became my favorite word when trying to come to terms with my predicament. I'd often drive by a local fitness club on my way home from work in Princeton, and think about joining—tomorrow. Then I'd take another drink. I'd get into yet another fight with Carol, and then promise her that "tomorrow" things would get better. The next day, I'd take another drink. The insanity of expecting a different outcome continued. For the suffering alcoholic, the most successful self-help program in the world has to be the "tomorrow program."

Amazingly, one day in March, "today" finally did arrive. Another bitter row the night before with Carol turned particularly ugly, and she let me have it. "You're drinking is out of control. Your kids don't know from one day to the next what kind of mood you're going to be in when you walk through that door. You're fat as a house, and I'm just not happy anymore. *You have to do something about it!*" My besotted brain could only absorb so much, but the "fat as a house" line was really over the top, I thought. I got the overall message, however, and promised right then and there to stop drinking.

The next morning I went to see my doctor, and I joined that gym. I told my doctor that I was quitting booze for the first time in over 20 years. He gladly wrote out a prescription for Valium and wished me luck. "Your wife and your liver will thank you," I remember him saying as I was leaving his office. The pills helped greatly those first few, shaky days, and I immediately started working out at the gym with a vengeance.

Within weeks, everything was better. I was already losing weight, and my home life was happy again. By the time school ended in June, I had lost 20 pounds, and all three compartments of my little life were properly stowed. I felt strong enough in my sobriety to still frequent The Ivy Inn in Princeton, and other local drinking establishments without fear of relapse. I drank club and cranberry in large quantities with Tom Patterson while he continued his astounding, controlled vodka intake. He was impressed with me, and so was I.

A big test came in late June when Carol's parents took the entire Smith clan to Sweden for a long holiday. Carol's parents, Ken and Margie, well-off and extremely generous, had a policy of taking each of their seven children to the destination of their choice on the occasion of their 40th birthday. Indeed, two years prior in 2002, Carol, Katie and I joined a few others on a magnificent cruise on a private yacht in the Grenadines to celebrate Carol's 40th. This year, it would have been Carol's sister Jody's 40th, but she had died tragically of AIDS in 1991. The decision was made to celebrate it anyway with a trip to Sweden, where Margie's entire family had originated and where many of her relatives still resided.

And so it was that the first night in Stockholm, Ken organized a sumptuous dinner feast at the renowned Nobel Hall in the center of that ancient city. There were over 20 of us present, and the two, vast tables in the grand hall were adorned with all the finest accoutrements. At each adult place-setting stood at least four different crystal glasses, each filled with a different type of local alcoholic specialty. A small army of tuxedoed waiters stood by, ready to refill any empty glass. I took a seat, and faced a dilemma.

I immediately looked to Carol for consultation. I knew I could easily be blasted in about 10 minutes if I wasn't careful, but, on the other hand, I also wanted to join in the fun. I asked Carol if it might be okay to just have a glass or two of wine. She gave me a shrug, and kept a keen eye on me throughout the entire evening.

After the succulent remnants of the Reindeer tenderloin were cleared away, it was apparent that I had passed the test. I felt great with my small portion of red wine, and didn't feel the need for anything else. Carol was pleased, many of the others were pleasantly sloshed and didn't give a damn, but I felt good. I had cleared a major hurdle. This sobriety business was not going too badly at all.

Chapter Nine

From an actual AA meeting...

Group Leader: "Do we have any announcements?"

Member: "Yes! Dave, alcoholic."

Group: "Dave!"

Dave: "Yesterday, with the grace of God, and with the help of AA and so many of you in his room, I celebrated five years of sobriety. It's been the best five years of my life, and it just keeps getting better! That's it!"

Group: (Wild applause)

Leader: "Yes?"

Member: "I'm Joe, and I'm an alcoholic."

Group: "Hi Joe!"

Joe: "I picked up yesterday, and I don't know whether I want to live or die."

"VITALS!" a loud and harsh voice shouts. The overhead light in our room switches on and I'm immediately blinded.

"Jesus, Mary and Joseph!" Mike Cass wails from his bed next to mine. "What time is it? Christ! I thought we were done with that middle-of-the-night shit." His voice is raspy and muffled, as he's covered his head with pillows.

"I don't need 'em from you and Ebby," the unwelcome female voice says flatly, "but I do from the newbie. Come on Eric, get some pants on." Squinting, I see a large, black woman hovering just inside the open door. She's got her hands on her hips, and is holding a stethoscope.

I sit up and glance at my watch. "Four o'clock? Are you kidding me?" I ask, bewildered. I shiver uncontrollably, and grope for my sweats on the floor next to my bed.

"Every—four—hours," the woman states, placing plenty of space between each word. "You know the rules. Until your numbers get right, you gotta get 'em done every—four—hours."

"Yeah," Mike Cass mutters in a southern, *Cool-Handed* drawl, "until *you get your mind right.*"

I hear Ebby laughing under his pillows. I bark out a quick guffaw and slip on my pants. As soon as I'm decent, she comes over and sits next to me on the bed. She takes my pulse, temperature and blood pressure, jots down the results, then quickly gets up and leaves.

As soon as she hits the light and shuts the door, Mike says, "Damn! I wish we could lock that fucking door. First two nights it was me. Now they come back like the friggin' Gestapo for you. What's next, God-damn flashlights, sirens and dogs? Vitals! Vitals! Ach Tung! Freakin' German Shepherds froth-ing—RARR, RARR"

Giggling, I lay back on the bed. Mike continues. "She ruined a perfectly wonderful sex dream—the bitch! Put her on the list, too, Ebby."

"Uh huh," Ebby acknowledges distantly. He's already slipping back into unconsciousness.

Lying there, I realize that I've only slept for about three hours, but it's been dreamless and deep. I'm amazed to discover that, although quite groggy, I actually feel refreshed. I can't remember the last time that I felt this good with so little sleep. I also suddenly realize that I have to pee badly.

I get up and start feeling my way for the door. I can't see anything and quickly bounce chest-first into Mike's dresser at the foot of his bed, making a loud, thudding noise. I hit it so hard that I hear some of Mike's stuff rattling around from inside the dresser. "Ouch! Shit! My bladder's gonna blow."

"What the hell is going on?" Mike yells from his bed. "If you knocked over my cup of teef you're DEAD!" Without his front teeth, Mike's words come out with sort of a lisp.

"Just trying to find the door," I say, laughing so hard my insides are aching. "God, I could use a shot of your Aqua Velva right about now."

Our wild laughter must have the neighbors awake by now. "That'th my Buddy Boy!" says Mike.

I make it to the door, and start gasping and stumbling down the empty hallway toward the bathroom. I'm just about there when the overnight nurse steps out of the station doorway and looks at me. "Hey!" she says, quietly but sternly. "Get back to your room and put a shirt on."

I look at her pleadingly. It's not the black woman, but a tiny, Asian lady. She's less than five feet tall, and now *she's* got her hands on *her* hips. I'm sure I look anything but attractive with my big gut hanging out all over the place. "Oh, shit! But, I have to pee," I beg. "Pleeese?"

She's unmoved, and points her hand down the hall, over my shoulder. "Get back there—now!"

I make another gasping noise, mumble something, and turn around. I open our door again, and make it to my bed without banging into anything. I grab what I assume is the Phillies tee-shirt that I wore yesterday. Mike says, "That was the quicketh pith I ever thaw."

"Didn't make it that far yet," I blurt out, still nearly doubled over in laughter and pain. Mike's lisping is hilarious. "That Chinese nurse made me come back and get a shirt."

"She's not Chinese, that's Tokyo Rose!" Ebby chimes in. Somebody's now banging on the wall from the next room, but we don't care.

"Yeah," Mike says, "The Japths and the Nathis run this fucking plathe at night!"

I finally make it to the urinal, just in the nick of time.

About three hours later, I'm sitting alone in the Darcy Room finishing up a breakfast of cool, rubbery eggs and toast that was brought in from the cafeteria. I'm on my third cup of coffee, and have spent some time making notes in my journal, and watching a bit of TV.

I tried to go back to sleep, but found it impossible. The four o'clock disruption and the ensuing events made any attempt at that a useless exercise. In addition, my brain was racing thinking about how I was going to handle the upcoming call home. Mike and Ebby had no trouble getting back to sleep, however, and I lay in my bed enduring their snoring chorus for almost an hour before getting up for good.

It's almost 7:30 and a small number of patients are sitting around talking or watching TV. I walk over to another table where the day's *Star Ledger* is sitting, and look at the sports page. After only a minute, I suddenly realize the extent of how bad things have been for me in the last few weeks. I see that my Phillies won and are off to a strong start at 8 and 2; and that the Flyers had beaten the despised Devils the night before in game one of the Stanley Cup playoffs. For the first time since I was a small child, I recognize, I have no idea at all of these developments.

In my insanity, I've even left behind the small but vital minutia of my everyday life. My liver might be beyond repair, my marriage may well be too, and Lord knows how many students I have left; but not being aware of what's going on with my teams? *This* is almost too much to take in. I shake my head in disgust and self-loathing, and put down the paper. I sigh and attempt to take a look on the bright side. Matters could be even worse, I reckon. Imagine how bad I'd feel if they both had lost?

A tap on my shoulder snaps me back to reality. It's Nurse Sharon holding an empty plastic container. She's looking bright and cheery, hair neatly in a bun, and her glasses fixed in place at the end of her nose.

"How are you feeling today, Eric?" she asks, earnestly.

"Not too bad, thanks," I reply. "I'm still jittery and my back hurts. But I'm surprised how good I feel, really."

"Good," says Sharon quickly. "The vitals line is already starting, so get that done and see me. You need to go over and get your blood drawn again at 11, so don't forget."

"I won't," I assure her.

"Here!" she hands me the container. "Go pee in this and bring it to me—pronto."

I look at her and start to open my mouth.

"Everyone gets tested in here the first few days," she tells me before I can speak. "We throw out anyone who tests positive for drugs and alcohol. Don't forget, we don't *have* to keep you here."

"Ah!" I say, nodding. "I don't plan on doing anything wrong. I'm in enough trouble as it is."

"That doesn't stop some people," Sharon says, looking around at the milling patients. Her tone is casual but serious.

"Do you catch many cheaters?" I ask.

"All the time," Nurse Sharon responds flatly. "Some people just can't help themselves." She turns quickly and walks back toward her station. I like her. She's not on *my* list.

I enter the bathroom and start for the urinal. Just like yesterday, Mike Cass and Ebby are busy at the sinks, hair-teasing and shaving, respectively. Henry is also standing there just behind them. He's talking to them, and seems to be agitated.

"My God-damned brother is running the business into the ground, and I can't do a fucking thing about it in here," Henry tells them. He seems more with it this morning; as if some of the heavy-duty meds have worn off a bit. This, I see, is probably not a good thing, because his anger level has definitely increased. "Then, my idiot wife tells me last night that she's signing all these fucking papers from the bank. I told her over and over not to, but she did it anyway! I can't BELIEVE her!" he shouts. He slams his fist into a door of a nearby toilet stall.

Mike puts down his comb, turns around and faces Henry. "Hey, calm down! Listen Henry," he tells him. "You can't worry about that now. You're stuck here, and that's that. You think I wanna be in this fucking nut-house with the likes of *him*?" He points his finger at me standing at the urinal and gives me a wink. Henry glances at me, and Mike answers his own question. "No! I don't. Now just calm down, go get your vitals taken, and see Nurse Ratchitt. She'll make you feel better, I guarantee it! Okay?"

They stare at each other for a long moment. "Maybe you're right," Henry says. He glances my way. "No offense, Eric, but Mike's right. I *don't* want to be here in this shitter with you." He says this not unkindly, and I smile. I don't particularly want to be here with me either.

"None taken," I say, screwing the top closed on the pee-filled container, and flushing the urinal.

Henry had started for the door, but now stops and turns to face the wall. He starts counting off metronomically: "One...two...three..." He cues the urinal like a conductor bringing in a brass section: "*THWONK*!" The timing is perfect. It's the deep, metallic belch coming from inside the wall. We all laugh. "I love that," Henry says, beaming, and walks—not shuffles—out the door.

Holding my fresh specimen of pee aloft, Mike and Ebby gladly get out of my way when I head for the sink to wash up. "Another 15 minutes for your hair?" I ask Mike, who's again attempting to get it *just so*.

"Aren't you supposed to be making a call, Buddy Boy?" he asks with a bit of an edge in his voice. This changes my mood instantly, and I simply grunt and nod.

"If things go like I think they will with her," he says, "just let her know I have three inches of Jersey blue steel ready to go if she wants."

Doubled over after that offering, I almost drop my pee container. After the tumult subsides, Ebby says, "Why don't you call your mom first? That will probably be more pleasant."

"That's a good idea!" I say, smiling. "You're a smart dude! Thanks, Ebby!"

"Of course he is!" Mike says, putting an arm around his neck and head-locking him. "This is *my* roommate! And, Buddy Boy, don't mention the blue-steel thing to your mom."

"Hello?"

"Hi, Mom! Happy birthday!"

"Eric, how are you, dear?"

"I'm better than I should be. How are you?"

"I'm fine. Thank *God* you're getting help. We've been so worried about you. We got your message yesterday. How is it there?"

"They're taking care of me. I'm exactly where I need to be. I've got two great roommates; and thank God for that, because you should see some of the people others get stuck with."

"Oh, that's wonderful. Dad's out walking, but I'll tell him you called. We're all praying for you. Do you have your bible?"

"No, Mom, but I'll try to get one. They really know what they're doing here at Carrier. 100 years they've been treating drunks like me."

"Oh, don't say it like that. You know your grandmother was there in the 70's when her medicine got all messed up. They fixed her up nicely, too."

"I remember. I came up here a couple times with Dad to see her."

"Do you think you're going to *finally* quit drinking this time? We didn't even know you *were* drinking."

"Mom, I've been sick. I'm learning about the disease. It's starting to make sense. I *have* to quit. I just *have* to. My liver is in bad shape and Carol…"

"Your liver? Oh my God! How bad is it?"

"Pretty bad, but they think I might be okay. I'm getting another blood test today. I'll keep you posted."

"Good. Please do. We're all praying for you. Do you think you will stop smoking too?"

"Mom, please, one crisis at a time. I have to get off and call Carol…"

"Eric, I talked with her last night. You've got a lot of work to do, I can tell you. She's very mad. All that money wasted, the car, the lies…"

"I know, I know. I have to call her anyway and find out…"

"Just be patient, and don't expect much."

"I won't. I love you, Mom."

"I love you, too, Punkers, and we'll keep praying. You pray too!"

"I will Mom. Bye!"

"Bye."

I hang up and take a deep breath. *That went well*, I say to myself. I glance down the hall and see about 10 people still in the vitals line. *I have some time yet.* Nobody's waiting for the phone, so I better call home now. *Here goes.* I enter the number, then all the numbers on the calling card, and wait. It's ringing.

"Hello?"

"Hi honey, It's me."

"Hey, how are you?"

"I'm doing pretty well. I'm where I need to be, thanks to you."

"You need help, that's for sure."

Her tone is dark.

"How are things at home?"

"Eric, I'm late for work, and I gotta get Natalie on the bus, so I only have a minute; but you left me with a huge mess here. There's no money in the bank. That thousand-dollar check Andy wrote you bounced; and there's only about 50 bucks in checking."

"What? How can that be?"

Andy, who wrote me that check has over $30,000 in his account. He was worried about his shaky signature, though.

"How the hell do I know? I don't know anything about all your dealings. I was completely in the dark about the money."

This is not going well.

"Well, the bills are mostly paid, and there's money coming in. I somehow felt the end was near for me, and cashed in some more shares of stock, and my mutual fund. Money will be arriving."

"And food in the meantime? I'm *so* angry right now. I feel *so* stupid. Do you know the home-equity line has gone up $25,000 in the last two years? You're closed out of the bank account, and I shut down your credit card."

"I, I don't know what to say."

"And now you left me with a smashed-up car to deal with. How you didn't get arrested I'll never know. I almost wish you would have."

"Oh, my God. Then I got here and fell, and spent five or six hours in the ER for nothing. My liver's in bad shape, too."

Try the sympathy card?

"I know, I know. Scott told me everything. How long are you going to be there?"

That didn't work.

"At least a week; I don't know how long my insurance will cover me, but I'll pay for a few days if I have to. I *can't* go back to living with those guys. That would be…"

"Eric, I can't talk about that right now. I hope you get better, but, right now, I'm too angry to discuss anything else."

Leave the "coming home" business for later.

"Thank God, I have two really great roommates. They're helping me a lot. And I'm going to AA meetings every night. This time, I know I've said it before, but *this time,* I have to stop—for good!"

"Yeah, well words don't cut it anymore, Eric. There's been nothing but lies for years, so I don't want to hear it. I have to go."

This is torture. Change up again?

"How are the kids?"

"They're okay. Natalie misses her daddy, and so does Matt."

"Tell them I love them. And…I love you, and I'll be home…"

"Bye, Eric. Get well."

I'm standing there holding the dead receiver in my shaking hands. Although my physical condition seems to be improving, I'm well aware that the alcoholic poison is still present in my system. Then there's my mental state, now in tatters. My insides are churning, and I don't even notice the tears trickling down my face until they drop, one by one, on the floor. I wipe them with my sleeve, hang up the phone and slowly make my way to the vitals line.

I'm surprised to see Eva. The last I heard she was in the ER. She's getting her numbers checked, and Stanley—the only friend she has here, it seems—stands guardian-like above her. She must have finally stopped puking, because, although she still looks pale and weary, I notice her hair has been brushed, and she's finally shed her pajamas in favor of jeans and a loose -fitting sweatshirt. And, possibly for the first time since she arrived half-dead from heroin abuse, she's not draped in a comforter.

She finishes and Stanley helps her up. She glances my way, and gives me a comforting smile. I try to return it, but find it difficult. There's something about the way she's looking at me. Although I haven't spoken a single word to her, I get the distinct impression that somehow she knows exactly what I'm going through, and that, despite everything, there may still be hope—for the both of us. After the shit-storm she's been through, I figure, if she can harbor the slightest bit of opti-mism, then maybe I can too.

My mind is still racing as I sit down and get my vitals checked. Not surprisingly, my blood-pressure and pulse are still through the roof; and Nurse Sharon frowns and shakes her head when I show her my paper at the station. She again reminds me of my blood-work appointment, and tells me to ask the doctor about upping my BP dosage when I see her after the results come in. I'm grateful for the Librium, and down it greedily along with the other items she gives me. My mood is subdued, to say the least, and the keenly observant Sharon picks up on it.

"Are you okay? What's the matter?" she asks.

"Tough call home," I say, and turn towards Darcy. "I'll be okay."

I walk absently into the lounge and, not knowing why, head straight for the pathetic-looking upright in the far corner. I sit down on the creaky bench and glance around. Only a few patients are in the room, as most are over in the cafeteria eating breakfast. The TV is off, and no one is playing ping-pong. I hear only a few quiet conversations going on, and, for the first time in months, begin playing.

For some reason, I start in on Beethoven's *Moonlight Sonata*. The haunting, melancholic strains fill the near-empty space. I think about the Master's condition when he wrote the piece. He was a wreck, too. It was composed around the time he was contemplating suicide because of his increasing deafness. He was near despair trying to come to terms with a malady that was robbing him of his most vital faculty. But, in a letter to a friend at the time, he vowed to "seize fate by the throat," and carry on despite the realities of his impending hearing loss.

In the music itself, there are less-than-subtle motifs that, at least to me, signify the man trying to accept his ever-darkening existence. The "DAH—da DAH" theme is particularly telling. I see the accented notes amidst the gloomy, fearful rumblings as simply the reality of his present state: muffled noise, with occasional bursts of clarity. I see the accented notes penetrating the murkiness, and leading, ultimately, to a new, safer place.

As the piece continues—with wrong notes, and awful tuning in abundance—I see myself in somewhat related circumstances. I cannot despair, and must get through what has been *my* ever-darkening existence. I can never return to that hopelessness of the past, and must start anew. Despite the terrible fear of what may lie ahead, I can begin to see my way through, and must try to heal what is now broken. Regardless of all the pain I have caused, I must do all in my power to make well and overcome the past. This is what I'm contemplating when the music ends, and I draw my still-trembling hands from the keyboard.

The first morning group meets in the smaller lounge area adjacent to Darcy, and is mostly a nuts-and-bolts affair run this day by Carley, the attractive brunette with a thin, yet elegant aquiline nose. She's pleasant enough, and even jokes a bit with us, but, as with almost everybody who works at the institution, she will not abide even a small portion of bull-shit.

When Jason, "Mr. T," as Ebby refers to him, frequently interrupts and makes crude remarks, Carley simply stops talking and calls him out. I'm amazed to see that it even works on him to some degree; and the Neanderthal has to retreat for a few minutes into a largely unknown region for him: silence.

Carley goes over the many rules and regulations, and takes notes on patients' problems and concerns. She invites those of us new to introduce ourselves, and asks those who are leaving to say a few words, if they desire. She goes over the work-list, and gives out jobs to those who want one. I raise my hand and volunteer to help Ebby take care of the Darcy Garden out back. "Just make sure not to throw butts in the garden, please," Carley implores the group. "Can't you all have just a tiny bit of respect?" I see Mr. Testosterone smiling and shaking his head.

Mike Cass, sitting next to me, of course, leans in close. "That jack-ass is *really* on the list." I nod.

The meeting concludes with a reading from *Daily Reflections*, and then there's a short break before the next group begins.

Mike taps me and asks, "Cup of tea and a smoke?"

"You bet," I reply, and follow him into Darcy.

We make our tea, and go out back into the smoking area. The April morning is bright and crisp, and we take a seat atop one of the picnic tables and light up. Over half of the patients in Blake are smokers, I reckon, and about 15 of us are now present in the designated area.

"How did the call home go?" Mike asks me, with uncommon seriousness.

I take a drag and a sip of tea, then say, "She's pissed. She has every right to be. I just need to do what you told Henry earlier."

"What's that? I forget."

"Just get better, I guess. And only worry about things like being in this fucking nuthouse with people like myself, I think."

Mike chuckles and takes a drink. "Tomorrow's call will be better, I predict," he tells me. I notice Ebby walking over to us.

"My roommate!" Mike calls to him, and Ebby nods and smiles. Ebby asks me the same question, and Mike moans. "Does this whole fucking world revolve around Buddy Boy's home-life? I got problems too, ya know."

I manage a smile, and tell Ebby, "Not good. I'm afraid of what might happen, but…"

"*But* you can't worry about that!" Mike interrupts harshly. "Deal with getting better. Shit, your liver might be about to explode, for Christ's sake!"

"Mike's right," Ebby says in his calming, more even tone. "Just take it one day at a time, like Frank was saying last night. What did you think of him, by the way?"

"Powerful," I say. "That guy told it like it is. That's the message I need to get into my thick skull."

"Was that the ex-cop?" Mike asks.

"Yeah," Ebby says. "He got put on disability for drinking on the job, and other things, I guess. He didn't really tell us all the things that happened."

"Yeah, cops get away with everything," Mike Cass says with distain in his voice. He suddenly thinks of something and sits up. "Well, *almost* everything. My cousin told me about a friend of his who was a cop down in South Jersey. Man, did this guy have a problem." Mike takes another drag and continues. Ebby and I are all ears. "Get this: he replaced the washer fluid in his cruiser with vodka."

"Get the hell out of here," I say. "No way!"

"No, it's true. Listen to this," Mike says in all seriousness. "He took the tank out, washed it out, then he filled it with booze. Then, he rigged the spraying end to come through the dashboard, and every time he wanted a drink, he put the end up to his mouth and hit the button. Honest to God."

"Did he get nailed?" Ebby asks him.

"Of course he did, or I wouldn't be telling this story. It was getting serviced or something and they discovered it. He lost his job, pension—everything!"

"It might be Frank," I say, not completely in jest.

"Nah," says Mike. "Although this guy could be running AA meetings down in South Jersey somewhere. He might be dead."

"Damn!" Ebby says. "The things we do for a drink.

I nod in total agreement.

The next group is run by Tim, a slightly built, bearded man of about 30. Although his demeanor is professorial and prim, he immediately lets it be known that he himself is a recovering alcoholic; and that only a few years prior was a patient here at Carrier.

The subject of this particular group is "people, places and things," and Tim stresses how important it was in his life to drastically change up these areas. "After leaving here," Tim says, "in order for me to maintain my sobriety, I had to turn away from my so-called friends, avoid bars and other places that served alcohol, and also look at the things in my life that triggered the abuse. You will discover—if you haven't already—that returning to the people, places and things that you associate with your past life, will more often than not lead you right back to your addiction." He looks out at the group, eyes moving from one unfortunate to another, letting the words sink in. "This is an extremely important factor in your recovery. Any questions?"

Kara Alcoholic's hand shoots up. Mike sits back with a heavy sigh, and I hear Henry, seated a few chairs down, groan. Bobby Brooklyn, sitting on the other side of Mike, is madly scribbling some caricature in his sketch-book. I can make out a head with some impossibly large hair at the top of a page in his book, and assume that it's Kara. Maxine, sitting faithfully next to Karen, has buried her head in her hands.

"Yes," Tim says, and points to Karen.

"Hi, Kara, alcoholic. How do I avoid myself? That's a good question. I'm my biggest enemy, I think. Most of my drinking was done alone. Of course, my dogs were with me, but they don't count, do they? I don't think my husband should be included either, because…"

At this moment, a tall, skinny kid of about 20, slowly shuffles through the door and moves unsteadily toward an open chair. He's wearing baggy jeans, barely clinging to his scrawny hips, and of course they're all bunched up at the ankles. He's also sporting an oversized, white hoodie, and is topped with a crooked ball-cap pulled down over his eyes. He's carrying a cup of coffee in one hand, and an unlit cigarette in the other. His painfully slow movements attract the attention of everybody in the room. That is, everybody *but* Kara Alcoholic, who just keeps *rollin' along*.

"…What about bowling? I *love* to bowl. Do I have to quit this, too? I mean, I still have to live, don't I? I'm not sure whether I associate bowling with drinking, but I guess I do. I don't know. I'd love to get some feedback as to whether…"

Only Tim and a couple others are paying much attention to runaway Kara. Most eyes are directed at the unsteady newcomer. Mike leans over close to my ear. "I love this kid," he whispers. "He's all twisted out on something."

"I love his hat," I respond secretly.

"That's it, Buddy Boy! He's 'the hat!'"

I laugh quietly and continue watching him.

Tim holds a hand up like a traffic cop and mercifully halts Kara in mid-sentence. "Okay, Kara, listen," he says, as many in the room exhale thankfully. "Of course, you have to keep living, and many of you will find yourself in uncomfortable situations. But, what you were doing many times, and who you were with; these things were causing you to make the wrong choices. And that's why you're here. It's about choices. Now, what about going to places or events that serve alcohol? Take a wedding, for instance. What do you do when you find yourself at a reception, and the open bar is sitting right there?"

He looks around for a reply from the group. I'm looking at the new kid who found a seat, but already seems to be drifting off. He's leaning forward precariously, and his cup of coffee is tilting.

Henry breaks the silence with this dead-pan bomb: "Walk over to the bar. Order a double-scotch."

The room erupts and the kid drops the coffee directly at his feet. The mess is instant, and Ebby, seated next to the door, jumps up and leaves the room. "The Hat" looks up, a vague, empty expression on his placid face.

"Shit!" Tim exclaims. "Morris? What are you doing, Morris?" he cries in a whiny, high-pitched voice. "You know you're not to drink coffee in group, Morris. Are you there, Morris? Hello?"

"Huh? What?" Morris the Hat replies with sincere puzzlement. No coffee or soda in group was definitely one of the rules that Carley mentioned earlier. Also, we're not to wear hats in group. I glance around and see at least a dozen cups of coffee and cans of soda scattered on the floor under seats, and along the long window-sill. Also, many of the men and a few of the women—yours truly included—are wearing hats.

Sharon comes in, followed closely by Ebby who's got some paper towels. She takes the over-medicated Morris by the arm and slowly leads him away. She looks over her shoulder at me and says, "Blood-test," and gives me a 'get going' gesture with her free hand.

My right arm is all black and blue at the bend in the elbow from my first blood test two nights ago, so the nurse in the lab tries my left. Of course, she misses the vein on the first try; and after she finally draws what she needs, I'm left with two, glaring "track lines"—one on each arm. After leaving, I look at them and shrug. *Who the hell cares, anyway?* I offer a quick prayer for my damaged liver. I hope the test shows signs of improvement, otherwise, well, *don't think about that.* Although my belly is still bloated, it doesn't really hurt, and that must count for something.

I walk out into the chilly midday sun. Should I walk the short distance back to Blake and catch the last 15 minutes of Kara Alcoholic's speech? No. I think a walk is in order before lunch. They told me I could cover the grounds, and I'm certainly excused, for God's sake. I figure it's time to take the first tiny step at getting back into shape.

I turn to the right—north, I think—and hop to. As I begin, I realize something. In just one morning, I've identified three important areas of my life that I've completely abandoned in my recent insanity: sports, piano, and exercise. All three were always daily necessities for me. But they've been completely absent lately—all swallowed up by alcohol and my spiraling obsession with cocaine and Xanax. I attempt a smile as I lengthen my strides. *Today, I start to get my life back.*

Much later, I'm sitting on my bed making notes. After my "long" walk (about a mile was all I could muster), and a turkey roll sandwich, the afternoon groups were led by Carley and

Kevin, a grey-haired, 70-something counselor who's been working at Carrier, I'm told, for ages. His group was most enlightening, as it centered on the root-causes of addiction. He worked the blackboard vigorously, listing many of the common issues that plague potential and real addicts and alcoholics. There followed a lively give-and-take on the particular subjects. Kevin's vast expertise was evident, as he was able to cull important personal elements from many of the patients, and then see how those factors played a role in their addictions. Once again, and certainly not coincidental, I found myself nodding in full agreement at many of the points made.

After two full days, I finally had a decent meal, having been cleared to travel to the cafeteria. Afterward, Matt, a tall, lean and extremely serious young counselor, who doubles as a kind of one-man, roving security force, conducted the evening group. This was the guy who helped me to bed the other night, I realized.

Just before the group started, he had to break up a scuffle between Mr. T. and another young, overly-anxious druggie. They got into a lively wrestling match after a questionable call at the ping-pong table, and it all ended well-enough with the two of them warily shaking hands. Matt, with his military buzz cut and looming presence, warned them against any more outbursts, and all the patients soon shuffled into the group lounge room.

On the blackboard during his group were written three sets of numbers, one on top of the other: 1234, 360 and 220. We soon discovered that these were the daily death-tolls in America for tobacco, alcohol and drug-abuse, respectively. Matt discussed each figure in detail, and the group weighed in on related subjects. I kept focusing on the 360 number. My church in Elizabeth, a large and ornate structure built 100 years ago, holds just about that number. On past Christmases and Easters, I've counted over 300 in attendance, and it certainly would be possible to squeeze another few dozen into the building.

I kept imagining 360 people filing into *my* church every morning, as if attending a funeral. The only problem was that for every one of them, it would be their own funeral. Each and every day, I'd be standing above the poor wretches in the choir loft, as they filled the church—all destined to die that day from alcoholism and related causes. Perhaps one day soon, I'd join the long cue of walking dead, waiting to file in for my own date with destiny. I may still be on the list, but, if I keep that vivid image in my mind—"remember the pain," as Frank put in the night before—I may get a reprieve.

Mike Cass strolls through our open door at about a quarter to eight. "Here's Johnny!" he bellows, ala Jack Nicholson, and then heads directly for the small mirror on the inside of his dresser. He's still wearing those same blue denims; and that dyed-black, "Elvis" hair hasn't budged a millimeter all day. That fact doesn't stop him from fussing with it, though. "You ready for vitals, and…?" he asks me, leaving his sentence dangling, but the meaning implicit.

"Yeah," I reply, making a few more notes.

"Yeah, because if you screw it up, you're…"

"I know, I know," I cut him off, "DEAD!"

"No, no," he says, gazing at me with an evil air. "I'm not gonna hurt you, Wendy. I'm not gonna hurt you." Here comes "Johnny" again. I start laughing. "I'm just gonna bash your—fucking—brains in!"

"You are too much!" I cough out, sides aching. "What *would* you do if you killed us all off, anyway?"

"Finally get some peace and fucking quiet around here," he states evenly, again at the mirror. "No more psychos like Mr. T. or that rambling loon, Kara. No more Nurse Ratchitts constantly hounding me with 'Put a sleeved shirt on! Put a sleeved shirt on!'" He sighs expansively. "It would be just me and the key for the mother-load in the nurse's station—the King's ransom."

He pauses and seems to snap out of his reverie. "Xanax." The one word is spoken with utter distain. "Oh, shit, how am I *ever* gonna stop that *fucking* Xanax?" He sighs heavily and drops on his bed. He puts his hands to his face and slowly rubs his eyes. "I can't stop thinking about it," he says with pain in his voice. "It was killing me, but I just can't stop. It's fucking torture."

I don't know what to say to my new friend. I'm in the same boat, but my obsession seems to have left me—at least for right now. Mike still seems to be totally under his drug's spell. After a long pause, I manage, "You can do it, Mike. Can't you?"

He looks up at me. "We'll see, Buddy Boy," Mike Cass says without conviction. He nods his head. "Yeah, we'll see." He gets up and touches his hair one last time. His happy-go-lucky smile returns. Mike Cass is back in frivolity mode. He takes one last look in the mirror and says, "Let's go cause some mayhem."

I'm standing at the station waiting for Donna to emerge from the drug room. Mike is standing right next to me, and

Ebby, Bobby and Henry are chatting behind us. The AA and NA meetings are only minutes away as Donna shows herself.

"Oh, boy, Mutt and Jeff. To what do I owe the honor?" She looks like she's going to a dinner party: bright-colored pants suit, blonde hair just so, and *all that* jewelry.

"Just looking for my pill, Donna," I say, and hand her my sheet.

"Hi Donna," Mike says brightly. "Can I have the nose-spray? I haven't been able to breathe all day."

Donna is studying my sheet, and doesn't even look up when she says, "Well, despite not breathing all day, you're still standing there, aren't you? Can you please wait until I'm done with your roommate?"

"Yeah, sure," Mike Cass says, and then adds, "You're looking very nice this evening."

Donna looks up at Mike. By the look on her face, I don't think she trusted that last remark. She addresses me. "I see your BP is finally a little lower," she says. "And, the results of your blood-test should be here first thing in the morning."

"Good. I hope they improve like my pressure. I finally cracked 150 on the systolic. Or is it the diastolic?" I respond proudly.

She ignores the question, and instead asks me, "How are your jitters?"

"Better—a bit," I say somewhat truthfully, but holding back the real truth that the Librium has worked wonders with my nerves. I don't want to make it seem that I'm feeling too much better, lest they pull the plug on my saving med. I am an alcoholic, after all!

"Okay, I'll be right back," she tells me and turns around.

"What about the spray?" Mike asks again.

"In a minute, for God's sake," Donna says, annoyed.

She returns and hands me the paper cup. I down the pill, drink the other cup filled with water, and look down at her hand. "Those are beautiful rings. Are they emeralds or diamonds?" I ask sincerely.

Donna bends over and points to the biggest one. "This is actually cut glass from the Mt. St. Helens' volcano," she tells me eagerly. "All this," she stands up and points out her gaudy necklace, "is from a collection of volcanic glass."

"Wow," I say, "it's magnificent!"

"Donna, can I have the…" Mike points to his nose.

"Oh, all right." She steps back, grabs the spray-bottle and hands it to Mike. "Three puffs only—three!" She holds up three fingers, and then returns to her hand.

"But how did they get it out of a volcano?" I ask stupidly. "It must be terrifically expensive."

"Oh, not at all," she tells me. "When it blew in 1981, this stuff was lying all over Washington State, and many locals cashed in on the bonanza. I got the entire collection for less than $200. This round one…"

I don't see Mike, of course, but hear him: "Sniff, sniff, sniff," in quick succession. Then the other nostril: "sniff, sniff, sniff." The rhythmic sniffs continue every few seconds.

Donna is completely absorbed in the telling of her Mt. St. Helens' volcanic cut-glass collection. "It comes in all shapes and colors: gorgeous reds and blues. Here, look at my bracelet." She stands erect and holds out her hand, but then sees Mike convulsing with the spray bottle and explodes herself. "Hey! What are you doing with that? What the hell?"

I turn and see Mike sniffing away—a wild expression on his face.

"Give me that!" Donna lurches for the bottle and grabs it from Mike. He staggers back, and looks like he just did a two-foot line of Coke. His hair even appears to have sprung out away from his head an inch or so.

"Sorry, Donna," Mike gasps. "But it was stuck. I couldn't get anything out of it."

"Stuck, my ass!" Nurse Donna snaps. "That stuff's addicting! Get the hell out of here before I have Matt throw you out!"

Mike moves away unsteadily and I follow him into Darcy. We both just about fall into a couple of chairs—crippled with laughter.

"Wow, that was beautiful, Buddy Boy," he says breathlessly. "I hope it *is* addicting. It's bound to be cheaper than Xanax."

"What is it, anyway, Neo-Synefrin, or something like that?" I ask.

"I don't know what the hell it is, but it helps me breathe if I get enough of it. Of course, like everything else, I seem to need a lot more of it than most people." He keeps sniffing, and his passages do sound clearer.

"So that's what happened with the Xanax?" I ask more seriously, wanting to hear that story. "I mean, the amount just kept increasing?"

"Exactly," Mike says, his breathing becoming more regular. "Like I told you—I think it was you, I don't know—it really did take the pain away with my eye, but then I was doing more and more. After I did a large quantity, it was great for a while. I could do anything: I was washing my mom's car, chopping wood, you name it. Then, the crash would come, and it was awful." Mike puts his head in his hands again, remembering the down-side feeling of the drug. "I couldn't do anything but lie in bed. 3:00 in the afternoon, and I was useless for the rest of the day. This was happening more and more—every day at the end. Mom would come to my door," he pauses and looks at me. "You know I live with my 83-year-old mother?"

I nod. "I think you told me."

"And she'd ask me what was wrong; and I just laid there like a fucking zombie—unable to even speak. She was heart-broken." I see Mike Cass' eyes moistening. "When my dad died," he goes on, "I promised him." He's beginning to lose it now, I see. There's a box of tissues on the table next to us, and I grab it and pass it to him. "Thanks. Anyway, just before he died, I promised my dad that I'd take care of my mom. And, and, it had gotten so bad that I couldn't even do that any-more." The last few words come out in sobs, and I feel myself welling up, too.

Mike blows his recently cleared-out nose, takes a few breaths and continues. "This went on for weeks until my brother finally convinced me to get help, and I ended up here. It was absolutely killing me." He looks at me again, and shakes his head. "But, that's not even the worst part, Eric." I look at him, and he stares back—a mix of fear and sadness written all over his plump face. "The worst part is that it's going to be waiting for me when I get home; and I don't know if I'll be able to lay off it. It's that powerful."

"I know what you mean," I tell him. "It's not going to be easy for me, either. Everything I did in my life revolved around taking a drink. But, that's why I'm here. That's why you're here. I really should be dead, but I'm not. I simply can't go back to that. It sounds like you can't, either Mike. So, let's learn how to live life without that shit."

Mike looks at me and slowly nods his head. A partial smile appears, but the fear and sadness haven't completely left his face. "That's what I need to keep hearing, Buddy Boy. There is hope, right?"

"That's all we got," I say.

Mike and I look around Darcy. The chairs are set up for the meeting, and more than a few people are taking their seats. I look at Mike and see that his real smile is back again. "That, and lots of fucking AA and NA meetings," he says, and pops-up out of his chair and quickly strides away. "See ya later, Buddy Boy."

Chapter Ten

"We are like men who have lost their legs; they never grow new ones. We tried every imaginable remedy. In some instances there has been brief recovery, followed always by a still worse relapse. Physicians who are familiar with alcoholism agree there is no such thing as making a normal drinker out of an alcoholic. Science may one day accomplish this, but it hasn't done so yet."
—Pages 30 and 31, *Alcoholics Anonymous*

Although I had promised Carol and myself to completely quit drinking in March of 2004, the reality of the situation was slightly different. Yes, for 18 months I totally swore off vodka and bourbon, and yes, for a long time I rarely even took a glass of wine with dinner; but, the green-light she gave me on that festive night in Stockholm—to go ahead and have just a little bit—kept my mind in the hunt for other opportunities. The mere thought, however small, of taking a sanctioned drink, was never completely eradicated. The seed was never removed from the soil—it lay dormant, as if during an extremely long, *dry* winter.

...le conscious realization of these ...the vast improvements, both physi- ...nt, were enough to severely suppress ...apse. I was thrilled to be 98% alcohol- ...omething special, I thought. I was the model of ... nal, moderate drinker," and what could possibly be wrong with that?

I continued to take and pass one test after another. Every night after teaching the big test was the drive home. This is where my drinking was born and raised, after all. It was my true comfort-zone, and I had known for years that I could get away with almost anything behind the wheel of my car. But, I held firm, and it was Diet-Coke in the cup-holder, not the vodka-mix. To be sure, those first few days and weeks were a trial, and I needed every ounce of will-power I could muster to stifle the intense cravings. The Valium helped.

My doctor gave me the prescription the very day I quit in March, and it immediately helped quell the urges. I'd take one in the morning and then another after work when my cravings were strongest. The drug arrested my agitation during these critical, few hours, and the final dose late in the evening administered the knock-out punch I needed. He balked at refilling it more than once, but my pathetic pleadings convinced him to add just one more refill. "That's it, Eric," he told me in no uncertain terms. "The last thing you want to do is trade one addiction for another."

To an extent, however, that's just what happened. After over three months of daily use, I did become somewhat addicted; and those first few days after my last dose were not pleasant. This time, I had nowhere to turn for help, and simply white-knuckled it. I was squirrelly and agitated, pacing the house, and constantly going outside for a smoke. It took a couple days of frayed nerves and lost sleep, but for the first time in 25 years, I was truly—*finally*—alcohol *and* drug free.

Regarding the Valium, honesty with Carol again was lacking. To be sure, she knew about it, and was supportive in every way, but she didn't know the extent of it. I would never tell her that I tried pressuring the doctor for more prescriptions, knowing the potential risks. That would give her more information than she required, I figured. I see now that my secretive thinking, developed and finely-honed during my drinking career, was also perfectly at home when dealing with a potential drug addiction. Carol would surely have helped if I had been honest with her, but I didn't see it that way. I'm sure that I would have taken as many prescriptions of Valium as my good doctor would have given me, but I never would have told her. It all came down to me. I was self-seeking once again, and I was fearful of discovery. It wouldn't be the last time.

At the time, I knew little of AA and was ignorant about most of the important suggestions and guidelines that help its members stay sober one day at a time. Around then, it was suggested by Carol and others that I attend some meetings, but that wasn't going to happen. I had a problem and I was dealing with it. That was all. There was no need for draconian 12-step programs.

Of course, *everybody* knows that life as you know it ends when you step into those rooms. On top of that, it was a cult, right? And people only go there to find babes or other drunks to party with. And, of course they were all a bunch of disgusting messes anyway. Everyone knows that their idea of a good party was pissing themselves and blacking-out in their puke. I had never been like that. There was no way I could possibly consider associating with any of those brown-bag-toting, falling-down *losers*.

One aspect of the program that was completely foreign to me, was the idea of avoiding the "people, places and things" that trigger cravings; and so I continued to visit them. I seriously doubt I would have paid any mind to that tenet anyway had I been aware. After all, I was a success story. I had stopped drinking, and that was enough. My life was better, my wife liked me again, and my kids were wonderful. Compartment number two—work—was better than ever now that I didn't have to teach or play church services with hangovers or the threat of debilitating panic attacks.

Everything was fine, so I didn't see any reason to stop hanging out with friends who drank, or going to the Ivy every Sunday in the fall for the games, or golf or parties, or any of that. I often stopped at Tom Patterson's in the evenings and drank club and cranberry to excess, while the two of us discussed everything under the sun. I'm sure I felt a bit of resentment as he went at his vodka with that controlled zeal that I could never master. But that was okay. I simply continued doing everything I always did in area number three of my life, without the booze.

Another key to my apparent success was my exercise regimen. I found that it was absolutely vital in filling the void created by abstinence. I became a fitness-club fanatic, and often found myself sweating on the cross-trainers and rowing machines at my gym two times a day. The evening workout, I found, was a fantastic substitute for my nightly binge, and I'd often push myself to the breaking point on the machines in order to vanquish any remnants of the thought of a drink. It worked, and Tom Patterson was impressed indeed when I'd present myself at his door. It seemed every week meant another lost pound; and by the time of the big Sweden trip in June, I had already dropped 20—weighing in at a respectable 215.

It felt great to have that 80-proof, toxic gorilla off my back, and my attitude and behavior at home continued to improve. More and more, Carol and I and the kids were doing things together, and I didn't fly off the handle the way I did during the drinking days. The Sweden trip was followed by a summer drive to St. Louis; and we had a fabulous time with Carol's family there. I'm sure I had a glass of wine or two with Carol's father and the rest of her large family, but that was no problem. By the time school started in the fall, life at home was peaceful and happy. I had a full-plate of over 40 students waiting to be taught, and I was approaching the 200-pound mark for the first time since our marriage.

Slowly but ever-so-surely my "occasional" drinking started to become more frequent. For the first six months of my new, nearly-sober life, the occasions where I took a glass of wine with dinner were few. During the next six months, they were more than a few. By the time the summer of 2005 rolled around, I looked forward to my weekly glass of wine *or two* at the Sunday dinner table. On top of that, after a sweaty golf match with one of my pals, sure, I'd have a cold beer—just one, though. It didn't make a difference if the frequency of the events were coming closer and closer together, I thought. At least I wasn't drinking the hard-stuff, and I wasn't drinking to excess.

At Houghton family gatherings, my mother and father, who held the same belief as me that my "little problem" was solved, worked on me to marry my success with the drink with the smoking issue. "I'd much rather see you have a drink or two every day, and quit smoking instead," my dad kept telling me. He was correct, of course, but I knew that any type of daily alcohol intake was bound to cause adverse consequences; and I had no desire to quit smoking anyway. Little comments like that by my father and others, however, did foster in me a sense of over-confidence, and my infrequent, controlled drinking continued to become more recurrent.

A photo from a Caribbean cruise the Houghton family took in July of 2005 now sits on my refrigerator, and is a clear reminder of the time. I'm standing arm-in-arm with Carol on the balcony of our ocean-side quarters, and we're both beaming. Carol appears tanned and gorgeous as ever, as the sun shines down on the azure gulf in the background. I appear almost skinny, having achieved a weight of slightly over 190. It was a high-water mark for the two of us in our marriage, and although I got an ear-full from her after consuming my third glass of wine at the Captain's dinner, the trip was full of love and good-feeling. The snap-shot for me tells a story of clarity and happiness, of peace and devotion. It speaks of love, and a future bright with boundless possibilities.

So, when "it" happened less than two months later, just following hurricane Katrina, I felt that somehow, all my success of the past 18 months, and all the hope and promise for the future represented in that photo, were now at risk. I didn't know to what extent the future ramifications of the event would entail; but, without any doubt, I knew deep down in my heart that the mistake I made was going to have consequences. I still think about what happened on that mild, September evening all the time. It was nothing, really, but would soon become *really something.*

It was the day after Labor Day, and I had just finished teaching my private students at their homes in the area. I had a full load of over a dozen kids lined up for my Monday and Tuesday travel schedule, and even a few on a waiting list. I had a full-slate of students waiting to be taught at Williams as well, and finances were looking great for the upcoming year. On top of that, I had gone out on a limb and started a small vending business, financing at great expense—and much to Carol's justified concerns—five snack and soda machines. I would soon be installing them at the Music School where I worked and a few other local businesses. Carol was always saying that I needed to fill up my days more, and try to pull in a little extra income, and this plan seemed to fit the bill nicely.

Although what occurred that day was completely spontaneous, looking back, I had yet another good reason to feel somewhat justified in my actions. Natalie, my littlest sweetheart, was just shy of five, and was to begin kindergarten the following morning. For me, this would mark the end of three triumphant tours of duty as Mr. Mom. Matthew, now 11 and Katie, 14, were coming along beautifully; well-adjusted and happy in every way. I was there for all of them, and would continue to be so no matter what circumstances arose. My heart was swelling with pride.

And so, with all these things bouncing around in my brain, when I saw the small bistro in Hopewell coming up on the left, I decided to pull in. I parked and walked into the crowded barroom. I sat down and bartender approached. I ordered a club and cranberry, but, when she turned away to make my drink I heard myself ask quietly, "Could you put a little Absolut in there, too?"

My palms began to sweat. Distant alarm bells went off in my head, and I briefly considered getting up and walking right out of there. I'd go to the safety of Tom Patterson's, where I was heading in the first place. He and Cindy were moving to Florida in a few weeks, and I needed consultation—now! I watched my bartender pouring the vodka, and the thought of leaving vanished. I didn't budge.

When the drink arrived, I stared at it for a long moment. *This is **not** a good idea*, I thought. It wasn't just an innocent-looking cocktail, but more like a bomb waiting to blow up all the will-power I had accumulated over the past 18 months. I was completely torn and tried to weigh the pros and cons. Satan put in his two cents: *Go ahead, my boy. You deserve it. Celebrate your success! You've been so good for so long, after all. Live a little!* My God probably looked at it a bit differently: *You can do whatever you want, my son. But, you're risking all the positive gains that you've made in your life.*

It was really no contest. *One drink won't do a damn thing*, I told myself with finality, earning a proud nod from the Prince of Darkness. I drank. That first sip was something beyond glorious. It glided easily down my throat, and settled into a grateful belly. I immediately felt that warm, numbing sensation that I had been missing for so long. It was back. I was back.

I watched the TV above the bar broadcasting the non-stop misery of New Orleans, and lost myself. I felt awful for those poor souls who were suffering beyond imagination. I felt so helpless for them—all of them. The bartender came back. "Yeah, sure, just like the last time. Can't fly with one wing!"

They were stuck in a horrific tragedy that could easily have been avoided if proper precautions were made. Life was just so unfair. And why do the poorest people always seem to get shafted even worse when events like these occur?

When CNN went to break, I snapped back to my reality. The bartender was standing right there and I downed the rest of my drink. Well, why not? In for a penny…I ordered one more and started to think. *This is an isolated incident,* I told myself over and over. *Three drinks is nothing,* I convinced myself. *Tomorrow, it's back to Diet-Coke. I **cannot** return to daily drinking. It's **not** an option.* I left the bar and went straight home.

I kept it all to myself, and tried desperately to put it aside. *Tomorrow is another day*, I kept telling myself. But, I soon couldn't escape a terrible fear—paralyzing and real. This fear was now with me, and it was overwhelming. I had been successful at controlling my drinking, and now, all bets were off. If I could fall so easily tonight, I figured, then how could I say no tomorrow? Those few drinks felt so good, but could I have just a few the next time? Like—tomorrow? Well, whatever happens, the most important thing was that no one—Carol, especially Carol—would know what I was doing.

The next night after work, I didn't go to a bar, but instead bought half-a-pint of Smirnoff from the liquor store in Princeton, and made a few concoctions for the ride home. The following night it was the same, and the next and the next. For weeks, the half-pint was enough, and four drinks was no big deal at all, I rationalized. By Christmas, I was supplementing the half-pint with an airplane-bottle or two.

Also, as the weeks passed, and the slow progression required just a tiny bit more to achieve the feeling I was looking for, I kept trying to focus on the positive. I was able to temper my fear, and the accompanying lies and deceit, with the knowledge that I was a faithful, loving husband and father. I worked hard in and outside the house, and had dropped over 30 pounds, for goodness sake. I still made it to the gym every day, albeit not so often in the evenings anymore, and that was only because of my increased teaching load. Well, that wasn't completely untrue. I was working until 8:00 on some nights, just not 9:00 or 9:30, as I typically told Carol.

The way I acted at home afterward was of paramount importance. My behavior, so vital to a happy home-life, was still good; and this was something that I simply had to keep a close eye on. If I started acting out again—yelling and cursing at Carol as I had before—then the real truth about my return to alcohol was bound to come to the fore. And that must be avoided at all cost.

Had I learned how to balance it all? Could I keep everything under control, and keep juggling all those balls successfully? Despite my returning obsession, and the increasing amounts needed to satisfy my thirst, I was going to give it my all, and that was for sure. My only other option was to come clean, and I didn't want to go there. And, I certainly wasn't ready for AA and all those sanctimonious blow-hards. But how long could I sustain this charade and manage what was already becoming somewhat of an obsession within a few short months?

I certainly couldn't forever, but, perhaps over time I could find that even-keel—that neutral-ground—that I was able to achieve for a time with the help of Tom Patterson. He was gone now, though, and I had no idea how I could manage this problem. I needed to buckle down and be strong and careful. Strength of will counted for something, I knew, and I wanted to keep on drinking. I must proceed with extreme caution.

And so, I took a drink.

Chapter Eleven

"*Men and women drink essentially because they like the effect produced by alcohol. The sensation is so elusive that, while they admit it is injurious, they cannot after a time differentiate the true from the false. To them, their alcoholic life seems the only normal one...After they have succumbed to the desire again, as so many do, and the phenomenon of craving develops, they pass through the well-known stages of a spree, emerging remorseful, with a firm resolution not to drink again. This is repeated over and over, and unless this person can experience an entire psychic change there is very little hope of his recovery.*"

—Page xxix, *The Doctor's Opinion*, "*Alcoholics Anonymous*"

I'm standing on the back deck of my childhood home in the Jersey Shore community of Harvey Cedars. It's a mild, summer day, and I'm looking out over the scenic lagoon panorama. Boats are everywhere, and I have a strange, unsettled feeling when I notice that many of them are anchored.

Literally dozens of people are out of their boats, I see, treading around in the chest-deep water digging clams. They shouldn't be doing that—that's illegal! I want to call the marine police, or something.

I glance over and see Mike Cass seated over by the picnic table. He's about two feet in front of my grandmother, and he's gesturing wildly, making point after point. I can't make out what he's saying, but Mimi, my dad's mom, is just nodding her head as Mike carries on. She's smiling, but I'm troubled when I notice the breathing tubes up her nose. He leans over and lights a Lucky Strike for her. What's the matter with him, anyway? After all, doesn't he realize that the Lucky Strikes ended up killing her back in 1986? He shouldn't be bothering her like that. I want to tell him to knock it off. Instead, I turn and go inside.

The TV is on, and my dad and two brothers are seated in front of it watching the Phillies intently. I look at the screen, and I'm immediately frustrated because I can't see the players, don't know the score, who they're playing or anything at all about the game. My brothers bark at me to move, and Dad shoos me aside. I want to ask them the score, but for some reason, I don't.

I walk the few feet to the kitchen counter where Mom greets me with a big smile. She's wiping down the counter, and I reach for the bottle of vodka sitting there right in front of me. Before I can grab it, Mom asks me to go wake up Carol, as dinner is almost ready. This angers me, because she didn't give me time to make a drink first. I want to tell her to leave me alone; that we should let Carol sleep so I can sneak a few. But, again, I simply turn and walk away.

I enter my parent's master bedroom. It's almost pitch-black, but I can clearly make out my dog, Tammy lying on the bed at the foot of a slumbering Carol. I walk over to them. Tammy got run over by a car in 1982, and she greets me with her typical, bright face and wagging tail. She shouldn't be on the bed, I think. Mom will be pissed if she sees this. I lean down and pet her. A sense of calmness washes over me as her flapping tongue administers about 50 rapid-fire licks to my face.

My annoyed, frustrated feeling changes even further as Carol opens her eyes and looks at me. This particular look gives me a feeling of total tranquility. There's a welcoming and forgiving sentiment in her eyes, and I want nothing else but to crawl into that bed and hold her in a long, loving embrace. She beckons me with her hand.

"VITALS!" a voice pummels me back to consciousness. I open my eyes and I'm once again blinded by the over-head light. "I'll be back, Honey," I think I say in my stupor.

"Oh shit! Not again." I hear Mike Cass groan in the bed next to me. He picks his head up a few inches. "And who the fuck are you calling Honey?"

I sit up and put my feet on the floor. "Go back to sleep, Mike," I tell him, yawning and laughing at the same time. I grab a tee-shirt and a pair of shorts lying at my feet and slip them on. Not wanting to repeat the shock of the previous night, I had mentally prepared myself for this 4 AM visit when I turned in a few hours ago; and within seconds I silently motion the night-nurse to come over and take my readings. She comes over, sits next me and takes my pulse, blood-pressure and temperature. She whispers in my ear, "138 over 85." I smile faintly and nod. The trend is good.

Unable to get back to sleep, I walk down to Darcy just before sunrise. Sitting there with my notebook, I recall last night's AA meeting. The three older guys who ran the meeting were on their monthly commitment from a nearby group. They've been coming to Carrier for years, joking and telling wild stories from their vast experience in the field of drunkenness.

At the end of their alcoholic careers, they all found themselves at differing degrees of desperation, and finally came to the conclusion that AA and a higher power were the only things standing between life and a horrible death from drinking. They regaled us all with what they called their "drunkalog," and the hour passed in what seemed to me a matter of minutes.

Between the three of them, I think they had something like 75 years of sobriety, and they had all the slogans and acronyms of AA down pat. Everyone knows some of the more clichéd phrases like, "one day at a time," or "keep it simple," but the acronyms were new to me.

They told us to "halt" that if we felt "hungry, angry, lonely or tired." Any one of these sensations can trigger a drinking spree, they said, and we should be constantly vigilant. "Halt what you're doing and get to an AA meeting, or call someone in the program if one of these four emotions should strike you," they said.

They told us that if we felt "fine," we should "push." Many of us looked around in puzzlement at this suggestion. Kara A., of course, shot her hand up, but was thankfully ignored. I think these guys might have remembered her from one of her previous stays at Carrier, and so spared everyone the pain.

"I'm sure you all feel *fine*," the leader then told us sardonically. He then made himself clear. "That is, 'fucked-up, ignorant, neurotic and emotional.'" He ticked off each one on his fingers. I knew that with the possible exception of neurotic, I certainly qualified. He looked at us for a long moment, and then he continued.

"This is when you have to *push*. That is, 'pray until something happens.' God is the key," he told us. "And it can be any God you like—as long as it's not you. Many of you have tried to play God, and look where it got you." He stared around at all of us. "I found my higher power, and I talk to Him on a daily basis. Many times, He's the only thing standing between me and a drink; so I better talk to him. I suggest that today—and more importantly when you get out of here, and things are better—you do the same." I took a lot of notes.

Around 7 AM, I'm sitting out in the smoking area with my coffee, enjoying the cool, morning light. A few people have been up and about, but I'm surprised to see Eva open the door of the group lounge and slowly make her way toward me. She's wearing a gray sweat-suit, and, for the first time that I can recall, is not accompanied by Stanley. She walks right up me holding an unlit cigarette.

"Got a light?" she asks with a gentle smile. Eva looks halfway decent—a thousand times better than when I first laid eyes on her—but she's still extremely pale. Her brown eyes are slightly blood-shot, and her face is puffy, as if she's been in a fight or something; but the change for the better in only two days is remarkable. I take out my lighter and hand it to her.

"I've seen you around. I'm Eva," she tells me, lighting up.

"Eric," I say, and stick out my hand. She shakes it, and hands me back the lighter. I say, "You're looking much better. Are you feeling better?"

"Definitely," she says, taking a drag. "I *really* thought I was dead."

"That makes two of us," I say. Eva frowns at me. "That's not what I meant," I try to explain. "I mean, I thought a couple days ago that I was dead too, but—here we are!" I hold out my hands and give a quick laugh. Eva smiles and takes another puff.

"I'm sorry, Eva, but you *really did* look like you were dying," I say, trying to be honest, but not too much so.

"Heroin," she says flatly. "Another trip on the merry-go-round; but this was the worst yet. They had to pump fluids into me twice. It was touch and go there for awhile." She says it matter-of-factly, almost casually.

"Wow," I say, shaking my head. "We knew it was bad, but… Have you been able to eat yet?" I ask.

"Yeah, since yesterday; I think the worst is over." Her voice is steady and almost confident.

"For me too, I hope," I tell her, but not so confidently. "I'm waiting to see the doctor about my blood-test—my liver." I point to my right side.

"I thought maybe you were in for heroin too by the look of your arms there." She points to my "tracks" on both arms.

"Nah, booze," I say, smiling and holding out both of my bruised arms. "She just kept missing. I was like a friggin' pin-cushion! It's does make for good conversation." Eva smiles again.

"At least they found your veins. I couldn't find mine at the end." Eva looks down at the ground, and brings the cigarette to her lips. I do the same. "I've got to find a way out of this," she says in a low, somber tone. We're quiet for a minute. Eventually, she looks up at me. "I saw you were in pain after that phone-call yesterday. Is everything alright?"

I'm surprised by the question, but I do recall the knowing way she was looking at me at the time. "Well, actually, no," I say, recovering. "I don't know if I'll be going home to my family." I pause, then add, "I, I could tell you kinda knew something. It was in your look," I meet her eyes again. "It was like we were sharing our pain or something."

"I could see you were really hurting," Eva says, smiling. "I hope it all works out."

I'm trying to understand how she was able to read me like that, and how I picked up on the look in her eyes yesterday. I can read Carol like that, too, I realize, though lately, and for good reason, it's been *all* bad looks from her. My mood darkens.

Suddenly, a wild shriek off in the distance breaks the silence. It's a piercing, high-pitched "Ah-EH! Ah-EH! Ah-EH!" And it seems to be coming from the general direction of a few out-buildings visible about 500 yards away.

"What in the hell is THAT?" I say. We look at each other.

"It's a bird of some kind, I think," Eva says.

"Even the birds are nutty around here," I say, chuckling.

We listen intently as the noise continues in intervals of three for about a minute or so, then it suddenly stops. The piercing noise sounds like a cross between a rooster's call and a hawk's. I know I've heard the sound somewhere before, but I can't place it.

"I saw some guinea-hens while I was walking yesterday," I say, "but I don't think they sound like that."

"Eric H!" a voice calls from the door. I turn and see Nurse Sharon waving to me. "Go see the doctor, please."

"Okay!" I call back, and snuff out my butt. I turn and start heading back toward Blake. "Great to finally meet you, Eva," I say, leaving. "I'm so glad we both might live!"

"Yeah, good luck Eric!"

Dr. Shariff greets me with a caring smile as I walk through her door near the exit of Blake. She's dressed in business black, and has her long, jet-black hair pulled back in a neat pony-tail. She motions me to have a seat on the exam table.

"Well, you're looking a little better," she tells me, her deep -brown eyes bearing into mine. "How do you feel?"

"I can't believe how good I feel," I tell her. "I'm getting less sleep than I did when I was drinking, and I still feel better. It's amazing."

She picks up a file and looks at it. "Your liver numbers have improved," she says. "The enzyme readings are below 1000—still *way* too high, but better. I like the trend. We'll take one more blood-test before you leave" She looks at another page. "I think that will be…Saturday. Your insurance is paying through Saturday, I believe. Talk to Carley about all that; but, I think you're on the right track."

"Well, that *is* good news," I say, sighing with relief. "I'm still feeling jittery, but nothing like I imagined," I tell her. "That Librium sure does the trick."

"Today is your last day for that," she says flatly, making a note. "We'll put you on some milder stuff tomorrow. Your blood pressure is also a little better, but I'm going to up your Lisinopril to 10 milligrams. When was the last time you saw your doctor?"

I have to think about this one. "Maybe, about a year and a half ago," I say unsurely. "That's when he prescribed it for me. He also gave me Ativan, because he told me it would help me quit drinking."

"Well, did it?" She asks me.

"Of course not, because I didn't want to stop." I look away from Dr. Shariff in disgust. "I just kept taking it as long as he would give it to me. It helped me relax, and I just drank right along with it. I ended up getting mildly addicted to that, too, just like the Valium another doctor gave me six years ago when I 'stopped' drinking then."

"Eric," she says forcefully. I look at her. "That's why we stop the Librium after three days. No drug will keep you from picking up that first drink. Actually, it often works the other way around. *You* are the only one who can do that. But you need help. Are you getting the help you need here?"

"Doctor, it's exactly the help I need." I smile at her. "The groups are great, you've been great and the AA meetings—well, I'm going to be going to *a lot* of those when I get out of here, I can tell you."

"Good," she says. "You know, as a profession, we doctors don't officially endorse AA; but we know how it's helped millions overcome alcoholism over the years. Drugs can help you with the symptoms, but the cause—the drinking?" Dr. Shariff holds out her hands and shrugs. "At the end of the day, it's all up to you. A program like AA gives you a better than average chance, if you really work it."

I nod enthusiastically.

"After you get out of here in a few days, go to a meeting, and do what they tell you to do," she tells me, "*and,* don't pick up that first drink." She changes the subject. "Are you getting along with the other patients and nurses?"

"Again," I respond, "it's amazing! I have two great roommates, and the others are just trying to do the best they can, like me. We're all together in this—drunks and addicts. Sharon and Donna are fantastic. It's kind of weird, though," I say.

The doctor cocks her head. "What?"

"Sometimes I feel I'm having too much fun in here. So many things and events keep popping up that are just hilarious to me. My roommate, Mike, you know Mike Cass?"

"Oh, yeah," she rolls her eyes. "We all know Mike—very funny guy."

"That's putting it mildly," I say with a laugh. "I don't know. It feels like some kind of demented, sleep-away camp or something." Dr. Shariff laughs out loud. "God, five minutes ago I heard a wild bird shrieking outside," I say. "It's just crazy."

"Oh, that's the peacock," she says matter-of-factly, making a few notes on my file.

"The peacock?" I laugh. "Oh, of course, the peacock," I say, suddenly realizing where I've heard that sound before. "I can't wait to tell Mike."

"Listen Eric," Dr. Shariff says, looking up at me seriously. "Just try to stay focused on why you're here. You're sober and feeling better in this controlled environment, but you've got a long way to go. The last thing you want is over-confidence. Remember, 75% of the people you see in here will go back out and continue using. There's nothing wrong with staying upbeat, and even having a bit of fun, but remember that this disease almost killed you. And, if you start up again, it probably will."

"I really don't want to end up like Joe Darcy, Doctor," I tell her, and mean it. "I think I get it this time."

"Good," she replies. "Everybody knows about him in here, but there are hundreds of other Joe Darcys out there dying because of this disease every day." She looks at me. I continue to nod slowly. She finally says, "Do you have any questions?"

"No," I say. I feel my empty stomach rumbling.

"Okay," she says. "I'll arrange for another blood-test on Saturday. Oh, and Eric," I tilt up my head, "losing 25 pounds will help your blood-pressure and everything else, too. That might be a good next step."

"I'm hearing a lot about steps in here. It sounds good to me."

I see Nurse Sharon, who gives me my increased dose of Lisinopril, and my penultimate dose of Librium. I'm extremely thankful when she informs me that, because of my improving blood pressure readings, I won't have to endure 4 AM vitals anymore. "This calls for a brisk walk!" I announce to her gleefully. "I want to go see that Carrier mascot, the peacock." Sharon laughs. I grab my jacket from the room and head out the door.

Mike and Ebby are nowhere to be found. I assume they are already over in the cafeteria, but despite my hunger, I resist the urge to join them. I have a good half-hour to kill, and I need to get my blood moving. I make a right after exiting Blake and walk smartly in the same direction I went yesterday. The road winds through the massive grounds of Carrier, and I notice a few other buildings housing other types of patients, I assume.

The road ends at Rt. 601 about half-a-mile down, and I turn and retrace my steps. I wonder how many patients have come to that intersection over the years, and have either stuck out their thumb or simply kept walking. *Damn!* I think to myself. At the pace I'm taking, I'd probably be in Princeton in two hours—maybe three and I'd be home in Ewing. I lose that thought, put my head down and pick up the pace.

I make it back to Blake, but instead of making a right into the admissions building where the cafeteria is, I continue down the road. Yesterday, this is where my feeble walk ended, but today I'm determined to forge ahead and fill the entire half -hour.

The road bends to the right, and I pass the main entrance where I entered the other day. I notice the tree that "moved" on me the other day, causing me six hours of hell at the ER, and sigh. That event somehow seems distant to me. It's like a bad dream that happened weeks ago, I reflect. For that matter, the last three months seem like a nightmare—and they were— for me and especially those who care for me. *Should I call Carol today? No—first thing tomorrow. Concentrate on recovery!* I increase my stride even more.

The road eventually winds past a few of what must be the original buildings—their withered exteriors and broken windows plainly evident. Just past the last of these, I come upon a tennis court. It hasn't been used in years, I assume, by the look of it. It's partially hidden by untended forsythia, but I can plainly see that the fence surrounding it is rusted and broken in places, and there's no net, of course. The court surface is cracked with weeds pushing through everywhere.

Passing the dilapidated court, I'm startled to see that there is some activity going on. I'm probably 100 yards or so from it, but I can plainly see a lot of guinea hens milling around it. I walk over closer and I'm astonished to see that many of them are actually trapped inside the court trying to get out. They resemble little, gray basketballs moving around the court. There are at least a dozen of them pecking at the fence from the inside, some of their friends pecking furiously on the other side seeming to say, "How the hell did you get in there, Molly?" Or, "You *must* have flown in, Harry, well just fly out then!" I smile. Maybe they're in there for a tick-gorging addiction! *You are powerless against the tick. Your lives have become unmanageable.* I smile again. "When you get out, better get to a meeting," I say out loud to them, as they peck, peck, peck. The guys back at Blake will never believe me.

The road inside the vast grounds of Carrier, I discover, is perhaps a mile-long semi-circle, and this portion also ends at Rt. 601. I come to the end, turn and start back, taking a wider, northerly tack toward a large, empty parking lot. This way leads in the general direction of where I heard the peacock's call.

At the end of the parking lot, I continue straight onto a dirt path that ends within view of Blake. The maintenance building and another, smaller structure stand at the end of the path. A fenced-in enclosure surrounds the smaller building, and, coming upon it, I see many chickens and a huge, white turkey inside that area. As I approach the fence, the chickens scatter, and the big gobbler becomes agitated, puffing out his chest and strutting peevishly. I pause at the fence, and what has to be a 40-pound bird comes over, sticks his bearded head through an opening and makes a wild stab at me. I wisely back off, as he gobbles maliciously. I'm a little put-off by this. After all, I'm not there with an ax, for God's sake, so, as I turn to leave, I provoke him even more with a few, choice gobbles of my own. This pisses him off even more. I shake my head. He and Henry should have a talk, I think.

Starting the final 500 yards or so back, I take one last look around, and—*there he is*. The grand peacock is standing at the tree-line bordering the grounds about 100 yards away. He's not shrieking or showing his magnificent plumage, but I can plainly see that he has it. He's slowly walking down the tree-line, pecking at the ground; and I make out his long, trailing retinue of brilliant feathers bunched up behind him. The trailing plumage must be five feet long, I see. I'm fascinated by the sight—and a bit confused. Why the hell is there a peacock at Carrier Clinic, anyway? I shrug and continue to watch him for a few more minutes. I finally turn and cover the last few hundred yards to the cafeteria.

Before I reach the back door of the large main building holding the cafeteria, Mike Cass, Ebby and Bobby Brooklyn burst out and start heading across the road to Blake. Mike turns his head and sees me coming. "Hey, Buddy Boy! Hurry up with breakfast. You don't want to be late for the beautiful Carley and all those rules and regs."

"Were you walking?" Ebby asks me. "If you want, you can join Kara, Maxine and I now if you like. We've got a little time until group starts."

"No thanks, I just finished about two miles," I say. I tell them all about the incarcerated guinea hens, the pissed-off turkey and, of course the peacock. After I mention the peacock Mike says, "Get the fuck out of here! Peacocks? No way!"

"No, it's true, Mike," Ebby says with excitement. "Remember I told you about him? They take the messed-up kids over there to see all those animals—therapy, they say."

Mike nods and makes a grunting noise.

"I think we should get some of those peacock feathers and make a head-dress for Mike here," Bobby puts in.

"What, are you part Indian or something?" I ask Mike, puzzled.

He starts to answer, but Ebby beats him to it. "No, Mike is a proud member of the Awopaho tribe." Ebby puts his arm around Mike as he says this.

"A-what?" I stammer.

Mike smiles broadly. "A-WOP-a ho" he says, slowly emphasizing the "wop" part. He then adds breezily, "It's the Native-Italian-American tribe that's ruled the New York/New Jersey area for generations." He reaches up and touches his immoveable hair. "I probably could use a head-dress. Good idea, Bobby."

We all laugh. Ebby and Bobby start to walk away. I hear the Brooklyn boy telling Ebby that he wants to go for a walk, too. "I wanna see those fucking guinea-hens. That sounds like a riot."

"Mike," I say. He cocks his head. "Do you remember that scene in *Papillion* when Steve McQueen is escaping and they're in the jungle, then that bird screeches and I think they get captured?"

"Yeah, sure do. That was a peacock—trapped, I believe," Mike says.

"Exactly! Well, I heard that same noise about an hour ago out back having a smoke with Eva, and I thought I'd heard it before. Now I know where. It's unbelievable."

Mike nods. He then snaps his fingers and smiles. "Do you remember later in that movie—the dream-scene?"

"Yes," I nod, trying to think. "What were the lines?"

Mike quotes verbatim: "McQueen says, 'I'm not guilty! I didn't kill that pimp!' Then the judge says, what, 'You're accused of something far greater,' or something like that. 'I accuse you of a wasted life!'

'Guilty,' McQueen mutters and mopes away. 'Guilty!'"

"Wow," I say, impressed. "That was great! You got it exactly right."

"Well, Buddy Boy" Mike says, as he pats me on the back and starts walking away, "*are we guilty*?"

I walk into the cafeteria and chew on that for a while—along with my breakfast.

Two meals and about 11 hours later, I'm sitting in Darcy making notes and considering calling home. All day Mike has continually advised against it. "Just wait 'til the morning," he kept telling me, "You're doing better. Let her cool off some more with another night's sleep." I think I agree with him. I'll let her know in the morning that I'll probably be leaving here on Monday. Then I'll beg, plead and cajole her to let me get back into my home. "Just don't push it, for God's sake!" Mike counseled me. "Just put it out there, and have her think about it, that's all." He's absolutely right.

God, I miss her. And, I miss my kids terribly: Matt and Natalie—and Katie. I wonder how Katie's doing. She's a freshman at Princeton, and we haven't really spoken much since we moved her into her dorm room back in September. I'm sure she's disgusted with me, and why wouldn't she be? I sadly recall that she was witness to one of the last big blow-ups before I moved out in January. Once again, I was out of control, screaming at Carol and dropping the "fucking bitch" bomb left and right. *What a complete asshole I am.*

Carley confirmed the fact that my insurance coverage will end on Saturday. Five days is about the norm for private insurance companies these days, she told me. I'm willing to pay the $500 for the extra day, however, and I already worked that out with the business office. I also learned from Carley that my deductible is $1500. Despite my devastated financial situation, I'm resigned to this reality, as well. I'll work out a payment plan, and stretch the monthly recompense as far into the future as they'll let me. This is, after all, money well-spent. I completely wasted all those thousands before, and now I'm absolutely determined not to waste the money spent here.

Carley also advised that Carol and I have a joint-counseling session when—and if—she picks me up. I hope and pray that Carol goes for this idea. After all, she's been after me to go to joint and even solo counseling for months. This would be a perfect opportunity to help clear the air. I'll mention it to her in the morning, and then, if she agrees, Carley said she will host the session. If nothing else, I'm sure it will give Carol a chance to vent. "It will give her a chance to put her foot up your ass!" Mike predicted, in his usual "underplayed" manner.

One of the morning groups, hosted by "Professor" Tim, was a surprise and a godsend. He informed us at the start of the meeting that we were going to have a group meditation. The 30 or so patients gathered around the room seemed to have about 30 different reactions to this news. Henry, seeming much more docile today now that his meds were kicking in, sat back and smiled. Mike and Bobby, seated on either side of me, groaned audibly in apparent opposition to the idea. Mr. T, Jason, being a well-seasoned veteran of four or five other respectable rehab facilities, started a side lecture on how to *properly* conduct a successful group meditation. And, of course, as if on cue, Kara Alcoholic's hand shot up; but Tim ignored her because, at that moment, Morris the Hat shuffled in.

At the start, Tim had told us to remove all our caps and take out of the room all drinks, water excluded. We did as instructed, but "The Hat" missed that part, and was now in violation of both regulations—Again! "Morris!" Tim almost shouted at him. "Get rid of the coffee, and remove your hat."

Morris, adorned with the same loose-fitting hoodie and sweats as yesterday, took a moment to stop. He slowly turned his head in the general direction of Tim and said, "Huh?"

"Yes, you Morris!" Tim was losing patience quickly. "Out with the coffee and off with the hat." Tim pointed to the door. Morris was still just looking at Tim. "Today, Morris! Are you there?" It took Morris more than a few seconds for all these words to sink in, I guess, but he eventually turned and started making his way for the exit. Ebby, in his usual seat by the door, opened it for him, and watched carefully as The Hat slowly passed by. At this moment, Mike wrote a note on his pad regarding Morris and showed it to me: "Whatever he's on, count me in!" After what seemed a few minutes, The Hat returned hatless and we finally began.

Tim had the lights dimmed, and made us all relax our neck and shoulders. He also had us sit up as straight as we could, but in as relaxed a position as possible. He then had us picture a large tree standing solitary in a clearing. We were now to become that tree.

"In through the nose, out through the mouth," Tim kept intoning, chant-like. He liked to repeat the line two or three times in a row, in a kind of slow sing-song—his voice dreamy and distant. "In through the nose," would rise slightly in pitch, un-resolving. And then, after a pause of three or four seconds, came "out through the mouth." His voice would fall down and dissolve with our collective exhalations.

The result in only a few minutes was almost magical. The simple act of controlled breathing was so utterly calming I almost didn't bother paying attention to his narrative about us all becoming this tree. In between his intonations, Tim started bringing us up through the roots of the massive tree, into the trunk, and then finally out through the limbs, branches and leaves. Always between each section of the tree we were becoming came the eerily sublime, "in through the nose…out through the mouth," repeated over and over again.

40 minutes never passed so quickly, and the results were soon obvious, at least to me. When the noon vitals were taken my pulse was down to 68, and my pressure was a childlike 124/82—both Carrier Clinic lows for me! I told Mike Cass that if I used the meditation technique at appropriate times, I might never lose my temper again. He said, ala Professor Tim, "In through the nose…out through the mouth. Ahh!"

After lunch, Mike and I were out back having a smoke when Mr. T approached. He swaggered up to us dressed in his faded-blue hoodie, a huge smile pinned to his handsome face. "You guys need smokes?" he asked. "My girl brought me up a carton last night. Seven bucks a pack."

We declined his offer. All morning I had been telling anyone who would listen about my "wild kingdom" adventure of earlier, but when I mentioned it to Jason, he simply brushed it off.

"Yeah, I've seen all those animals," he said, adding, "Where I'm going, they've got armadillos and wild hogs and such."

"Oh yeah, and where's that?" Mike asked.

"Texas!" Jason responded with a certain amount of excitement. "I'm getting married down there, and there's a good job waiting for me. I just need to clean up my act."

Mike and I shared a quick glance. We both see Jason's chances for "cleaning up his act" as nil. At the ping-pong table, or before and after groups, we hear him constantly waxing longingly of the wonders of "Oxys" and "Speed-balls" and the like. We know this is at least his fourth rehab, and that it most likely won't be his last, if in fact he makes it to another one. He's even shared openly with the group the fact that he's infected with hepatitis C from sharing needles; but soft-pedaled the revelation with the casual assurance of receiving "a cure whenever he's ready." It seems that so many of the young addicts—indeed many of all of us—raise their one hand in groups and meetings and freely proclaim their addiction, while the other hand is hidden behind them, fingers crossed.

Despite his boorish, overburdening nature, I like the kid. He's got style and chutzpah, and he adds a certain color to our varied group of unfortunates. He's young and strong, and obviously has a tremendous personality and self-confidence. If by some miracle he *can* clean up his act, he could have a bright future, I reckon.

I recently had read a book on Davey Crockett, another brash and impetuous individual who went off to Texas to face his own destiny.

I said to him, "You know what Davey Crockett said about Texas, don't you?"

"Who's that?" Jason replied, a puzzled look on his face.

"One of the Alamo guys back in 1836 or something," I said.

"Yeah," added Mike Cass. "John Wayne played him in that movie."

"Okay," Jason nodded. "I've heard of the Alamo. What did he say?"

"The reason he went to Texas was because he lost an election to Congress in Tennessee. Just before he left he said, 'The good people of Tennessee voted me out; well, they can all go to hell! I'm goin' to Texas!'"

At this minor punch-line Jason almost doubled over. He found this quote absolutely hilarious. "I hope I do better than him!" he declared, moving away in hysterics. "They can go to hell! I'm going to Texas!" He just kept saying it.

"It's not that funny," I said to Mike, as we watched Jason bouncing around from person to person like a ball, repeating the quote.

"I wonder if his girlfriend brought him anything else besides smokes?" Mike replied, quite suggestively I thought.

Tim also conducted the 4 PM group, and I came in a few minutes early after vitals. I asked him if we might have another meditation group at some point, and he shrugged and added a non-committal "perhaps." He was fooling around with the VCR, and after he pushed a button, a quick glimpse appeared on the screen from "Indiana Jones and the Last Crusade."

"Are we gonna watch a movie?" Kara A. asked with eagerness.

"Actually, yes!" Tim replied, but then qualified his statement. "Well, a little bit of one."

Henry was the last to arrive for this group. Even The Hat, now even droopier and more forlorn than ever, beat Henry to a seat. Nurse Sharon and Dr. Shariff must have given Henry something powerful to settle him down, because he was "out there." He seemed a bit calmer earlier, but now he was practically trance-like. He shuffled in the room like a zombie, his face blank and expressionless. More than a few of us were watching him intently as he plopped down in a seat, his half-closed eyes dropping to the notepad he gripped. *There was no way that Henry was going home tomorrow*, I thought, and that was probably a good thing. Tim, also watching him carefully, finally got things started.

He pointed to the chalkboard where the first three steps of AA and NA were written out. We:

1.   Admitted we were powerless over alcohol/drugs—that our lives had become unmanageable.

2.   Came to believe that a power greater than ourselves could restore us to sanity.

3.   Made a decision to turn our will and our lives over to the care of God *as we understood Him.*

Tim had underlined the words "powerless" and "unmanageable" in the first step, "power greater than ourselves" in the second, and "turn our lives and will over to the care of God" in the third.

"Notice the underlined words and phrases," Tim said. "Without even realizing it, Steven Spielberg in *Indiana Jones and the Last Crusade* employs aspects of these first three steps of the AA/NA program quite well actually," he continued. "We'll watch the climactic grail scene, and I think you'll see what I'm talking about."

Tim pushed a button, and the video began with the Nazi character aiming his gun at Harrison Ford. The guy said something, and then pointed the gun at Sean Connery—Dr. Jones Sr.—and fired. The loud report was followed by a shocking silence on the screen and in the room. But Henry, that driest of all wits, came to life. Out of nowhere, he offered in his "James Bond" best: "Shaken, not stirred!"

The room erupted and Tim scrambled up and shut off the machine. "Come on," he implored us. "Calm down!"

Henry wasn't even smiling, but rather, had his head tilted in a slightly bemused way.

"That's my Henry!" Mike Cass exclaimed above the tumult. After a minute or two, Tim tried again.

This time, he made it through uninterrupted. As Indiana made his perilous way to the grail's lair, Tim stopped the video several times to make points. The first stop was when Indy thought quickly about "kneeling" before God, so as not to be decapitated. "At this point," Tim said, "Jones is completely alone and powerless. In a way, his life is unmanageable. He must turn, not entirely *to* God, but rather to his knowledge *of* God." He started the movie again.

The next stoppage was when Jones nearly fell to his death after failing to correctly spell "Jehovah" with his feet. "Relying more on himself," Tim said, "Jones 'slips,' so to speak, and nearly dies. He then thinks more about God and realizes that Hebrew, not Greek is the correct way to go. He's restored to sanity." This seemed a bit of a stretch, I thought, but, after all, it is Hollywood.

Another pause comes when Indy is faced with the famous "leap of faith" over the gorge—all with John Williams' burgeoning score underneath. It does make sense, at least to me, that in all three of these micro-scenes, Jones was powerless and had to turn to a power greater than himself for vital help.

Tim concurred. "He *accepted* the fact that he was *power-less*, and he was *willing* to ask for help." He stopped the tape at the precise moment when Indy was stepping out over the chasm. "Look at his face," Tim commanded us. "If that's not turning over a life and will to the care of God, then I don't know what is." Well, if he says so.

After starting up the film again, he emphasized this fact even more when Indiana is faced with the fateful choice of which grail to pick. The Nazi, aided by the gorgeous Elsa, had "chosen poorly," and, with the help of special effects, had turned to dust. "That guy obviously thought he could do it on his own. *He* was God," Tim said. "Again, this is where Jones has to really turn his life over to God." Jones makes the "wise choice," and takes a drink. With liquid dripping down his chin, he looks up with uncertainty. As we waited for Jones' reaction—Henry reacted.

"Is it Ketel One or Absolut?" He deadpanned, again sending the room into chaos.

It's now ten to 8, and Ebby and a few others are setting up chairs for the AA meeting. Mike Cass comes over and takes a seat across from me. He opens a pack of twinkies and stuffs one in his mouth. "Why are you always writing?" He asks me thickly through a mouthful of sugary goo.

"Just working on my grand opus," I say. "I might call it 'Carrier Daze,' D-A-Z-E,"

"I was thinking more like," Mike pauses to swallow, then immediately slips the second cake in his mouth, 'Two Flew Over the Carrier's Nest.'"

"Hey! That's great! I'll make a note of that." I do.

Mike swallows hard, and takes a large swig of chocolate milk. He then lets fly a tremendous belch. "Put that in your book!" he tells me.

I laugh. I'm grateful Mike didn't offer me what the wagon master offered Lt. Dunbar in "Dances with Wolves."

"Hey, The Hat is gone," Mike informs me.

"What? No way!" I say. "How could that be? He's a mess."

"He's out, Tom! He must have had shit in his urine—so to speak. Matt the enforcer just walked him right on out of here. They might be putting him in another unit—a lock-down or something."

I shake my head. "Sharon told me they kick them out of here all the time. But how did he get the shit?" I ask. "Matt goes through everything when we get here, right?"

"Maybe a visitor or maybe he had it all along," Mike says with a shrug. "He might have had it up his ass when he came in, I don't know."

"God, I pray he gets help," I say, frowning. "There're so many screwed up people."

We sit there in silence for a minute. Finally I say, "I'm leaving Monday, I think. I'm calling Carol in the morning to see what's up with her. I hope she lets me back."

"Well, good luck with that," Mike says. "I'm out of here Sunday, Buddy Boy. It's back to Manheim and my poor mother."

"What about those prescriptions waiting for you," I ask him delicately.

Mike puts his head down. "I don't know."

The AA meeting is being hosted by a young guy, no more than 25, who appears almost as beaten down and haggard as many of the 15 seated in front of him. He introduces himself as Jay, and he gives his sobriety date as February 21. His face is flush and puffy; his eyes, partially obscured by an oversized ball-cap, look to be blood-shot; and when he starts speaking, it almost seems that he's slurring his words.

Ebby and Bobby are present, as well as Karen, Maxine, Sal and others. Henry is seated at the end of the line of chairs, and, well—he's gone. Just a few minutes into the meeting, after the introductions and the *Serenity Prayer* are recited, I look over at him. His head is slumped, notebook teetering on his lap, and he's already fast asleep. Nurse Donna appears from behind us, wakes him up and slowly escorts him off to his room. No more one-liners from Henry today.

Jay talks for only a few minutes, giving a brief overview of his meteoric rise and fall in the world of drinking. He speaks in fits and starts, not so much slurring, but struggling to find what should be easily accessible word choices. While Jay is speaking, I shoot Ebby a quick look, raising my eyebrows. He returns a similar glance and shrugs. He obviously is thinking the same thing. Whether Jay is on the sauce or not is a question that will never be answered; but he quickly runs out of steam, and then passes the ball to one of the two older men flanking him on either side.

Both of these men, each with over 15 years of sobriety, speak at length, not so much about their drinking careers, but focusing more on their experience, strength and hope as regards steps one, two and three outlined in the "Big Book." On top of the "Indiana Jones" step-work, this is great reinforcement, I think.

The second of these guys, Jim, really seems to catch the group's attention. "Step one is the only one of the 12 that I have to do perfectly each and every day," he tells us. "If I'm to stay sober today, I have to admit my powerlessness over alcohol—period. All the rest of the steps are works in progress. It's all about progress from here on out—*not perfection*," he tells us forcefully.

"Step two brings in the 'power greater than ourselves' to 'restore us to sanity,'" Jim continues. "This is when we call upon Him—the all-important God of your understanding. Step three is when we turn this entire mess over to this God. Look," he tells us, "it's as simple as this: '*I can't—he can—so let him do it.*'" He checks off all three on his fingers. I love the simplicity.

Jim concludes his talk with this, "I can only tell you what's worked for me. It would be so easy to sit up here and preach to you that you need to do this, and this, and that; but that's not what it's all about. I can only speak for myself. These are only suggestions," he emphasizes. "AA is not about intolerance, because all that leads to resentments, and guess what that leads back to?"

Many of us nod, and Bobby blurts out, "A drink!"

"That's right," Jim says. "A drink is where all that leads. It says in the Big Book that 'not one drinker in a thousand likes to be told anything about alcohol,' and that 'if our attitude is one of bitterness or hostility, drinkers will not stand for it!' After all, it says at the end of the *Working with Others* chapter, 'our problems were of our own making.' Ain't that the truth!" He tells us. Most heads are nodding, I see.

"You're all wondering," he continues, "How in the hell am I gonna stop drinking? I wondered that same thing when I sat in one of those chairs 16 years ago. I found AA and my higher power, and I was able to stop—one day at a time. That's all I got."

We all give him a hearty round of applause. Michael, seated on the other side of Jay, interrupts the clapping. He had spoken for about 15 minutes prior to Jim. "Excuse me for double-dipping, but I want to say one more thing," he says. "In *The Doctor's Opinion* at the beginning of the Big Book, Dr. Silkworth talks about the importance of avoiding that first drink. This seems so obvious, but it is of vital importance. The doctor says that when we take that first drink, we succumb to what's known as the 'phenomenon of craving,' and that whatever willpower or desire we may have to quit the drink, it all goes out the window when this craving—this obsession—takes over. Get better, get out of here, and I strongly suggest that you get involved with AA," Michael tells us. "AA stopped me—at least for today—from picking up that first drink. And it's been the most wonderful 15 years of my life. Thank you."

After the meeting, I sit alone in my room and think about what Michael just said. *The Doctor's Opinion* rings a bell with me. I have a Big Book, and it's been gathering dust at home for over two years. Regis, the man who gave it me, told me to read that chapter. He said it would "get me off the hook," or something like that. I read it, and then, being "off the hook," proceeded to continue taking that first drink—day after agonizing day.

I sadly recall the fear and repercussions following my actions on that fateful September night in Hopewell almost five years ago. *That* first drink at the bar was the one that sparked the alcoholic onslaught that eventually led here, I realize. Although I told myself over and over again afterward that I would not return to the way things had been, that is precisely what came to pass. Within only a few weeks of that first drink, I was at it again—full throttle. If I am to live, I must *not* take that first drink. If I am to have a family, I must *not* take that first drink.

I want to live. I want a family. I get down on my knees—and pray.

Chapter Twelve

"The less people tolerated us, the more we withdrew from society, from life itself. As we became subjects of King Alcohol, shivering denizens of his mad realm, the chilling vapor that is loneliness settled down. It thickened, ever becoming blacker. Some of us sought out sordid places, hoping to find understanding companionship and approval. Momentarily we did—then would come oblivion and the awful awakening to face the hideous Four Horsemen—Terror, Bewilderment, Frustration, Despair. Unhappy drinkers who read this page will understand!"

—Page 151, *Alcoholics Anonymous*

I think it's safe to say that most people who have a tendency toward alcoholism can easily trace direct family members who struggled with the disease in one form or another. Just like hair and eye color, there seems to be no doubt that the tendency toward alcoholism is passed on from generation to generation. This genome thankfully missed my mother and father, but both of their fathers certainly displayed this trait— one more acutely than the other.

My dad's father died in 1960, two years before I was born, but had given up booze years before. In his drinking days, he was more of a weekend user, but when he went at it full-tilt, he often became a roaring beast. My dad, although small at the time, remembers episodes between Gramps and my grand-mother, Mimi, that he'd prefer to forget. After a number of excruciating bouts of pancreatitis back in the 40's, and perhaps more than a little thoughtful reflection, he wisely put the bottle down and was able to stay sober for the remainder of his life.

Mom's dad was different. Pappa was a daily, cocktail-party-animal for over 70 years, and a low-ball estimate of his lifetime total of rye and waters consumed must be in the neighborhood of 80,000. For him, every day at five the bottle came out; and it was then neatly stowed away after dinner. He would over-imbibe on occasion for sure, and his fierce Prussian temper would come to the fore; but right up until the end, at age 92, Pappa was able to keep his drinking in check.

I like to think that my drinking career represents a not-so-neat amalgamation of these two individuals. On the chronic side, I worked hard for years trying to keep the disease at bay, drinking daily, but only after work or around the dinner hour or two. Unlike with Pappa, however, over the years it started to become too much. I found that I was beginning to lose control and exhibit acute bad behavior; and the drinking started eating away at other areas of my life, as well. With the help of Carol, I was able to identify this alcohol problem, and I decided to stop. However, unlike Gramps, I was unable to stay stopped, and the consequences over time would be far-reaching.

The unfortunate "first drink" episode that occurred in Hopewell in September of 2005 was behind me. Yes, within mere weeks I was back at it again, full bore, but everything else in my life was still on the right track. Rationalizing the big lie about my return to booze, I weighed all the pros and cons, and I still came out way ahead on the plus side.

Finishing out 2005 and continuing throughout all of '06, my piano teaching was going better than ever, and my work playing at the church was secure and fulfilling. My little vending business was up and running, and that brought in a bit of extra money and helped fill up my days more. I kept up with my gym membership, and, although my evening work-outs were now a thing of the past, I still managed five-to-seven good sessions per week. I was in good shape, and my weight, as long as I continued to make it to the gym, was holding steady.

Life at home was mostly good. I continued to perform all the little things that needed to be done on a daily basis. I did all the yard work, the food shopping and laundry, and I paid all the bills. I was always there for Katie, Matt and little Natalie whenever they needed a hug, a ride, help with homework, bedtime stories—anything at all.

I strove to please my wife, and went out of my way to show my love. I had identified my bad behavior associated with the excess drinking of the past, and redoubled my effort to avoid those same types of conflicts with Carol. I understood that if I were to drink the way I needed to—in my secretive and excessive way—I simply had to behave, because if I started acting like a jerk again, all bets were off. This, for the most part during this prolonged period, I was able to accomplish. I was walking life's tightrope like a Flying Wallenda, and I was able to stay balanced on the wire.

I like to sum it up this way: I thought I deserved every good thing in life. I was a good person with a wonderful, loving family. I had a secure livelihood and a comfortable home in suburbia. Hell, I was born white and well-off in the latter half of the 20th century; in the richest and freest country God had ever put on this planet. Why should I be deprived of anything? Why can't I have it all—including my daily dose of alcohol? Well, why not indeed?

The inescapable answer to these questions would be revealed soon enough. Over time, the unstoppable progression—the never-ending increasing dosage needed to sustain me—marched ahead unchecked. Before I even realized it, the madness created by too much alcohol started to bear down on me.

At some point in 2007, I started drinking in the mornings again. At first, it was the occasional "eye-opener" on days that I didn't have to work. I took a drink or two to stop the inner tremors of withdrawal from the previous night's spree; and I found that, just like in the old days, it worked splendidly. Because most nights were more or less becoming the same now—10 to 12 strong vodkas on the long, winding road home—the mornings tended to greet me similarly; and therefore the morning buzz soon became the norm.

I knew this was a bad thing to do. I was hanging out again with old drinking buddies around town and at the Ivy Inn in Princeton, and I knew that none of them were morning drinkers. This was total alcoholic behavior, I knew. Each day I'd wake up and promise myself not to drink until after work. But, not unlike Bill Murray in *Groundhog Day*, I'd find myself trapped inside the same day—only with me it was the drinking, over and over and over again.

My weekday morning workouts at the gym were getting shorter and becoming less frequent. After I'd finish there, or after getting Natalie on the bus, my first stop in the car would invariably be the liquor store and the morning pint. I found that about three quarters of this would be required to put me in a good place. I'd travel around doing food shopping and other errands, or simply driving the back roads of Mercer County listening to books on tape, all the while drinking my concoction of flavored water and Smirnoff.

After the equivalent of about six drinks in about two hours, I'd call it a morning and return home. The routine was then lunch, three Advil and a long nap. With the hour or two nap, I found that I could then make it through an afternoon and evening of teaching without too much trouble. My drinking engine would then cough back to life after my teaching duties were done, and I'd limp home in the safety and secrecy of my mobile bar.

In my increasingly besotted mind, the control aspect of my drinking was still very important. However, I now had to adapt to more intricate controls. In essence, my drinking had become a full-time job. The pressure of masking its effects and covering all the tracks became all-encompassing. I now had to control and hide two drinking sessions each day, and this reality slowly started to eat away at all the positive gains of the previous three years. Even before the advent of 2008, the edges of my life started to fray.

The first casualty, as mentioned, was my strict adherence to an exercise regimen. Even though I was still showing up regularly at my gym, the number of calories being burned was steadily decreasing. This was in stark contrast to the number of daily alcoholic calories being consumed. Hence, the pounds slowly started to reappear, and by 2008, I was looking more and more like I did before I stopped drinking almost four years prior.

Carol noticed this, of course, and wanted to know why. I put the blame on my increased workload and worsening diet—both at least somewhat truthful explanations. I also told her that lately I had been more slipshod as regards to my workouts, and I would try to redouble my efforts in that area. This was also partially true, but I knew the awful, *real* truth: My morning drinks were gradually replacing the workouts. Whatever reasons I gave Carol, I suppose she believed them, and I felt somewhat mollified in the knowledge of not having to lie about the primary reason for the weight gain.

My quality time with the kids began to suffer. On weekends and days off, I was taking off more and more to satisfy my obsession rather than spending the time with them. As one might expect, for the last few years of my drinking career, I missed countless games, recitals and school events, all in the name of King Alcohol. Getting home later and later because of "work," (I'd generally teach until 7 or 7:30, but rarely return home until 9 or 9:30) I'd often miss tucking Natalie into bed, or any real quality time with Matt and Katie. I'm not proud of much of anything going on in my life around this time, but this is especially true concerning my attitude toward my wonderful children.

Work remained largely unaffected for the time being. Although alcohol was certainly in my system during much of my teaching, I was never what you might call intoxicated. None of my co-workers at Williams or at church on the weekends ever displayed an inkling of knowledge in this area, and I was extremely wary of anyone smelling alcohol. I was never confronted, however, and I took solace in the fact that vodka, with its limited bouquet, could be easily masked with a generous quantity of gum and mints.

I continued to take care of many of my household duties, but, for *some reason*, the monthly credit card bills began to rise significantly. I complained to Carol that living in New Jersey was simply too expensive, and this was true enough. I also pointed to unexpected car repairs and other unforeseen expenses, but she was no fool. She knew that our combined monthly income was more than enough to cover all the bills— including the unanticipated bills and the steadily rising property taxes. On top of that, she knew that there should have been some money left over for our meager nest-egg and the theoretical children's college fund. There wasn't any.

Of course, I knew that the $150-$200 per week being poured down my throat was the real reason for the rising credit card debt, and lack of surplus funds. Nevertheless, I started to react with indignation when the family finances were discussed. I would cleverly throw out the itemized statements showing my 20-30 monthly charges at the liquor stores and bars, and then quarrel with Carol about her apparent spending sprees at department stores and the like.

Carol would then turn it around, bemoaning my reckless vending business venture that cost us $30,000, and would probably take 10 years or more just to recoup that initial investment. She was correct, of course, and I was even skimming some of the small, weekly profits and applying them to "other" areas. But, I never told her that. I just got mad.

This criticism of my financial dealings and bill-paying was, I thought, a direct slap in the face, and I would inevitably react when confronted. After all, didn't Carol know that our credit rating was impeccable, and that all of our bills were being paid—if not in full—at least on time? The arguments about money started to increase in frequency, and, just as I feared would happen, they often ended in slamming doors, broken TV remotes and screaming, expletive-laced tirades— all at Carol's expense.

These episodes, at least as of early 2008, were still the exception rather than the rule in our marriage, and they probably occurred about once a month or so. As spring turned into summer, however, my outbursts were becoming more commonplace, and often over the most trivial of matters. There were the money flare-ups to be sure, and fights about politics and all the free time I had during the day. Carol resented the fact that I could get a nap on most days, and continuously fumed about that. Many times the flare-ups were over ridiculous, petty things. It was all happening more often and I knew it was *all* about the alcohol.

Despite my remorseful, morning-after apologies follow-ing the fire-storms, I could see that Carol was once-again becoming weary. Although I realized the danger of exploding the way I did, and knew that continuing to drink the way I was would certainly do nothing to end the violent outbursts, I found myself completely incapable of stopping myself. One moment, all would be well, and then, following a few seem-ingly innocuous words or even a casual look that I'd perceive as threatening or insensitive, the switch would go on, and I'd blow. With alcohol always fueling my rage, the filter would disappear and the horrible words would flow.

One might ask how Carol missed the fact that I was drinking again. How could she not know, after all? Didn't I look or smell drunk even once in a while? The sad truth in this regard is that I was just too good at hiding or masking it. Each day, my planning reached almost diabolical levels. I invariably knew how much liquor to buy, how much time I had to safely consume it, and then cleverly cover all my tracks. I always stopped drinking 10 or 20 minutes before I got home, and was careful to dispose of all evidence. The gum or mints were an absolute necessity, and if I found myself lacking these on the way home, I'd go 10 miles out of my way to secure them. My careful planning always seemed to work.

Also, and most importantly, my tolerance for booze was more than considerable. Many of my drinking partners over the years had marveled at my ability to appear absolutely sober after a two or three-hour drinking bout. I almost never slurred my speech, and was able to conduct perfectly reasonable conversations after consuming massive amounts. I could walk a straight line with a cop standing right there—and had! And driving? Well, I was in a whole different league where driving drunk was concerned.

In late summer of 2007, I played golf with a couple drinking buddies in the annual Ivy Inn Open in nearby Cranbury. The three of us had played in the tournament for years, and we always had the food and drinks planned out to the letter. We preferred the first tee-off time, and this time was no different. We had our cart fully stocked by the time we hit our opening drives at 9:00.

We started with prosciutto and melon to go along with our jug of mimosas. After a few holes we cracked open the beers and the colossal shrimp cocktail. By the time we finished the round, we had consumed more alcohol than most of the normal-drinking players would the entire day. But, unlike them, we had just begun.

Vodka flowed in the clubhouse for an hour or two, and then we travelled—drinks in hand—clear up to New Brunswick for some go-go activity. Three hours later I was driving my nearly passed-out cohorts back to the Ivy for the afterparty. After about an hour and a few more there, I had to scoop up the two "light-weights" and take them home. At this time, one of them hazily slurred out these words: "God-damn, Eric, you're the best fucking drunken-designated-driver I've ever seen!"

I dropped them off and made it home with no trouble. Still only 7 PM or so, I then mowed my entire lawn. Carol and the kids were down the shore at my parents' house, so I didn't have to worry about any tricky confrontations. Feeling the need for more, I decided to take a trip down to Atlantic City and a bit of gambling. Before taking off, I showered and called Carol. We had a perfectly splendid conversation, and I told her about "some" of the fun I had that day.

Restored somewhat by the shower, and buoyed by my successful conversation with Carol, I left the house in fine fiddle. Drinking all the way down to the casinos, I then proceeded to hit the black-jack tables, and actually won back all the money I had spent that day. I then made an about-face and drank all the way back home.

After a monumental pig-out, I passed out in my bed after midnight—and then rose in agony six hours later to travel up to Elizabeth to play the Sunday masses. Thinking about the previous day on my way to church, I calculated my intake of the day before at well over 30 drinks—all taken with complete impunity.

As if I didn't already have enough to handle with booze, I found something else to add to the mayhem. In early 2008, I started becoming friendly with a bartender at a local club. Trevor was a good looking, slender black fellow of about 40. I liked him immediately. He made great drinks, was quick-witted, and I soon found that he and I shared a love of 50's and 60's Frank Sinatra music. We started hanging out a bit after work. I'd go to his apartment, he'd pour the booze and I'd put on some swingin' classics. One day he asked me if I liked blow. For some reason, I said, "Sure, line-em up!" And so it began.

I hadn't touched cocaine in over 20 years since my graduate days living high in the city with Nancy. The end for me and coke came just after budding-basketball sensation Len Bias keeled over after a night of heavy snorting. One night in Manhattan, after about 20 lines, I thought I was going to be next.

The terrible fall from the monumental high of cocaine can be awful, and this night would prove to be the worst for me. I remember pacing up and down 75th street on the Upper East Side, back and forth past Nancy's apartment waiting for my heart to give out. It was a panic attack times 10, and I was sure that I was going to end up as dead as the hoop star. For what seemed hours, my heart pounded, my body trembled and the sweat poured off of me in the sultry, summer heat. Eventually, the effects wore off and I started to settle down. But, I swore then and there that I would never again put that stuff up my nose, and risk that helpless, desperate feeling again.

That was 20 years ago, though. Maybe this time around it would be different. And, unluckily for Eric, it was! Possibly because of all the booze that was ever-present in my system, or because the cocaine was "cut up" more and lacked some of the heavy punch that it used to contain, I found that I didn't have to endure the terrible crashes that affected me all those years before. The high was still that amazing, "leap tall buildings in a single bound" state of euphoria, but the mild, down-side was what kept me coming back for more. It was a gentler landing than before, and I needed that. After a session, it would still take hours to get to sleep, but my heart didn't race, and I didn't feel that awful, panicky awareness that nearly killed me up in New York.

I started buying some from Trevor, and by the summer, I was using at least two grams per week—or about $160 worth. I realized the cost, combined with the mounting booze-tab, was not at all good. In order to protect my secret life, I found myself turning to a pattern of creative bookkeeping that was deviously elusive to Carol right up until the bitter end. We had some mutual funds, life-insurance policies and stocks, but it was the all-important Home Equity line of credit that eventually took it on the chin. I'd need every penny I could get from these—and more—to satisfy my obsessions over the next year-and-a half.

For me at that time, there were two other significant reasons for using cocaine. First, I found that after a session with Trevor or even by myself, I could go home and behave. It sounds crazy, but I was able to relax and be a well-mannered husband and father on the stuff. I know many people go wild after using, and go on rampages and such, but that wasn't the case with me. I'd be all revved up, for sure, but when I got home, I almost always put the excess energy to good, not bad. I went to work doing laundry or dishes, washed floors or did outside work. I did anything at all to keep moving. And, more importantly I wouldn't pick fights with Carol or even respond if she got after me about something.

Secondly, in my twisted mind, I liked to believe that cocaine was a useful dietetic. I can't tell you how many delicious meals I passed on because of cocaine's amazing ability to completely block any desire for food. As an appetite suppressant, coke is in a class by itself, and I actually thought I could lose weight on it. Of course, many people do by using it every day, but I never achieved that level of insanity. My nutty weight-loss theory would never work, I soon discovered, because the day following a binge, I'd usually eat enough for both days.

Whatever the reasons, my daily booze-brother now had a young protégé; and now, during the summer of 2008, especially on coked-up days, I was continuing to *act* as if I were sober. Without the blow, however, my behavior continued to deteriorate. I wasn't just getting mad about things, I was exploding. Carol saw the trend toward rage occurring more and more, and often asked me point blank the obvious question. "*No! I have not been drinking!*" I'd lie over and over again.

She was at her wit's end trying to figure out what was going on with me. She hadn't broached the subject of divorce as yet, but I'm certain it was starting to cross her mind. She did suggest anger management and/or marriage counseling sessions as a way to help the situation; but I brushed off these suggestions, knowing deep down what really had to be done to improve my behavior. During relatively sober moments, I'd simply make promises to try, try again to be a better, more stable husband and father. I told her truthfully that I loved her more than anything, and things would be better. "I promise," were two very popular words around this time.

The promises were broken and the battles continued, however. Carol's typical response during one of my outbursts would go something like this: "What is the matter with you? Why are you so angry all the time?"

I'd say, "You're always nit-picking everything I do. I can't do anything right! Don't you appreciate all the little things I do every day around here?"

"Eric, I do, but, how about doing a few of the big things, like not calling me a fucking bitch?" This response always knocked me for a loop, and I'd retreat to a neutral corner for a time.

I knew that this situation couldn't continue on indefinitely. Carol was very unhappy and before long she'd be after a divorce. This was the last thing I wanted, and I knew that I had to face the real possibility of quitting the drink once and for all.

But, how could I? Booze had become a full-blown obsession and I had no idea how to proceed. The coke was a passing fancy, I thought at the time, and no big deal. Hell, I never even wanted to touch the stuff if I wasn't drinking anyway. I still had enough sense to know that we'd all be out on the street—at least I would be—if I started buying eight-balls every other day, so cocaine's impact would tend to be limited. *It was always about the alcohol.* I knew that I'd be absolutely miserable without drink in my life. Tom Patterson had told me about his father-in-law, Dusty, and what he had to endure following his last drunk.

Dusty was a big boozer for all of his adult life, and health problems and near-insanity finally convinced him that he couldn't do it anymore. For him, as it eventually is for all alcoholics, the choice was clear: live without it, or die with it.

He chose life, but at what cost? Every night after dinner, Tom told me, Dusty would sit stewing in his easy chair, longing for his old friend. Every half hour, on the dot, he'd make a notch in the arm of his chair, signifying another period of time endured without a drink. The way Tom told it, Dusty suffered horribly from sobriety until the day he died. Was this to be my destiny?

The end seemed to come on Labor Day weekend 2008. The situation with Carol had been deteriorating fast for weeks, and the long weekend at my parents' house at the shore had become one, prolonged fight. I felt as though every conversation with Carol somehow turned into a bitter accusation or a slight of some kind. I would explode, and she would aggravate the situation by calling attention to my inability to control myself. My rage would then escalate further.

On Sunday, after sneaking a bunch of drinks in the afternoon and ruining yet again another wonderful repast with blistering sarcasm aimed at Carol, I stormed out of the house. Re-upping at the local liquor store, I travelled over the bridge and drove up and down the 18-mile stretch of Long Beach Island, trying to cool my jets and getting completely wasted in the process.

After a couple hours, I noticed a holiday party going on at my life-long friend, Scott Seward's sister's house and pulled in. I wobbled to the door and walked in. Scott and his wife, Anne, took one look at me and told me to grab a cup of coffee and sit down. Wanting no part of that nonsense, I grabbed a beer instead and made my way for the pot of whole-lobsters being served. After making a complete fool of myself for about an hour or two, I decided to leave. Scott had wisely taken my keys, however, and he had no intention of giving them back to me.

I surrendered. At that moment I simply decided to give up the whole deal. I called Carol. Instead of waiting a few hours, drinking coffee, sobering up, and then driving home; or simply spending the night at my old friend's house and telling Carol nothing about my condition, I went ahead and spilled the beans. I told her the news that I was stuck on LBI with Scott and Anne and they weren't letting me drive home because I was drunk. There, I said it! It was a freeing experience, but it was a fleeting one. The fear—that awful fear—not unlike the fear I experienced that fateful night in Hopewell, was back—big time!

After a miserable night spent contemplating my decision to be honest, I went back to my parents' house, apologized to everyone—Carol first and foremost—and we all took advantage of the gorgeous weather and headed on over to the beach.

Carol and I went for a long walk that day on the sun-soaked Harvey Cedars beach. It was all clear to her now: the weight gain, the puffy, red face; the disappearing money and the late nights; and, of course, the awful behavior. She was controlled in her tone with me, but there was no hiding her frustration, anger and complete disappointment.

She had some important questions to ask me, and if I didn't answer them to her satisfaction, our marriage would soon be over. How much had I been drinking, and when did it start up again? Would I now promise to go to AA and quit booze forever? Would I now agree to marriage or anger management counseling? Would I now allow her a closer look into our financial situation, as I had been blowing all that money in the recent past?

As we walked slowly up the beach, I nodded and listened carefully to all her questions. I was going to be completely honest, I thought. I wanted things to get better as much as she did, after all. But, that fear of a miserable life spent without alcohol was there, deep within me. The thought of Dusty stewing in his chair kept popping into my head.

The disease had taken hold, and it did not want to let go. I found that with each answer I gave, some truth came out of my mouth—but the fear and the disease was holding something back and telling *me* something quite different.

Yes, I was drinking eight or 10 cocktails every day, and I had started up a few months ago.

No, the number was higher, much higher, and you began almost three years ago to the day!

Yes, I was sure that I was now an alcoholic, and I would begin hitting AA meetings tomorrow when we got home. I know that I can never drink again.

No, you're not so bad. You just screwed up. You can control yourself if you really try. Temper your intake, that's all. Go to some AA meetings to appease her, and just be more careful. Just remember, you didn't get caught. You gave yourself up.

Yes, I'll do any counseling you suggest. I love you, and I must do whatever it takes to regain your trust and love.

Good answer. Counseling will help you to regain that lost trust. This is all good.

Yes, I have been spending too much money on drink. It's your money too, after all. Please be more vigilant as to the credit card bills, checking accounts, etc.

There are many accounts, many other avenues of funds. It will all work out. Just take it easy. And don't breathe a word about the coke, for God's sake!

We finished our walk, and she gave me a big hug. She was still extremely pissed, for sure, and it would take a long time to regain a bit of trust, and love. But, she was giving me another chance, and I was determined not to blow it.

And so, that Labor Day in 2008 I quit drinking. For the entire day I avoided that first drink that can cause so much trouble, and I felt good about myself.

It would be my last sober day until April 13, 2010.

Chapter Thirteen

From an Actual AA Meeting...

Leader: "Yes!"

Member: "Yeah, I'm Lawrence, and I'm still an alcoholic."

Group: "Lawrence!"

Lawrence: "I said to my wife of 43 years the other day, 'I'm going out to a meeting.'

She says, 'What, again? Three meetings in one day? Can't you just stay home?'

I say to her, 'Let me ask you a few questions. Do you still hide your purse under your pillow?'

'No,' she says.

'Do you still put all your cash and credit cards in secret hiding places all over the house?'

'No,' she says.

'Do you still lock me out of the house when I leave?'

'No,' she says.

'Well, why not?' I ask her.

She thinks about it for a minute, then says, 'On second thought, you better go ahead to that meeting!'

That's all I got."

"Time to get up!" The voice is clear but not harsh. I open my eyes. The sun is already shining brightly through the lone window of my room, and I squint at my watch. It reads 7:00, and I begin to sit up. I see Carley standing at the door holding the doorknob. "Everything okay?" she says.

"Yeah, I'm up. Thanks, Carley." She leaves. I look around and see that Mike and Ebby are already up and out. Yawning, I rub my face. *Wow!* I think. This is only my fourth day here at Carrier. My fourth day without a drink and I'm feeling unbelievably well. I slept close to seven hours, I realize, and that is the most sleep I've had in one night in weeks. And, it was that deep, knock-out sleep that I know my body has been craving. I stand up, fish around in my clothes drawer, and put on my last clean pair of jeans and a sweatshirt.

In the bathroom, Ebby is at the sink shaving. "Hey, Eric, how you doing?" he asks me as I head for a stall.

"Great!" I say. "I didn't even hear you guys get up this morning."

"Well, I guess you didn't hear all the noise earlier then, did you?"

"No, what happened?" I ask from the cubicle.

"It must have been around five," Ebby says. "Mr. T. was yelling and screaming. They threw him out."

"What?" I respond, flushing the toilet and heading over to join him at the sink. "They threw him out?"

"Yup!" says Ebby, washing the shaving cream from his face. "He must have failed his urine test or something."

"I bet he did," I say nodding. "Yeah, he was bouncing around outside yesterday, and he told Mike and me that his girlfriend came to see him. Mike suspected as much. He was acting all fired up."

"That must have been it," Ebby says. "So they woke him up, and marched his ass right on out of here. He was pissed! He was yelling 'fuck this place! You guys don't know how to run a rehab!' and shit like that. It was pure Mr. T. Mike and I were laughing our asses off, but you just kept snoring away."

I splash water on my face and laugh out loud. "Well, let's hope he has better luck down in Texas. You know that's where he says he's going, right?"

"Yeah, he told me that the other day." Ebby looks up and cocks his head. "I think he yelled something like that this morning: 'You can go to hell, I'm going to Texas!'"

I burst out laughing. "He loved that Davey Crockett line I told him. That's too funny!"

"That guy needs more than a change of scenery, I tell ya," Ebby continues. "He needs, what did the *Doctor's Opinion* say—'an entire psychic change?'"

I nod. "I think that's what it said—and he does."

Ebby shakes his head. "I tried the geographic change to cure my drinking and it didn't help."

"Well, good luck to Mr. T." I say, drying my face and hands.

"Good luck to Texas!" he says, more to the fact.

"Where's Mike, anyway?" I ask him.

"He's down talking to Bobby. He just found out he's leaving, too."

"Bobby? No! Did he…"

"No, nothing like that," Ebby cuts me off. "He was hoping to go to Florida, and an extended rehab center down there, but his insurance nixed that. He's got to go home this morning, and he's pissed. Let's go see what's up with him."

I look at my watch. "Okay, I need to call home, but there's time."

"What, is everybody getting kicked out of here?" I say, entering Bobby Brooklyn's room. Ebby is right behind me. Mike Cass is sitting on Bobby's bed, and Bobby's packing up his small suitcase. He looks at us and curses.

"Those fucking bastards," he says. "I was told they'd let me go down to Florida to another rehab, but the fucking bean-counters think different." Bobby still has the bandage on his head from the accident with the sawzall. He's throwing some socks and underwear in his suitcase. "Now it's back to the old neighborhood. That sucks!"

Mike speaks up. "Just try to make the best of it, bro. Who's coming to get you?"

"My mom will be here in about an hour," he says, shaking his head and tossing clothes. "I guess I'll be staying with them for a while. But I'm not ready yet. I need more time."

"How about your wife?" Ebby asks him.

Bobby stops packing and sighs. "I don't know. She doesn't want me back yet, that's for sure. It all depends on me not drinking; and God only knows if I can manage that."

"You can do it, Bobby," Ebby tells him. "Hit those meetings. Get a sponsor. You don't want to lose your family."

Bobby throws a few more items in his case and zips it closed. "I really needed some more time to get well. *Those assholes!*" he yells.

"Well, I'm leaving Sunday," Mike says, "and the snoring wonder here is out on Monday." Mike points at me, and then glances at Ebby. "Ebby's on the state's nickel, so he might be here 'til Christmas."

We all laugh, but the atmosphere in the room is grim. Clearly, Bobby is getting hosed by the system. I'm hearing all the time from the nurses and counselors in here that what typically used to be a 28-day stay at rehabs, is now about five, or even three days. Shit, I'm getting kicked out too early, and that's for sure. And, it's also true that when the state or the court system mandates a detox and rehab stay, they typically pay the enormous, 28-day bill—all on the backs of the taxpayers. With the recidivism rate for drug and alcohol abusers as high as it is, it seems short-sighted to me for private insurance companies to kick people out if rehab-centers so quickly. Ideally, there must be a middle-ground between the state and private systems.

"Yeah, well, I'm not ready," Bobby says glumly. "I guess we all have to get out of here some time, though; and try not to go back to the life we had. That's what I have to do—like it or not."

"It's not going to be easy for any of us," I say. "We either learn the things they try to teach us, and change, or…" I hold out my hands and shrug.

"That's right, Buddy boy," Mike says. "With you three it's the booze, and with me it's the Xanax." Mike puts his head down. "*That fucking Xanax,*" he says, stressing all three words. It seems that every time he says the word, it causes him a mental disturbance. Ebby and I look at each other. This room is depressing us.

I look at my watch, and then make an attempt to lighten things up a bit. "On the bright side," I say, forcefully a huge, faux smile. "I have to call my wife right now!" Mike groans, Ebby chuckles, and Bobby says, "Well, good luck with that."

I say, "If I don't see you, Bobby, best of luck," and shake his hand. "Really, I mean it. We're kind of in the same boat. We have to get our families back, and we have to not drink!"

"You are right." Bobby says. He gives me a sincere smile. "Good luck to us both."

I leave them and make my way for the phone. I see about 10 people in the vitals line further down the hall as I pick up the receiver. I notice Eva standing at the end of the line next to Stanley. She gives me a half-smile as I start to dial.

"Hello?"

"Hi, Natalie! It's your daddy!"

"Hi, Daddy! *Mommy, it's Daddy*! Are you getting better? Mommy said you're in a hospital."

"Yes, I'm getting better. I miss you SO much."

"When are you coming home, Daddy?"

"Next week, I hope. I miss you, too, Sweetheart. Is Mommy there?"

"She's right here. Bye, Daddy!"

"Bye, Honey."

"Go brush your teeth, Natalie; we're leaving for the bus in five minutes."

This was Carol. The teeth and bus duty were my jobs with Natalie right up until the last day, I sadly remember. I miss that.

"Hello?"

"Hi, Carol."

"Hey, how are you feeling?"

"I'm doing a lot better. I can't believe how much better I feel in only four days. How are things going there?"

"We're okay. I still only have about $50 in the checking account. You left such an awful mess for me."

"Did those checks arrive?"

"Yes, but the bank's holding them for three days. I can't access the money."

"Just charge what you need. Carol, it looks like I'll be getting out on Monday."

"Yeah, well everybody I've talked to says I shouldn't let you come home, and I kind of agree with them. I thought you were going to pay for a few extra days after your insurance ended."

"I *will* be paying for one day, but Carol, I'm going to owe $1500 as it is, because of the deductible."

"Oh my God! You're going to pay for all this for years, Eric."

"I know, and I don't care. I just need to start rebuilding my life. And, I need to come home to my family."

"Well, I really don't want to see you at all right now. Quite frankly, I want your $3000 a month, not you."

Ugh. That hurt.

"I, I really don't know what to say. I…"

"How about, 'I'm sorry' for a start? Do you know that you haven't even said that yet?"

Oh, God, haven't I?

"Carol, I am sorry—for everything. But, I just thought…I thought it would all be meaningless at this point. I've said that so many times before, and then, well, you know. I just thought if you gave me one more chance that I could begin to show you how serious I am this time, and really *show you* in actions how sorry I am. I don't know. "

"Yeah, well I don't know about it either. I've been looking into apartments around here for you. I found one for $900 a month."

I do not want an apartment. I'd rather drive 90 minutes every day from my folks' than try to live by myself. I better get dramatic.

"Carol, please, just think about it. I can't do that. The money, me being alone—I wouldn't make it. Listen, please, I'm learning more and more every day how to deal with my disease, and stop once and for all. I can't drink anymore, Carol. If I do, I won't have to worry about family or a job. I'll be dead!"

"They're just words, Eric. I've heard this all before. I have to get Natalie on the bus. About work, I talked to Sean at the school. Because of all your missed lessons and everything, they're going to put you on disability for the rest of the semester."

I never even thought about this. I just assumed I'd be going straight back to work.

"As long as I still have a job, that's fine, I guess. I don't think I'll miss more than one weekend at church, so that shouldn't be too bad."

"What about treatment after you get out?"

"Yes, Carley—the counselor up here—is setting up IOP, or 'intensive out-patient' at the Princeton House, I think, three mornings a week. I'll still need lots of follow-up treatment. And I'm willing to do whatever I have to do. Carol, *please* believe me!"

"Well, call me on Sunday and let me know about Monday. I'll pick you up, but I'm not making you any promises. I'm so pissed off at you! I can't get over all the lies, I'm sorry! I really don't want to see you at all."

"Carley also said she'd hold a joint-counseling session for us when you come. How does that sound?"

"That sounds good. Do they have a room there where they can tie you up, and I can beat the shit of you?"

I laugh. This dark humor is a good sign—maybe.

"That would be fine with me, if I can just get back home with you and the kids. I swear to God, Carol, things will be different this time."

"I don't want to hear all that! I'm looking after myself, and I'm doing just fine with that. I can't, I don't want to…"

"Carol, please, just think it over, that's all. Just think about it. Remember how it once was? You were happy once, remember? I'll do whatever it takes to make you happy again—anything!"

"Yeah, yeah. I'll think about it, that's it!"

"Okay, I'll call you on Sunday."

"Eric, I'm glad you're getting the help you need, but remember I am too. The type of help I'm getting might not include you. Keep that in your mind, Eric."

"Okay, okay. Carol, please say hello to Matt and Katie, and tell them I love them.

"I will. Good bye."

"Good bye, Carol, and…I love you."

She had already hung up before the last three words.

My mind is racing. I stand there staring at the phone. Carol will think about it, that's it. There must be at least a little love left somewhere. She must realize the importance of me getting back home. If I can just get my foot in the door—literally—I know I can make it right with time.

It may be too late, though. Perhaps all those lies have finally put things beyond repair. She's certainly preparing me for the worst. She's learned how to live life without me, and it sounds as though she's doing pretty well with that. She wants my money, not me. Divorce is a distinct possibility.

On the other hand, Carol's quick humor was a good sign, I think. The door may not be shut all the way. I'm feeling better physically, and I'm starting to grasp the tools I need to stay sober. At the very least, I hope I can get home and get my program up and running. Then, over time, if Carol is adamant about a separation or even a divorce, I think I'll be in a better position to deal with it. But, then what do I do?

Okay, okay, I think. This is not the time. I must stow these racing thoughts away for now. One day, one hour, one minute at a time is the only way to proceed. I feel okay.

I proceed to the shortening vitals line where Mike is regaling Eva and Stanley with his patented BS. By the look of his wild gestures and loud talk he seems to have recovered fully from his "Xanax moment."

I walk right up to him and bump him heavily from behind. "Oh, excuse me, sir!" I say.

"Hey, watch it! My eye!" Mike moans, then turns and sees it's me and smiles. "Oh, how'd it go, Buddy Boy?" he asks me.

"Not terrible, I think," I respond. "It's not like Mrs. Lincoln after the play, anyway. There's still hope. She's thinking it all over."

"You're out, Tom!" he says, but sees my pained expression and softens. "Just kidding, you'll make it, Buddy Boy." He puts his hand on my shoulder.

Eva, getting her BP checked, smiles up at me. "There *is* still hope, I know it. I can see it in your eyes."

"I pray you're right, Eva," I say, again wondering how this woman can seem to know such things. "Well, you certainly look much better."

"I do. I'm starving. Are you going over to breakfast?"

"After a walk," I tell her. "I want to go see my pets."

"Doctor-fucking-Doolittle over here," Mike cracks. Everybody laughs, including Carley who's taking the readings.

When it's my turn to see Carley I tell her about Monday. She says that anytime between 10 and noon is okay for a counseling session, and she'll make a note of it. She also says that she'll be in touch with Princeton House to arrange my first IOP visit, probably beginning next Wednesday or Thursday. "It's usually 9:30-12, three days a week, and they last anywhere from six to 12 weeks," she tells me.

I'm pleased to present Nurse Sharon with my best vitals report to date: BP, pulse and temperature all within normal ranges. Before getting my morning batch of pills, I ask her about Mr. T. and Morris. "I told you we throw them out of here all the time," she says. "We have a zero-tolerance for that kind of behavior. If you want to keep using, go somewhere else and do it."

After I down my pills, including the more benign and non-addictive Buspirone for agitation, she hands me an empty urine-specimen cup. "Now, fill that up and give it back," she tells me. "Let's see if you get to stay a few more days at the *Hotel Carrier.*"

I smile. "You got it!" I start to turn toward the bathroom.

"Eric," she says. I look at her. "Maybe you can play some more piano today?"

I'm taken aback. "I didn't know you heard me the other day," I say.

"Oh, yes," she says, a big smile appearing on her face. "That Beethoven was beautiful. I only wish they'd tune that piece of shit."

I laugh. "Today, Sharon, you'll get Joplin," I tell her, and mean it. "Ragtime is perfect on a clunker. After first group I'll give it a go."

After filling my pee-cup and handing it back in, I head out the door and make a right. The young, spring day is turning out to be a beauty. There's a spring in my step to match.

That first morning group after Carley's "news and snooze" session is led by Kevin, the white-haired counseling fixture at Carrier for over three decades, and confirms my positive inclinations about the day.

He passes out a sheet with a triangle taking up the entire page. At the top of the page it reads, "Maslow's Hierarchy of Needs." The triangle is divided up into five sections. The bottom, largest section, is labeled "Survival Needs," and the other four parts leading to the top are naturally smaller. These four "needs" sections reflect other goals in early recovery. Those four are labeled, bottom to top, "Safety Needs," "Belonging and Love Needs," "Esteem Needs," and finally "Self-Actualization Needs" poking up to the top of the triangle.

The meeting is moving along uninterrupted for a change, and that's because Mr. T. is gone. He's *goin' to Texas*, and God bless him. Bobby, thanks to his capricious insurance company's policies, is now officially gone, and I kind of miss Morris the Hat and all his weirdness. But, there does seem to be a fresh replacement for Morris at least. Her name is Tanya.

We met Tanya in Carley's initial group, when she was bemoaning long and hard about the confiscation of her precious cell-phone. Many of the younger patients here have expressed similar complaints about the strict rule completely banning the device, but Tanya's reaction was slightly different.

In her early 20's, bluish, spiked hair akimbo and no visible orifice un-pierced, Tanya was passionate in her arguments regarding the ban. "I like, need it," she opined, in the lazy, slapdash vernacular so common today. "You know, how can I possibly be, you know, without a cell-phone? It's like cruel and unusual punishment. I, like, have never even *used* a pay-phone." Many of us seemed fascinated and even slightly sympathetic to her pleas, but Carley was stone-faced and un-moved. Her response was an address to the group as a whole, but Tanya was the principle target. "All of you, in some form or another, used your cell-phones to enable your drinking and drugging; and if you're caught with one in here, you are out—period!"

Tanya sighed heavily and looked at Carley as though she was some kind of lower life-form. Carley, looking gorgeous and professional as usual, stared back at Tanya and cocked her head, waiting for some kind of rebuttal. Tanya offered nothing. Somehow, some way, she's just going to have to get along without texting for a while.

Right now, while Kevin gives us an overview about the "Hierarchy of Needs," Tanya is organizing her make-up—I think. All eyes in the room, except Kevin's, seem to be gravi-tating toward Tanya, as she spreads out her blush, lip-gloss, mascara and other assorted paraphernalia on her lap and on the floor around her feet. One beauty-aid at a time, she slowly lifts it to her face, checks a small hand-held mirror, and touches or makes a small swipe. It's difficult at times for her to find a spot not already ringed, hooped, studded or otherwise impaled in one form or another, but she keeps working on it with diligence. It is quite compelling to watch, although as far as I'm concerned, her make-up is already finished. To my untrained eye, her face is simply a grotesque mask of Goth-inspired black blotches and purple smears.

She seems completely oblivious to Kevin's existence, let alone his thoughtful lesson in Maslow's Theory of Needs, until he finally notices most of the people in the room looking at her, and not him. "Excuse me, Madame," Kevin says to Tanya with mocking politeness. "Would you be so kind as to put all that stuff—*away!*" He shouts the last word, and points to her huge shoulder bag sitting nearly empty at her feet.

"Oh, yeah, like—no prob," Tanya responds, sounding surprised and a bit hurt. It takes her a few minutes to gather everything up and put it all back in her bag. She then sits back and closes her eyes. Tanya is out for the remainder of this group.

I'm fascinated to learn from Kevin that the bottom two portions of the triangle represent the detox and immediate reentry needs of addicts and alcoholics such as us. "This is most vital for you all to understand," Kevin tells us. "You may be feeling better, but this is an extremely traumatic period in all your lives, and many of you will need to deal with basic survival and safety needs first and foremost.

"Those who jump right back into work, and expect their family life or relationships to immediately return to normal after such traumas are often making a big mistake. You need to employ an incremental reentry back to normalcy," he tells us. "It's as basic as hunger, thirst, shelter, clothing and sleep," he says, pointing to the large base of the triangle that he's drawn on the chalk-board. Inside this section are written these survival needs.

"You must allow more time to deal with those bigger issues of work and relationships—many of which have been damaged so severely, or even ruined completely," he says. "Your primary focus has to be on personal recovery. Without that, you can never recover the trust of loved-ones, successfully return to work, or—and this is most important—become the *person you are capable of becoming*. That is your ultimate objective and represents the top portion of this triangle."

The timing of this subject is perfect. Kevin is telling me exactly what I need to hear today at this moment. I had always assumed I'd just go straight back to work. I definitely realize the damage I've caused to my family, and that it will take a lot of time to repair that damage—if I can at all—but Kevin and this triangle explain it all to me clearly. The nurses, counselors and even Dr. Shariff have been telling me the same thing in similar ways, but now it's plainly obvious to me that focusing on my immediate recovery has to supersede everything else. The news of me going on disability fits perfectly with the needs triangle; and that realization gives me a huge sense of relief.

"In terms of rebuilding trust in your relationships," Kevin continues, "you will need lots of time to accomplish this. Regarding trust, the word "time" can be a very useful acronym. *This I Must Earn—'time.'*" Kevin writes the five words on the board and underlines each; I do the same on my sheet. He holds his arms out, and then says simply, "You have to earn trust back, and this will take lots of time."

Of all the acronyms I've heard thus far, none seem as important and apropos to me as this one. If my marriage can be repaired, I will certainly need plenty of time to do it. Over time, if I can stay sober and get myself fully immersed in a good program, like AA, I think it might be possible to earn back the trust that has been lost.

I look around and most of us are nodding vigorously and scribbling notes. Henry, looking more focused and well-rested today, is frowning. He's due to leave today, I realize, and from what he's been saying to us all along, I think I know what's going through his mind. His business is teetering and, like me, his marriage situation is not good. I know he feels he has to immediately jump back into his business and try to repair that aspect of his life, so the thought of a gradual reentry is most likely not going to happen there. Being sober for a few days in here doesn't seem to have helped his anger issues either. Only the mind-numbing meds have helped him in this regard, and that can't continue indefinitely. It's another tough situation.

But, they are all tough situations. Bobby was forced to jump right back into his life, and now it seems Henry has to, as well. Jason and Morris are out because they were using in here, for God's sake, so I don't hold out much hope for either of them. Mike has to deal with his Xanax demon as early as Sunday, and it will be my turn to step back into the real world on the following day. This disease takes no prisoners, and escaping from its grasp is a monumental task for anyone stricken. I'm under no illusions. Some of us, if not most, are bound to fail.

"Cup of tea and a smoke?" Mike asks me in the group lounge following Kevin's group.

"Yeah, but first I promised Nurse Sharon I'd play her a tune on the piano," I say.

Mike groans. "Nurse Ratchitt? She doesn't deserve anything! She denied me my nose-spray again this morning. She's DEAD!"

"Well, don't do that 'til I play her a little ragtime. Remember what Tim taught us," I tell him. "In through the nose...out through the mouth."

"Ah, yes," he says, and he stands up straight, relaxing his shoulders and arms. I do the same. Together we do a truncated version of Tim's soothing breathing technique.

Afterward, we walk past the nurse's station, and I see Sharon talking with Carley behind the glass. I motion to her and she looks up at me. I make like I'm playing the piano with my fingers and point toward Darcy. She smiles at me and nods.

Within two minutes, I'm pounding out a tinny, mistake-ridden rendition of *Maple Leaf Rag* on the battered upright. Patients are milling about, making coffee and tea and talking. Some are taking notice of me at the piano, but most aren't. It reminds me of the cocktail-parties and other related events I've played so many times in the past. At those affairs, most people don't listen to the music at all, and only speak louder to be heard. I never cared, though, as long as the bar was open and I got paid. Here I get neither—quite the opposite, actually—but I'm satisfied to see Sharon and Carley smiling and tapping their feet in rhythm in the doorway. Even Matt the Enforcer, standing behind them with his arms folded is nodding his head to the syncopated beat.

As the rousing Trio section commences, I'm amazed to see Kara A. and Maxine get up from a table and start dancing together. They join hands and bounce around, spinning and laughing. Eva and Stanley join in, although not as robustly. Mike, sitting with Henry and Ebby nearby, is shoveling cereal into his mouth, of course, and smiles at me and nods his head with the music. I laugh out loud over the din when he takes a lighter from the chest-pocket of his denim jacket and raises it over his head and ignites it briefly—as if at a rock-concert. This causes Henry, sitting across from Mike, to crack a big smile. Ebby smacks the table and nearly doubles over. The three of them then start clapping their hands in time to the music as they watch the four, impromptu dancers shimmy and shake with the raucous beat. For a brief minute or two, all is well in our little, screwed-up world. Over the years, in all types of situations, I've often found Scott Joplin capable of such things.

For effect, I've taken the piece at break-neck speed; and as it slams to an abrupt halt—not terribly unlike an out-of-control bike hitting a brick wall—many in the disparate group break into a hearty round of applause. I get up, give a slight bow, and walk quickly over to Mike's table and take a seat, hoping to quickly settle back into my anonymity. Within seconds, my hopes are dashed, as there's a tap on my shoulder. I turn to see Tanya standing above me.

She's smiling slightly, as she sticks out her hand and introduces herself. I take her hand and look at her. Beyond all the grotesque, Goth-inspired make-up and elaborate piercings, I see two beautiful, green eyes bearing down on me. I think of how much better she'd look if she got rid of all that phony crap distorting her face, and just permitted those wondrous eyes to rule. I get lost in reverie for a brief moment considering her eyes when she asks me, "Do you know any Weezer?"

"Any what?" I stammer, completely clueless. Ebby laughs out loud, Mike nearly chokes on his Krispies and Henry gives a loud, choking chortle.

Tanya eyes the four of us with suspicion. "Weezer, you know, like, the best band EVER!" she tells me, shocked at my ignorance. "Their keyboards dude is like, disgusting."

"I…don't know any Weezer," I say, shrugging. "My rock knowledge ended with Van Halen, sorry."

"Van who?" she says, mimicking my response and intonation. She gives a deep sigh, frowns at the four of us, and then slithers away. She seems to be wearing about 15 different articles of clothing, and every one of them is in a different color and state of intended disrepair. From her tattered, multicolored knit cap, all the way down to her black leather, knee-high stiletto boots, it's one loud attempt at a fashion statement after another. We all watch her as she slowly exits Darcy.

"My God!" Mike says slowly in wonder, "That is unbelievable."

"Spoiled bitch" adds Henry, his pudgy, red face staring after her.

"I thought Morris the Hat was bizarre," Ebby says. "She is *out* there."

"Oh, she's okay," I say with a shrug. "It's kind of typical for in here."

Mike Cass changes the subject. "Are you out of here, Henry?"

Henry looks at him. "My wife's picking me up after lunch. What do you say? *I'm out, Tom!*"

We all laugh. His tone is steady and controlled, not at all agitated. Perhaps the music and a better combination of meds have settled him down.

"Are you ready?" Ebby asks him.

"No, but I've got some meetings lined up, and IOP starting Monday," he says evenly. He looks okay with the situation.

"Well, I'm gonna miss you, Henry," Mike says, trying to lighten the mood. "I know I'll never be able to look at Sean Connery again without thinking of you. *Shaken, not stirred!* That was hilarious." We all laugh.

"You guys have helped me a lot," Henry says, addressing the three of us. "The little things you've been telling me these last few days have meant a lot. I'm gonna miss you guys, too."

We all give Henry some more words of encouragement and farewells. After a bit, Mike Cass looks at me. "Can we finally have that cup of tea and a smoke, Liberace?"

"Sure," I say, chuckling, as is everyone else. I get up and move toward the cups and teabags. Ebby and Henry get up and head toward the door.

"See you two," Henry says.

"Goodbye, Henry," I say, waving.

After they leave, Mike sits back and pats his ever-expanding mid-section. He belches loudly. Patients as far away as the TV turn their heads. "*Did you hear that?*" he proclaims, ala Buddy the elf, even louder than the burp.

I'm smiling as I make the tea, but I get a sudden pang in my gut when I think of Mike's inevitable departure. I realize how attached I've become to him, and the thought of his leaving fills me with dread. It's as if he's become a brother to me in only four short days. And then, just like that, he'll be gone forever. *First Bobby, then Henry, and then it will be Mike.* I consider this reality and sigh heavily. I soak the teabags, and then add the sugar and milk. During these last two days I'll stay even closer to Mike. And, thank God Ebby will still be here to help me with my state of affairs. I'll need his clear-thinking and steadiness in dealing with the Carol situation, that's for sure.

"Not too strong, Buddy Boy!" Mike commands me. "Last time it was too fucking strong! Do it again, and you're DEAD!"

"Okay, Al," I say. I walk over and hand him his cup. "*Here ya go, Don Vito,*" I say in my best Sicilian.

Mike stands up and heads for the door. "*Leave the gun. Take the cannoli.*"

The evening AA meeting is hosted by a trio of alcoholics from nearby Somerville. Jack, their leader, is a 50ish, attractive bald-headed man with a slick goatee. Seated on his right is an older, diminutive man whom Jack introduces as Harry. Lance, a heavy, 40ish-looking fellow rounds out the threesome, and is seated on Jack's left.

With Bobby and Henry now departed, only 10 of us are here in Darcy. The other 20 or so now in Blake are in the NA meeting going on in the group lounge. At the far end of the line of chairs, Maxine and Kara are seated next to one another; and a couple of younger women are seated next to them. Ebby is next to me; and Sal and a few other men make up the entire group.

After the introductions, Jack leads us in the *Serenity Prayer*: "*God, grant me the serenity to accept the things I cannot change, the courage to change the things I can, and the wisdom to know the difference.*" This being my fifth meeting at Carrier, I almost have the simple prayer memorized. I had forgotten it completely from my brief tour of 18 months ago, and it feels good to say it.

I ponder the word "serenity" as it's used in the prayer. The writer asks God to allow him peacefulness and tranquility when dealing with the imponderables of life. He doesn't ask God to grant him "intelligence," or "understanding," or even "audacity" to help him deal with things he cannot change, but only "serenity." I realize that, with me, it's accepting the simple fact that I am an alcoholic, and always will be. I've accomplished this, but I would not say that I'm serene about it. In these few AA meetings I've attended here, however, I have noticed many of the members and the way they present themselves. Many do have that serenity in their lives, and being sober has been a real blessing, not the tortured, gloomy existence I always envisioned. Aside from Frank in that first meeting, with his dark forebodings of "remember the pain," and his "scared straight" approach, almost all of the others have displayed some of this serenity. If they can get there, I think, perhaps I can get there, too.

Harry and Lance tell us their stories. Once again, I can identify with much of their experiences of suffering and isolation brought on by their drinking. They speak of lost relationships and disasters at work, and how close to death they were before finally making it into AA. And, they tell us how their once-shattered lives were then transformed. They talk about the importance of meetings. "Meeting makers make it!" Harry says with authority.

They speak of how vital it was to get in touch with a higher power; and how their daily sobriety is now based solely on how spiritually fit they are. "I know how easy it would be to pick up that first drink," Lance tells us at the end of his talk, "and so my sobriety today is based solely on the maintenance of my spiritual condition. I pray a lot!" he concludes.

Jack's story is a two-part tale. He made it into the rooms of AA at age 30, and lasted 12 years without taking another drink. "I got a sponsor, did the 12 steps and listened to all their suggestions," he says, and then adds, "Remember, everything you are told to do in AA, are only suggestions. The only requirement for AA membership is a desire to stop drinking." He then smiles. "Of course, my sponsor, an old-timer, used to say, 'Yeah, they're only suggestions. Like if Vito Corleone *suggests* that you *might* want to get out of the olive-oil business, it might be a good idea for you to listen.'" Everyone laughs.

"Anyway," Jack continues, "everything in my life was looking good. I had a good job, wife, house—everything that you could want. So, I felt I didn't need AA anymore, and stopped going to meetings. Soon, I felt that maybe I wasn't such a bad drunk after all, and that maybe I could drink like all my friends were doing. I decided that I deserved a reward. And this time it would all work out. So, out one night at a party, I had a drink." Jack pauses, and looks around at us. I'm spellbound. This is so much like that first drink I took in Hopewell nearly five years ago.

"Within six weeks of that first drink," he tells us with much emotion, "I was out of my house, out of my job, and out of my mind with booze! For the next five years, I bounced around from town to town, living in my van. I became homeless and hopeless. I didn't think I was going to live." He takes a deep breath, and continues. "Somehow, I made it back. I reached out to AA, and for the second time in my life they welcomed me with open arms.

"No one judges you in here," he continues. "We've all been there at the bottom—some deeper than others—but we've all been there. For eight years now I've been back and my life is better than ever. I have a new wife and a new life. I go meetings all the time, take lots of commitments from my home-group like this one, and I pray all the time." Jack looks around at us and smiles. "Ya see, when I stopped going to meetings, my program stopped. And that meant that my praying stopped, because I thought I could do it alone. We are not able to do it alone. Alcoholics Anonymous is a 'we' program." He points to the list of the 12 steps hanging on the far wall of Darcy. "At the beginning of all 12 steps, just insert the word 'we.' And God, as you understand Him, must be at the center of all this.

"If you have a problem with a traditional type of God, let me help you out with a couple more of our splendid acronyms," Jack says. Lance and Harry laugh. "Many think of the groups themselves as a higher power, and this true enough," he says. "So, how about using a 'Group Of Drunks' as your higher power—or 'GOD'? The power of the group—a collection of men and women who share your disease, and have come up from the bottom as we all have—has been recognized as a vital part of staying sober since AA's founding almost 75 years ago in Akron, Ohio. That brand of higher power has helped keep millions from that first drink."

Jack continues. "I believe many of you will need to change the way you think when you get out of here, yes?" My head's nodding, as are most of the others. I see Sal leaning forward in his chair, looking at his feet. "So, get out of here, get a sponsor and start taking some 'Good, Orderly Direction'—GOD! This can be extremely effective for some as a higher power.

"Whatever it is—and for me it happens to be all of these things *and* Jesus Christ; I need all the higher powers I can get—it must be something more powerful than you. I had to learn the hard way—twice—that Jack was not God, and I must continue to realize this every day in order to stay sober. That's about all I got. God bless you and good luck."

The three receive a warm round of applause. Jack checks his watch, looks around at us and says, "Before we end in our typical way, we have a couple minutes. Are there any questions you'd like to ask us?"

Many of us immediately look over at Kara. Her hand is already raised as she notices all the eyes bearing down on her. She seems to shrink a bit and a rosy blush appears on her face. She fidgets in her chair and starts to lower her arm. Before she can get it down, Jack calls on her.

"Hi, I'm Kara, Alcoholic," she says haltingly. "Uh, I just want to say," she smiles and squirms even more, and then blurts out, "I just want to say that I agree with everything you were saying. That's it." Ebby and I laugh out loud. God bless Kara A.

Sal raises his hand. "Yes?" Jack says, pointing to him. Sal has been frowning and looking at his feet and watch ever since the meeting started. I think Sal feels he just doesn't belong here at Carrier, that somehow he's been done wrong.

"Yeah, I'm Sal. I don't know. It all just seems so repetitive. We keep hearing the same shit over and over again. All this AA business seems like a lot of brainwashing to me."

Jack looks at him. It's a sad kind of look. "Why are you here, Sal?" he asks him in a soft voice.

"I was drinking too much, and it was causing a few problems. That's all." Sal's sitting back in his chair, arms folded. Something tells me that Sal hasn't reached his bottom yet.

Jack nods his head and asks him, "Did you find yourself, perhaps doing *the same shit* over and over again, day after day?" Ebby grunts. I chuckle a bit. Sal loves to stick his chin out.

Sitting there, Sal has that same perplexed look of a couple nights ago when he was concerned about making 90 meetings in 90 days. "Um, well, yeah. And, yeah, I was drinking every day—probably too much, yeah."

"Well," Jack says, quite casually, "I can only speak for myself, but I'm an alcoholic, and I need to keep hearing this same message over and over again. I would be dead right now if it weren't for what you call *brainwashing*. My brain needed a good washing. Does anybody else here feel that way?"

Every hand in the room shoots up, except Sal's. I know my brain needs to be washed. My brain needs some steel-wool taken to it, for God's sake. Alcohol has taken every fiber of my once-normal brain and twisted and tied it into a bird's-nest of insanity. At this point I'm ready for anything up to and including an exorcism to help rid me of this alcohol demon. As far as I'm concerned, Sal can take all his negativity and denial and go pound sand.

Jack is more compassionate. He gives Sal a small smile. "Look, I think you'll find that we are not a glum lot. Get out of here and join our merry little tribe. Bill Wilson, our co-founder and author of *Alcoholics Anonymous*, wrote, and I can confirm this to you from my vast amount of sometimes painful, personal research, 'Rarely have we seen a person fail who has thoroughly followed our path.' And, it was said that on his deathbed, when asked if there was anything he would change in the 'Big Book,' Bill said that he wished he had changed the word 'rarely' to 'never.'

"Sal," Jack says, and then he turns his head and scans the rest of us, "you never have to feel this way again."

Sal continues to frown and looks down at his feet again.

Jack sits up and smacks his thighs. His bald head is gleaming—a shining beacon of hope, as I see it. "Well, that's all we got! We have a nice way of closing." Everyone stands up, and all but one join hands.

"Our Father who art in heaven…"

"Stop wiff fa peacockths and fucking triangleths for Chrith'th thake!" Mike Cass moans later in our room, his pronounced lisp sending Ebby and I into paroxysms of laughter. It's well past midnight, and Mike is on a roll. "Who givths a shit about your liver, and your mother and your wife, anyway? Wiff all the shit you put her frew, she's probably banging the mailman for Chrith'th thake! I got my own problemths. Can't you thee what a nervouth wreck I am?"

Ebby and I have been in bed for close to 30 minutes waiting for Mike to finish his never-ending nightly rituals. It's been the same every night: the pleading with Nurse Donna for nose-spray, extra sleeping pills and other various meds; the incessant back and forth to the bathroom for water to soak his bridge, his nightly shower and all that entails, more hair-spray, tooth-brushing, and then the all-important eye drops. He insists on shutting off the light every time he leaves the room, and then erupts in maniacal laughter after switching it on again each time he reenters. Now, after half-a-dozen visits to the can, he's back for what he's promised is the last time. Tonight, Mike Cass is wound up even tighter than usual, and Ebby and I are paying the painful yet hilarious price.

"Just turn it off and let us get some sleep please," Ebby begs Mike. "I've got to do my fifth-step tomorrow for you clowns, and I'm not looking forward to it."

Ebby has been working on his fourth-step moral inventory since before I arrived, and tomorrow's the day he lays out all his fears, resentments and other issues before the group.

"Fifth thstep? Hog piths! Shit, Ebby," Mike says. "Your rethentments are chicken-feed compared to my shit." Mike is standing in front of his open bureau making sure everything is in its proper place. His hair certainly is—it never moves. He's stripped down to his guinea-tee and boxers. Thankfully, this means he's making the final preparations for bed.

He turns and faces me. "How do I look?" His ever-expanding mid-section is pushing the tee to its limits. He gives me a big, gap-toothed grin. I can't reply right away because I'm being wracked by a laugh-induced coughing fit.

"You should listhen to your mother. 'Stop smoking! Stop smoking!'" He cackles what he thinks my mother sounds like.

I recover my voice briefly. "How did you lose those teeth, anyway?" I ask him out of the blue. "Was it Crystal Meth?"

"Oh, why did you have to ask him that?" Ebby cries, knowing Mike would be set off by the question.

Mike is indeed set-off, and launches into a stream-of-consciousness tirade covering a wide variety of issues. "Chrithst!" he starts. "Water balloonths, okay? Fucking water balloonths! I hit thsome guy at a party by accthident and he cold-cocked me about an hour later. Crythstal meth! Jethus, I'm hooked on Thanaxth, you know that! What am I to do about Thanaxth? My poor mother.

"I can't thsee becauthse of that fucked-up dog-leash. I'm gonna sue that prick couthsin of mine, I thswear to CHRITHST! HE'THS DEAD!

"Nurthse Ratchitt hounding me relentlethssly about every-little-fucking thing. 'Put on a thsleeved thshirt! Put on a thsleeved thshirt!' Did you know Donna livths about a mile from my houthse," he suddenly asks me in a more calm tone.

I'm laughing so hard I can only muster a wheezed, "really?"

Mike continues. "I told her I'd come by and vithsit her. I know ethxactly where she livths. You know what she thsaid? She thsaid if she sees me at her door, she's gonna get her shot-gun. The BITCH! Put her on the lithst, Ebby."

"I ran out of paper," Ebby snorts.

"Oh, yeah, and that fucking cleaning lady, Rothsa, or thsome Mexicano shit, put her on the lithst, too," Mike continues, spittle spraying from his half-toothless mouth. "She pretendths she doesn't thspeak any English, but she does. Oh, yes, she does! Eva and I were talking earlier, and she was eavthesdropping, the bitch! She's probably a mole for Ratchitt. And, she's been moving my shit, here." Mike gestures toward his open bureau.

"Did she steal anything," I manage, tears covering my face. My stomach is in painful knots.

"I'm thstill looking for thstuff. I don't know. But she understandths. Don't you worry about that!"

"Mike, please. I beg you," Ebby says desperately. "Turn off the fucking light, and let's at least try to get some sleep."

"ALRIGHT!" Mike screams. "You two are fucking killing me! Just don't pressure me! I'm gonna blow!"

Mike moves to the door. He's going to hit the light and move to his bed. Up until now, Ebby has been the last one to hit the light each night, but tonight, Mike's going to do it. His bed has been turned down for over an hour now, and he's got his good eye fixed on it. Mike eyes the lane carefully from the door. He's got about eight feet to get from the door to his bed, and his only obstacle is the bureau that sticks out a foot or so in his way. With one hand on the switch and the other facing his goal, Mike Cass turns off the light.

About two seconds and two loud footfalls later, there's a *tremendous crash*.

"For the love of God!" Ebby cries, and jumps up and turns on the light again. "You had eight fucking feet and you couldn't make it?" Mike is lying in a heap on the floor at the foot of his bureau. He broadsided it, and all his stuff, once neatly stowed—teeth included—is now scattered about him on the floor.

"Ahh!" Mike cries out. "Ahh! My eye! My knee! Chrithst! I can't thsee!"

The walls on both sides are being pounded by patients rudely awakened by the hullabaloo. I am in agony. We may never get to sleep tonight.

Chapter Fourteen

"I woke up. This had to be stopped. I saw I could not take so much as one drink. I was through forever. Before then, I had written lots of sweet promises, but my wife happily observed that this time I meant business. And so I did.

"Shortly afterward I came home drunk. There had been no fight. Where had been my high resolve? I simply didn't know. It hadn't even come to mind. Someone had pushed a drink my way, and I had taken it. Was I crazy? I began to wonder, for such an appalling lack of perspective seemed near being just that."

—Page 5. *Alcoholics Anonymous*

In retrospect, I can characterize the events surrounding Labor Day 2008 as somewhat liberating and cleansing. My admission to Carol about my return to the bottle, painful as it was, allowed me the opportunity to reboot my life—at least to a certain degree.

During that long walk on the beach, she was shocked by my revelation that I had been drinking not three or four a day, as she had suggested, but often eight or 10. She asked how long I had been back at it, and I told her a few months or so. This information, woefully thin on truth as it was—it had been closer to 15 drinks per day by now, and I had been back three full years—supplied the explanation she needed for my increasingly explosive behavior. With my promises to stop drinking completely, start attending AA meetings, attend marriage counseling, and provide a more transparent accounting of expenses, I vowed that the behavior would improve. Over time, I assured her, a happy, loving home-life would return.

Nevertheless, Carol was justifiably wary, and warned me that this was my last chance. She had been extremely unhappy in our marriage, especially during the recent months, and *this time* there would be no wiggle-room, she told me. If I returned to the bottle and the bad behavior continued, there would be little hope for us. I went along with it all, apologizing for my deceitfulness, wholeheartedly declaring my undying love for her and the kids, and promising to start life anew. The ball was now in my court.

Even as we walked that beach, however, and the voices of alcoholism murmured in my head, I knew that stopping drinking was not going to happen. Admitting to drinking was not the same as being caught, I thought. I knew that if I could make progress in the other areas—especially re-doubling my efforts in the behavior department—the drinking could be successfully hidden. I had drunk with impunity for three full years, hadn't I? With the help of AA and my doctor, if I could somehow cut back on my intake and find that elusive conduct-control mechanism, all would be well.

More to the point, I wasn't willing to stop because I hadn't suffered enough yet. The disease now had me fully in its grasp, and I wasn't beaten down enough to fully comprehend the direction it was taking me. Simply put, I wouldn't— or couldn't—stop, so my only viable alternative was to continue with extreme caution. At the time I accepted this, and, on the whole, I felt pretty confident. I had come clean, albeit incompletely, and it was now up to me to show what I could do.

I targeted one key area of my drinking for improvement. I needed to avoid morning drinking at all cost. To protect myself against further repercussions, I never mentioned this extreme alcoholic behavior to Carol. I knew that if she became aware of this aspect of my boozing, there would be only two choices: rehab or the door. I knew that twice before the morning drink had led directly to problems with Carol; and I was determined not to let it happen again. Even in my twisted, alcoholic mind, I knew that morning drinking was nothing but bad. I simply had to accomplish this one mission.

After all, for 30 years isn't this what I'd been trained to do? I had earned two advanced degrees in Performance, and this certainly qualified as such. I had performed hundreds, if not thousands of secretive booze adventures with few adverse consequences. I was a virtuoso in alcohol deception; and now with the bar was raised ever-higher, all my skills would be required. I understood that the concert stage—where the consequences of failure were measured merely in poor reviews and lackluster crowds—was nothing compared to this real-life recital. Without fully realizing it at the time, the type of performance now required put at stake not only the survival of my marriage, but also, quite possibly, my own personal survival.

At Carol's urging, I saw my doctor on the day after Labor Day. I was open with him, and candidly told him of my drinking history (conveniently omitting the part about morning drinking, of course) and my "desire" to stop. Having been sober for only one day, I was predictably jittery, and he prescribed Ativan for the symptoms. I started taking it immediately. It helped. After attending my first AA meeting that night after teaching, the few drinks I had on the way home helped even more.

I found the Princeton meeting online—a 7:30 affair at a church—and sat in the back row of seats separated from the "real" drunks closer to the front. At the start of the meeting, the leader asked if there was anyone new and I raised my hand. It was the first time in my life that I stated I was an alcoholic. He asked me if I wanted a meeting list with phone numbers, and I said yes. Arriving home, alcohol-breath fully cleansed with gum, I proudly showed Carol the list, and talked glowingly of the meeting.

For the remainder of 2008, I made lots of meetings and made sure to tell Carol about every one of them. I fell into a tolerable routine of teaching, meetings afterward, and then drinking *exclusively* in the evenings. During this time, I was strong enough to resist the urge to pick up the morning drink, and this, combined with better behavior and a few sessions with a marriage counselor, resulted in a relatively peaceful home-life.

When teaching allowed it, I often attended the 5:30 meeting at the 24 Club in Princeton. Here I met a couple members who gave me advice on how to not drink, but not in a preachy way. Regis and Payne, both about my age and sober for less than two years, were savvy enough to realize that I was merely observing the proceedings, and not ready to embrace the program, but they gave it their best shot anyway.

When I'd share at a meeting, I'd talk about trying to control my drinking; and then ask questions afterward regarding possible loop-holes in the program that might allow for reasonable drinking. Regis, with his angular features and raspy, nicotine-enhanced voice, knew that everything coming out of my mouth was ridiculous, but he was gentle with me. He tried to help me, but one method he used backfired, because I was desperate to find even the faintest of green-lights where my drinking was concerned. He approached me after a meeting early on, and handed me a copy of *Alcoholics Anonymous*.

"We give this to all newcomers," he told me. "I know you're struggling, and you're still out there doing more 'research,' but I want you to read *The Doctor's Opinion* at the beginning of this book. Read it carefully. I think it will get you off the hook."

I went home and read it. In it, William Silkworth, MD, a physician who had treated hundreds of alcoholics in the early 20th century, talks of alcoholics having an allergic reaction or sorts every time they pick up. After taking that first drink, he describes how a "phenomenon of craving" takes over and causes the alcoholic to obsessively get drunk. He talks about the fact that alcoholism has no cure and only total abstinence can be successful in arresting the disease.

The doctor writes in awe about how the fledgling *Alcoholics Anonymous* group was having a higher success rate in treating alcoholics than any medical or psychiatric hospitals ever had. The section at the start of the book is designed to give the organization a weighty endorsement for their program, and it succeeds totally.

After reading it, I didn't see how Silkworth's opinion affected me, though. It made no difference that what Regis and the doctor really wanted me to understand was that alcoholism was incurable and deadly; and that AA offered a time-tested program of recovery. Or, that this was Regis' subtle way of trying to tell me that it was impossible for an alcoholic to try to nibble around the edges with idiotic thoughts of control or moderation.

In my mind, the only thing I saw was Regis standing there at the 24 Club telling me that reading it would "get me off the hook" where drinking was concerned. So, therefore, I was off the hook. I could now appreciate some of the pathology regarding the disease, and I could continue to drink. That was it! I borrowed one of the program's slogans, "keep it simple," and, like the fool I was, simplified it even more.

This twisted sort of thinking regarding not only my own drinking, but also others and their drinking, had been with me for years. I remember my cousin, Mike, who was a fall-down, out-of-control lunatic when he drank, and my reaction to him after he went into the AA program in the mid-80s. Mike was bad, and surely would have died from the disease had it not been for AA. After he was sober, I remember seeing him at weddings and family reunions. He was calm and happy, at peace with himself and the world. He'd sit there drinking his club-soda while all the rest of us would carry on around him.

I remember asking him once, "Can't you have just a couple, Mike?"

His response was often something like this, "No, not today. Maybe tomorrow, though."

In my mind, Mike was saying that he might *really* start drinking tomorrow, and I latched onto that. At the time, I had no understanding of the "one day at a time" mentality of AA's who always say "yeah, maybe tomorrow," but never actually do pick up. Ignorant of this "just for today" style of thinking, back then I really did want him to pick up. It would somehow make me feel better to know that he re-joined the party. It would justify, in some bizarre way, my own excessive drinking.

Carol's Uncle Don was another example. He quit drinking in the 70's. There are stories of Don throwing people into swimming pools at weddings and other insane, alcohol-induced behavior; and he's been in the program for over 30 years.

Don and his wife, Peg, lived in New York City for years, and I'll never forget the absolute serenity Don possessed in the face of all the big city's craziness. Don always drove everywhere in New York, and he seemed to endure traffic jams, rude cabbies and the lack of available parking with an amazingly stoic pacifism that never failed to astound me. Rushing to get to a restaurant or show, everyone else in the car would be stewing and agitated over the traffic situation, and he'd just sit there behind the wheel, a contented, tranquil countenance always pinned on his face.

Back at their spacious, Upper-East-Side apartment, I once asked him how hard it was for him to quit drinking. "No problem," he told me simply. "AA made it so easy. Smoking was the killer, though," he told me. "Even to this day I miss that first cigarette with my morning coffee. I don't miss booze a bit, though." *Yeah, right*, I thought. I didn't buy any of that. I just knew that not being able to drink would be a torturous existence.

In his apartment hung a number of photos and quotes from various Hindu Maharishis, sages and other Eastern spiritual leaders. One photo showed some Guru staring back, trance-like, with two of the most piercing eyes imaginable. I remember thinking at the time that it had to be all these Eastern religious influences—the incense, chanting and other brain-washing mumbo-jumbo—that allowed him all that peacefulness.

As 2008 rolled into 2009, I began slipping on the meetings, and, predictably, the drinking escalated. As much as I tried to avoid returning to morning drinking, I found myself doing just that. I was sick about it, but I just couldn't help myself.

The hangover from the night before, combined with too much free time again doomed my resolve. I'd wake up feeling horrible and shaky, get Matt and Natalie off to school and say goodbye to Carol. It was then all me until teaching began six hours later. I needed the drinks first for recovery, and then to escape the feeling of total uselessness that morning drinking brought on. After about six or seven, I'd get where I needed to be, eat lunch, nap, and then limp off to work.

Just like every time before, I knew that getting mildly bombed in the morning was horribly destructive and alcoholic in the extreme; but with no accountability needed, and no immediate consequences standing in my way, I was powerless to avoid it. I had failed in this one, vital task, and I began to sink into the depths of self-pity. Performance degrees, my ass! I had succumbed once again to the disease, and that feeling of worthlessness started to infect what little normalcy I had left in my life.

Deceitfully, I now used the idea of going to meetings as a self-serving cover for added drinking time. If I taught until 7:00, I told Carol it was 8:00. Then there was an 8:30 meeting that I said I was attending. This cunning combination would allow for three full hours of "play time" in the evenings, and I made use of every minute of it. The bonus time also allowed me more time with Trevor, and I started hanging out with a couple of new friends who just happened to drink like me.

George and Andy were living across the river in nearby Morrisville, Pennsylvania. George, an out-of-work construction worker, owned a small, three-bedroom ranch in town; and Andy, a down-on-his-luck real-estate salesman, was renting a room from him. I knew both of them through mutual friends, and George's house soon became an ideal party headquarters for the four of us.

During 2009, I often arrived home late from work and a "meeting," ate some dinner, and spent some time with Carol and kids; and then used the excuse of going over to 7-11 for cheaper smokes in Pennsylvania. Procuring cigarettes had little to do with most of my excursions, however, and most of these nights were filled with lots of drinking and snorting at "HQ," as we called it.

I'd call Carol late from George's and invent some lame excuse for not being home. On more than one occasion, I had the audacity to tell her that I was counseling the both of them about how to stop drinking. *I,* now an expert on AA and sobriety, was simply trying to offer guidance on their drinking. It was beyond absurd, but she seemed to believe this nonsense for a time. As I returned home later and later, though, and my absences became more frequent, she started suspecting my return to drinking and grilled me on it.

"No, I have not been drinking!" I told her over and over again with all the sincerity in the world. "I promise you! I swear to God! May God strike me dead!" You name it, I said it. I lied to her on this point dozens of times during 2009, and, not having any proof to the contrary, she simply accepted it. She also was starting to accept the fact that the loving, caring man she married over 20 years ago was now a someone else. This was not the same man now living with her. And, drinking or not drinking, *this guy* was not making her happy.

As for the money trail, I was now using the home-equity line more and more to fund my addictions, and that wasn't easy for Carol to detect. I had always been in total charge of the finances, and no one had ever been calling about overdue bills; so, even though she had been keeping a closer eye on checking and credit-card expenses, the home-equity line was like an invisible cash-cow. I knew this, and milked it thoroughly right up until the end.

By attending occasional AA meetings and going to marriage counseling sessions I was able to buy myself a bit more time with Carol, but it was all starting to wear thin. Even though most of my meetings were now imaginary, I still attended the 5:30 at the 24 Club on occasion. I'd talk to Carol about stories told at the 24 Club, and important tips I'd pick up from Regis and Payne, and this would appease her for a day or two. But then I'd be out until 3 AM on the third night, and her disgust would mount.

I traveled to Princeton at least a dozen times for marriage counseling sessions, and I tried to say all the right things—attempting to use any information the counselor provided to help me with my troubled marriage. I must have heard dozens of times that it was okay to get angry, but it was necessary to control more positively the way I reacted when angry. There was that word "control" again.

By the time 2009 was coming to an end, any semblance of control with my drinking and drugging was gone, and I had come to believe all the alcoholic voices in my head. *My troubled marriage was now my troubled wife. My anger could never be controlled because Carol could not, or would not accept me for who I was. She was nagging me relentlessly about everything. She was becoming an old woman. Perhaps she was going through the change of life. I wasn't, though. She had changed. I wasn't going to.*

Active alcoholics are prone to experience many peculiar and potentially disastrous things as the disease worsens. As I look back at 2009, I had my fair share to be sure.

Ever since my earliest days drinking and driving, I had somehow avoided the law. Between the near-miss on Christmas Eve 1989 and 2009, there were plenty of other close-calls, but one night in February, 2009, I came within an eyelash of getting popped.

I had left Princeton early enough on this stormy night. It was always a good idea to do so after imbibing in that town, and tonight was no different. This night I had stopped by the Ivy Inn, and, after only two or three, I started winding my way back to Trevor's apartment on the back roads, "road-soda" in hand as usual. I was also carrying two grams of cocaine in my jacket pocket.

The winds that day were extreme, and as I passed a sharp curve on the narrow, darkened road, I saw flashing lights up ahead. Knowing that the road must have been blocked by a downed tree or something, I stopped and began turning around. While performing a K-turn, my front wheels got stuck on the edge of the narrow road. The lip of the street was at least eight inches higher than the shoulder, and my front wheels spun freely, unable to gain traction. I couldn't move, and I was a sitting duck for the law.

The cop car was a good 100 hundred yards in the distance, and I needed assistance to free my car—but, *please*, not from him. Luckily, almost immediately another driver came up behind me, and I asked him to get behind the wheel of my car and reverse it as I pushed the small Honda free. Just as we began to do this, I saw a flashlight's beam coming fast. I had remembered to pop a piece of gum, but I knew that the large, plastic cup sitting in the console was filled with my vodka-mix. If he investigated that, the frisk would be next, and then I'd be off to the pokey for sure.

I had to think—fast. As the cop approached, I seized the initiative. Before he had a chance to say a word, I barked, "Could you please give me a hand here?"

The young officer, barely 25, was caught a bit off-guard by my brazenness, and immediately stepped in next to me. We both heaved, and within seconds the Honda was free. I thanked him and the Samaritan profusely, and started to get back in my car. I wasn't out of the woods yet, however.

He approached my window and shone his light about the interior while asking me a few questions. "What happened here? Where have you been? Where are you going? Have you been drinking?"

I answered all his queries with sincere lies, and he bought them. I saw the light-beam hit the cup more than once, and my heart was galloping. Amazingly, he didn't ask me about it, though. He simply told me to be careful, and sent me back towards Princeton, even informing me of an alternate route back to Ewing. Of course, I was well aware of all 15 routes at this stage of my drinking and driving career, but I thanked him nonetheless.

For the next 15 minutes, I was barely able to breathe. I trembled with fear as the realization of what could have happened took hold. When I was finally able to pick up the cup without spilling it, I downed the entire contents in one, thankful gulp. An hour later, all tooted up at Trevor's, we both laughed about it.

Around Halloween I could have easily been killed.

Snorting massive amounts of cocaine at my age can be hazardous enough. I already had high blood-pressure to begin with, and the white powder surely sent my numbers into the stratosphere. I always could feel my head madly pulsing with blood during long sessions, and sleep was typically out of the question. In order to help with this problem, Trevor had given me calming, Xanax from time to time, and this night I had taken a double dose.

I got home around 3:00 that morning, and began wobbling quietly up the stairs toward my bedroom. Despite being completely polluted on vodka, coke and the muscle-relaxing Xanax, I tried to be as stealthy as possible.

At or near the top step, I missed the railing with my hand and tumbled backwards down the nine stairs. The crash that followed at the bottom must have shaken the entire house. Amazingly, I wasn't badly hurt. I landed on a finger, and the impact smashed the nail, and exploded a wound out the tip. I also had a tremendous bruise that extended from my lower back to below my ass; but aside from that, I was completely uninjured.

The most miraculous part of the near-catastrophe was that no one in the house woke up. If Carol had come to the stairs and seen me lying there, I would've been packing my bags that morning. As it happens, the next day I simply continued the insanity.

The week before Christmas, a massive snowstorm was due to hit. It was coming in on a Saturday, so I decided it would be prudent to stay the night up in Elizabeth in the rectory at my church. Every week, I usually travel the 50 miles each way to play the Saturday vigil mass, and then return to Ewing. I then repeat the process on Sunday, supplying the music for the other two weekend masses.

Carol, disgusted and unhappy as she was by now, was still treating me with a fair amount of decorum; and I consulted with her about this. She agreed that it would be wise for me to stay the night, but I'm pretty sure that by now she wouldn't have minded if I decided to move in at the church rectory permanently.

The impending storm had forced the cancellation of lessons at the Music School in Princeton that day, so I took advantage of the free time to do what I did best at this point in my life: drink. By the time I made it to Elizabeth, I was well on my way. By early afternoon the storm began in earnest, and another organist friend of mine called me and asked if I could play his 5:30 service at another nearby church. I gladly agreed—the $75 would pay for my dinner. Perfect!

For quite some time now, I had been carrying the easily concealed 50 milliliter vodka bottles around with me. If I were going anywhere that my drinking would be noticed, two or three of these minis in each pocket would be required. A simple trip to the bathroom was all that I needed to "relieve" myself.

The night of the storm at both churches, I employed this patented "airplane bottle stealth tactic" to a tee, I drank straight through both services without any noticeable problems (at least to me), and then made my way to my favorite Spanish restaurant a few blocks down the road.

The night was magical. Christmas lights were everywhere, the snow was flying, and my spirits couldn't have been higher. I was free for the entire evening, and I was going to get happily smashed. As I trudged toward the restaurant in what was fast becoming a blizzard, I wanted Carol to share in my George Bailey-type exuberance. I fired off a quick text to her: "It really is a wonderful life!" She didn't reply.

Four hours later, having somehow driven back to church, my attitude was *slightly different*. I was freezing to death and on my hands and knees near my car groping about for my keys in drifts of snow three feet high. I was all alone in a deserted parking lot in the middle of a full-blown blizzard. My phone was dead, I was out of money and smokes, and I somehow had lost my keys. I was being paid a visit by the "Four Horsemen" mentioned in the Big Book: Terror and bewilderment, frustration and despair.

What am I doing out here? Jesus, help me! I can't see. Think, Think! Exactly what did I do after leaving the restaurant? Did I go into church or not? I can't remember! Shit, it's so cold. Did I go in to use the bathroom? I don't remember.

Why is my mind not responding? Did I have three brandies after all that sangria, or was it four—five, perhaps? Oh, who the hell knows? Where are my fucking keys?

For over an hour, I was stricken with numbing panic and frozen in the elements searching all around my car for my keys. I really could have keeled over and frozen to death right there in Elizabeth. Something told me that I had gone into the church, and I stumbled through the drifts and wind, discovering to my drunken surprise that the church was unlocked.

My keys were sitting right where I set them over an hour before—on a table by the bathroom door. I huddled up next to a radiator and passed out for a few hours.

Long before booze appeared in my life, I loved to go off on "mystery walks," as my parents would call them. As early as age four or five, during the long, lonely off-seasons, when Long Beach Island was nearly deserted, I walked off by myself for hours at a time. On many occasions, my curious and wandering nature got me into trouble.

When I was only two, I escaped the house in the midst of a wild "nor'easter," and made a mad dash to the beach. I wanted to go for a swim! A woman neighbor—oddly enough walking the same beach during the storm—saw me floundering and fished me out of the crashing surf. If it were not for her, I would have surely drowned.

Later, I fell out of trees, went through the ice on our lagoon on more than one occasion, and also once nearly hanged myself by accident. I seemed to always return to the house soaked, bleeding or covered in bay muck; and my long absences worried my loving mother to no end. She was at her wit's end trying to keep tabs on me, and, being religious as she was, contacted God for guidance.

According to Mom, she learned, through Him, that I was to be assigned not one, but two guardian angels. One, it seems, was not sufficient in keeping me safe and sound. She told me that Will and Bill were now to look after me for the rest of my days.

During the final couple years of my drinking, Will and Bill would be on call 24/7. As the episodes of mayhem increased in frequency, I acknowledged this, and thanked God and my mother for keeping me alive and safe—but that was that. Sober or not, I prayed to God and thanked him for giving me another day. I prayed for forgiveness and for the strength to somehow try to do better. But, that would be the end of it. I would be all right, I thought, and He would then be left to go off and tackle some more pressing problems around the world. *Just be there when I need you*, I would pray. *For now, I can do it.*

The fear and frustration caused by my inability to manage my rapidly advancing disease was causing me to isolate more and more in my marriage. At the end of a day, all twisted as I was, I didn't want to face Carol for fear of answering difficult or even simple questions. My hair-trigger temper was back, and I desperately tried to avoid uncomfortable situations—like being home.

After all, I was trapped in a pressure-cooker existence. Imagine yourself in a daily situation where one wobbly step, one slurred word, or one whiff of alcohol might mean the end of a 20 year relationship. Being able to manage three jobs, a dynamic household and a marriage with three children was a daunting enough task. Now, throw in a full-time addiction that required absolute secrecy. I knew that sustaining such a life for long could never happen, but I kept trying. Violent collisions with Carol were unavoidable, however.

Not surprisingly, by the end of 2009 these events occurred more and more, and I'd blow up for any number of reasons. There were questions about money and bills, and my answers didn't satisfy Carol. I would explode. She would grill me on my whereabouts the evening before, and I would lie. That look of disgust would follow, and I'd explode again. Getting angry only threw fuel on the fire, and the result would invariably be even more violent language. I would storm out of house, and then try to patch things up the next morning when I'd briefly realize how wrong I was. As soon as I was boozed-up again, however, similar flare-ups ensued.

As mentioned, Carol was starting to realize that, drinking or no drinking, I was not making any progress in the behavior department; and, despite all my attempts at contrition, things were getting worse, not better. More and more, she just wanted me out, and I think I knew that.

On top of that, Matt and Natalie were being exposed to an enraged madman on an almost nightly basis, and this would not do at all. Katie, away at college, was largely spared the tirades, but Matt and Natalie, living in constant fear never knowing how their father was going to act when he came home, were now direct victims of the insanity. Something had to give.

In mid-January, with the marriage fast deteriorating, it was not Carol that provided the spark for a separation. Rather, it was my alcoholic voices that accomplished this. They continued to tell me with increasing certitude that Carol was the problem—that *she* was treating me unfairly. I would threaten to leave. *That* would set her straight.

After yet another brawl, I was carrying on over at George's retelling my latest installment of woe. It suddenly occurred to me that George had a spare bedroom. Knowing he was desperate for funds, I asked if I might move in for "a few weeks or so" if things didn't improve at home. He told me to come on over any time I was ready. *You now have a place to go if Carol doesn't start seeing things your way*, the voices told me.

The next night, Carol and I went at it again. I was stewing in Katie's bed trying to get some much-needed sleep. More and more I was sleeping in her bed, not just because of the fighting, but also because of my incessant snoring. Because of the drinking and coke, and also because I had gained so much weight lately, my snoring was driving Carol to near-madness. It was yet another tick on her mounting "disgust list," and I even brooded about that. *I can't even sleep in my own friggin' bed, for God's sake!*

Anyway, that night I got up out of Katie's bed and went to our bedroom. I said to Carol, "You obviously don't want me around anymore. George told me it would be okay to move in with him for a while. He's got an extra bedroom. I might just do that. How does that grab you?"

I'll never forget that look. I expected a surprised, wounded reaction. I imagined that this would upset her enough that she would now see the light and apologize for all her recent unfair treatment of me. However, to my shock and horror, her eyes revealed a look of utter relief. She didn't say anything, but she didn't have to. Her eyes said it all: "Please don't let the door hit you on the way out!" I went back to Katie's bed and seethed.

The end came a few days later. After another expletive-laced diatribe, I howled. "I'm fucking leaving! I'm not going to put up with this shit one more day!" Carol sat on the couch, staring at the TV, saying nothing as I stormed around the house gathering up belongings. Natalie was crying on her bed, and Matt was huddled in his room. I said my tearful goodbyes to both of them, and then made my way for the door.

Carol, standing somewhat calmly by the door, did say that after I cooled off bit—maybe in a month or so—I might be able to come home. At that moment, I was so pissed that I didn't care. "I can't believe you're kicking me out of my own, fucking house!" I boomed, slamming the door behind me. "*That will show her!*" the voices assured me.

I stopped at the liquor store and bought a big bottle of Maker's Mark bourbon. Not having to worry about the smell of booze was another freeing moment for me, and I drank a couple stiff ones on the way to George's. Later with Trevor, George and Andy, my alcoholic voices were flowing freely along with the bourbon and the lines of coke.

She'll come around, don't you worry about that! You're the king of your house, and she'll be lost without you. You wait, she'll be begging for you to come home before you know it. Everything will turn out just fine—just fine."

Trevor handed me another bag of coke. I handed him my empty glass. *"Pour some more, por favor!"*

Now, with nothing to hold it back, my disease was delighted.

Chapter Fifteen

"It may seem incredible that these men are to become happy, respected and useful once more. How can they rise out of such misery, bad repute and hopelessness? The practical answer is that since these things have happened among us, they can happen with you. Should you wish them above all else, and be willing to make use of our experience, we are sure they will come. The age of miracles is still with us. Our own recovery proves that!"
—Page 153, *Alcoholics Anonymous*

Carley wakes the three of us from a sound sleep at 7:00 on Saturday morning. After all the chaos Mike caused the night before, we were finally able to settle down enough to get to sleep sometime after 1:00 AM.

Ebby doesn't stir at all, and Mike groans, sits up and puts his feet on the floor. I nearly jump out of bed. Again astounded by how good I feel with only five days of sobriety under my belt, I greet the pleasant, April Saturday with the enthusiasm of a boy anxious for his first little-league game of the year.

"I dreamt about French toast and Xanax," Mike mumbles, rubbing his face. I give a quick laugh, and head for the bathroom.

After a shave and shower, I change into my last semi-clean outfit and then whistle my way to the vitals line. I see Mike down at the nurse's station, already bantering with Nurse Sharon. He looks down the hall at me and gives me a thumbs-up. *How did he get down there so fast?* I wonder. *It takes him forever to do anything at night.* The answer comes as I see him motion again my way. He repeatedly puts his hand to his mouth, and then points toward the cafeteria. *Ah, yes!* What else, but the thought of food would light a fire under his ass?

Eva, standing in front of me, also sees Mike and laughs. "Your buddy won't even wait for you?" she asks me. Eva looks amazingly well after nearly dying of heroin withdrawal and dehydration only a few days before. She appears well-rested, and is wearing just a touch of make-up. She's standing right behind Stanley, who's now getting his BP checked by Matt the enforcer.

"No, he won't wait." I respond with a chuckle. "He told me he was dreaming about French toast. If he's hungry, he's gone!"

Stanley gets up with his vitals sheet and walks over to me. He's holding the paper with both hands. Because of his MS, his movements are mechanical, and his entire body seems to shake constantly. He is wearing a broad smile, however, and his dark eyes light up as he says, "I think we should call him Maury."

I look puzzled. "Maury?"

Eva, now seated next to Matt, says, "Yeah, you know Maury from *Goodfellas*? The guy with the toupee?"

I laugh out loud. "You're right!" I say. "God, he's gonna love that!"

Matt reacts, too. The three of us are surprised when the always serious, tough guy grins broadly and says, "I love that scene where De Niro nearly strangles Maury with that phone cord." Matt drops his stethoscope and puts his arms in an imaginary head-lock pose. "I want the fucking money! Give me the fucking money?" he rants. We all laugh.

"How's the agitation?" Nurse Sharon asks me after I hand her my vitals sheet. All three readings are even better than yesterday.

"Much better," I say. "About a two or three, I guess."

"Good! The buse-bar must be doing the trick."

"The what? Booze-bar?" I ask. It certainly sounded like "booze." "You're not telling me there's alcohol in that pill, are you?"

Sharon looks up at me through the glasses perched on the tip of her nose and frowns. "Not 'booze-bar,' you idiot— BUSE-bar—Buspirone. It's the Librium substitute."

"Oh, yeah—huh!" I respond, chastened. "Yeah, it's pretty good." I lean in close and grin. "The Librium is better, though."

"Of course it is!" she barks at me, but not too unkindly. Sharon flashes me a look and shakes her head. "You addicts and boozehounds are all alike. I think you're roommate's craziness is starting to rub off on you."

She returns to the sheet. "BP is much better. That increased dose of Lisinopril is working, I see. I'll be right back,

Mr. piano-player." She retreats to the drug-room behind the counter, muttering, "Booze-bar, can you imagine?"

The Buspirone does help, but it *is* a far cry from the super calming Librium. Buspirone's effect is akin to putting on a light jacket in a snow-storm, as opposed to Librium's, which basically provides four layers and a fur parka.

Sharon returns with my cup of pills and another filled with water. "Take these, and then go over and get your last blood-test," she orders me. "Let's hope your liver continues to show improvement. You're leaving on Monday, right?"

"Yes ma'am," I say, downing the pills and water. Afterward, I say, "I hope to God I'll be going home."

"I hope so too, Eric." Sharon gives me a warm smile. "I don't say this to most patients, but I'm gonna miss you. But, please, I don't want to see you back."

"I'll be back to speak at meetings, Sharon," I tell her with confidence.

"Okay! You can do that. That would be great!" she tells me. "Now get out of here!"

I walk into the first group and take a seat next to Mike. I missed him at breakfast because of my walk and blood-test. He stretches and yawns as I look around. There are a few minutes to go before things get started, and patients are milling about.

I see Ebby huddling with Tim at the front of the room. This is his step-five meeting, I assume, and the look on Ebby's face confirms this. He appears sullen and pale, his head down looking at a stack papers in his arms. Ebby's chiseled, handsome features are lost in a mask of worry. Tim has his arm around him, and is whispering something in his ear.

Mike leans over. "Ebby's not looking forward to this."

I nod and frown. "Who would? He has to lay out all that shit in front of the entire group, for God's sake?"

"I heard that most people spill out their personal inventories to a sponsor or priest or something, not this group shit," Mike says.

I shake my head. "He probably thinks this is the best way for him to get it all off his chest, I dunno."

"My roommate's got balls, I'll tell ya that," Mike says, almost with pride. He turns to me. "You go out at find your animal friends?"

"Yeah," I say. "No sign of the guinea hens. I avoided the turkey. I'm sick of getting yelled at by him."

"What about the peacock?" Mikes asks.

"I heard him call a few times, but he must have been in the woods somewhere."

"The guinea hens are right out back pecking around for cigarette butts," Mike informs me.

"Really?" I ask. "I haven't been back there since earlier."

I get up and go over to the row of windows facing the open field behind Blake. Sure enough, there's 30 or so of them scurrying around, peck-pecking at everything. I actually see one with his head diving in and out of one of the butt cans.

I walk back to Mike, laughing. "One of them *is* going after the butts," I say. "Mom told me I used to do that when I was two."

Mike chuckles. "Somehow that doesn't surprise me." He looks at my bandaged arm. "Last blood test?" he asks.

"Yup!" I say. "She actually hit the vein on the first try. My liver numbers came down from 1300 to 900-and-change in three days. I'm betting on 500 this time," I tell him confidently.

Mike gives me a devilish grin. "Ten bucks it's not below 600."

I shake my head. "What a nice guy—betting against my recovery. Shit!"

He shrugs. "Just weighing my odds, Buddy Boy."

The group begins. While Ebby hands out three attached sheets to everyone, Tim starts talking. "When I met Ebby over two weeks ago, he told me that he was willing to go to any lengths to stop drinking. I am not his sponsor, but we've been doing some work together on the steps, anyway."

Tim, beard neatly trimmed and yuppily attired in white dress-shirt and dark tie, looks every bit the professor as he stands comfortably before us, papers in hand. "When I was a patient here," he continues, "I worked with another counselor, and went through all 12 steps for the first time during my stay. I was just like Ebby, beaten and broken by the disease, and I had to do something—*anything*—to find a way to stop. These 12 steps through the program of Alcoholics Anonymous helped me get my life back.

"We've been going over and over the first three steps," Tim continues, holding up a finger. "One, that we were powerless over alcohol, and that our lives had become unmanageable; two, that we sought a power greater than ourselves to restore us to sanity; and three, that we decided to turn our will and our lives over to the care of God as we understood him." Tim paces around the room a bit, holding out three fingers.

He starts up again. "I had a lot of trouble with the higher power business, as does Ebby. I'm sure many of you do, too. We didn't believe in God, per se, and we both thought we had enough power to manage our drinking all on our own. After failing over and over again, however, we finally had to admit that, without help from something more powerful, we simply could not do it. We came to believe in a power greater than ourselves. We found God, *as we understood him*, and asked him for help. Remember, the first three steps can be reduced to this: I can't—he can—so let him do it. It's as simple as that."

Tim sits down on the chair in front of the 30 of us gathered. Ebby is on his right. Tim says, "Having turned all this over to the God of his understanding, Ebby was then able to attack the fourth step: make a searching moral inventory of himself. You now have this inventory in front of you. Notice the columns. Resentment being the number one offender for alcoholics, the first column lists the many people, organizations, government entities, etcetera, that Ebby has had problems with throughout his life. The next column lists the cause of these resentments; and the third details how all this affected him, and the role he played in each."

Tim reaches over and pats Ebby on the shoulder. Ebby, slumped in his chair, head bowed, looks as if he'd rather be anywhere in the world right now, but here. Tim says, "This fifth step, admitting to God, to ourselves, and to another human being the exact nature of our wrongs, is of vital importance to achieving and maintaining sobriety. All these built-up resentments make us spiritually sick. Simply by telling somebody—you all for instance—about all these issues, we can overcome this spiritual illness and then begin to heal—from the inside out. Only then can we begin to live a new life, freed from the bonds of alcohol and drugs."

He leans in and speaks directly to Ebby. "It's painful and humiliating, I know, but I also know that after I did it—right here in this room as you are—it felt like the entire world was lifted from my shoulders. You told me that this is the way you wanted to go, Ebby. Are you ready?"

Ebby glances up at him, and makes a slight nod. Tim looks up and smiles broadly. "Ladies and gentlemen, I give you—Ebby." He gestures grandly with both hands towards Ebby, who exhibits a pained expression as we applaud.

This bit of showmanship is a bit much, I think. By the snorting sound he's making, Mike thinks so too, and he leans over close to me during the clapping. "I hate that prig, Tim. What is this, fucking Ringling Brothers? I'm sure Ebby would've put him on this fucking list if he could. I know he's on *mine*, the know-it-all, self absorbed…"

"Shhh!" I whisper, as Ebby, in fits and starts, begins his fifth step.

He starts with his parents. Ebby folks were divorced when he was very young, and he reads out resentment after resentment aimed at both of them. The causes for these are many, and Ebby mechanically plods through them all. How did it all affect Ebby? He ran away many times, stole from them, and ultimately turned to drugs and alcohol as an escape mechanism.

Other family members are then listed, as are friends, bosses—even the police. Again and again, Ebby reads aloud the painful resentments, the causes and then the inevitable angry, booze-enhanced responses that followed. Regarding run-ins with the law, Ebby resents every aspect of authority. After every arrest—and there were many—Ebby pins the blame elsewhere. Whether it was one of his five DWIs, or many of the other times he was hauled into custody, drunk and enraged, Ebby never seems to point the finger at himself.

We all sit there slack-jawed, listening as a jury of his peers would at trial. It's as if we're weighing all the evidence against him. But there will be no verdict other than guilty. There can't be. It's the only option. He's admitting his guilt right here in front of all of us.

When it comes to his wife and children, the list grows even longer; and we follow Ebby along this dark road, re-counting with him every lurid detail of his alcoholic behavior toward his family. There are the awful resentments and per-ceived causes; the chronic infidelity that the drinking and drugging brought on; and then the pathetic attempts at recon-ciliation that led to even worse binges and actions.

When he's finally finished, having taken up the entire hour, Ebby looks exhausted and beaten. Afterward, Mike and I go up and, not so much console, but congratulate him. By now, after the shock of it all has dissipated a bit, the relief on his face is monumental. Clearly, it was a harrowing experience for him.

I know it was tough for me just listening to it all. It was difficult to take in all the terrible things that this seemingly calm, steady and self-assured man has done. It's hard to believe it's the same person who many of us view here as such a stabilizing force. It just doesn't seem possible that he actually did all these insane things. From the cheating on his wife and abandoning his kids, to stealing from work and family, to constantly trying to outrun the law, the list goes on and on. How was it possible?

Of course, the answer was the alcohol. It was always about the alcohol. I was a guy just like Ebby, wasn't I? I was a mad-man, too. Sitting there all alone, after the group ends, I realize that what Ebby did out there under the influence, was no better or worse than what I had done for so long. I was just as guilty. I had all those same resentments, and they all made me drink. I lied and stole and cheated, too. Maybe not to the same degree as Ebby, but pretty damn bad, nonetheless. I totally identify with him. Before today, I had no idea what steps four and five were all about. I do now.

There are no group sessions during the afternoon. Many of the patients at Carrier are visited by family and friends on Saturday, and the rest of us are free to lounge around and do other things.

All of my clothes are dirty, and I ask Mike if I can throw some of his dirty stuff in with mine for a load of laundry. He gives me a few things, and I wash and dry them. Later, while I'm lounging out back on the picnic tables in the warm, spring sunshine with Ebby, and Eva, Mike saunters out.

"Hey, Buddy Boy," he says to me, "Your folded laundry is sitting on your bed."

"Oh, thanks Mike. I'm sorry. I forgot."

He's off to the races. "I give you one job—*one fucking job*! And you can't even handle that!"

I start laughing. This only gets Mike going even more. "Then Maxine starts *screaming* at me, 'You didn't clean out the lint-trap! You have to clean out the lint!' Jesus! You'd think the place was gonna fucking explode with all the mountains of lint piling up. And, if it does, it's all your fault, Mr. Piano player!"

Eva, laughing along with the rest of us, says, "You're too much, Maury."

Mike stares at her. "Maury?"

"Yeah, you know, Maury from *Goodfellas*," Eva says. "Stanley came up with that. I think it fits."

Mike, in typical fashion, giggles but appears angry. "Where is that Stanley? He's DEAD! His family—DEAD! If he wasn't all twisted out on speed-balls and such, I'd *kill* the mother fucker!" He touches his immoveable hair, and switches on a dime to a weird, British accent. "I'll have you know, my dear, that this is all mine—*all mine!*" The accent switches back again. "As for Stanley, Ebby—put him on the list!"

Ebby grunts and puts his head back, facing directly into the sun. "No more lists today, Mike. Sorry."

"Huh, I guess you're right," says Mike.

Eva, still laughing, says, "Mike, we even got a rise out of Matt earlier. I think he'll be calling you Maury from now on."

Mike lets out a honking laugh and looks at me. "That reminds me, Buddy Boy, tonight let's get that muscle-bound son of a bitch. Here's what we'll do…"

Just before dinner, I head out back for a quick smoke. I see Tanya sitting alone on a picnic table, having a cigarette. I haven't seen her around much today. I remember her sleeping during most of Ebby's big meeting this morning; and from the look of her now, that's probably what she's been doing the rest of the day, too. Her dyed-purple hair is all over the place, and, as I approach, I notice that she's not wearing any makeup at all.

She looks up at me. Those big, green eyes dominate her attractive face. They're like giant, emerald saucers, and they make her entire face glow. I don't think I've ever seen anything quite like them. Just as I thought yesterday, if she would only lose all that Goth war-paint and piercings, she could be a stunner.

I say, "Hi, Tanya. How are you feeling?"

"Oh, hi!" she says, taking a long drag. "I forget your name."

"Eric," I say, lighting up. "Are you settling in okay?"

"Well, no, like, *hello*? I'm in fucking detox, right? I did just have some pretty good news, though. I just found out my boyfriend got out of prison."

"That's good," I say. "How long was he in for?"

"Like eight months, I think. It was last summer when he went in." She squints and strains her neck, thinking. "Yeah, that's right."

"Was it drugs?" I venture, jumping right into her life. If she wants to say, "Butt out," she certainly can. She doesn't, though, and instead, let's loose a torrent of information regarding her incredibly dysfunctional life thus far.

"Yeah, like we had a real cool set-up with heroin in Scranton. We'd buy the shit in Newark, and then drive up there, three, four times a week. It was really stoking—like two, three G's a week. We rented an apartment up there, and after awhile I told the stupid shit that it was being eyed by the cops, but he wouldn't listen. He never fucking listened. Next thing you know, while I was making a buy back in Newark, the fucking SWAT team was breaking down the door, and he was hauled off to jail. It freaked out my mind, totally."

She pauses long enough to take a quick drag, and then plows on, mission-bound. "I really love him, man. He was like, *there* for me in my darkest hour. I was pulling trips with guys, speed-balling and really out of control before I met him. I've been completely lost without him. That's why I'm like—here, ya know?"

I shrug and stick the cigarette in my mouth.

She goes on. "With that awesome set-up we had now totally screwed, and with Todd put away, I went back out on the street. It was like, *so weird*, dude. Finally my parents found me, and threw my ass in here. They're worth millions, so I'll probably be in here for like, two months or some insane bullshit. I just want to get out and see Todd. They just don't get it, my fucking parents. What's your deal?"

I open my mouth and close it again. Then, I finally manage, "Uh, I'm here for booze. I'm a drunk. I'm leaving Monday. Did you say that you were—*pulling trips*?"

"Dude, like I'm not proud of it, but yeah, I was selling myself. Todd changed all that, until the fucking moron got popped. I'm gonna jack up his skinny ass."

I finish my cigarette, and try to think of something I can say to Tanya. Can I come up with a few words that might help her in some way? She can't be more than 21 or 22, for God's sake. Maybe all these counselors and nurses can somehow break down what seems to be an impenetrable wall of dysfunctionality, and set her out on a more productive path, but what can I say? Sadly, something along the lines of divine intervention may be the only thing that saves her. Todd certainly isn't the answer, I know that, but I don't want to go there. I think of the *Serenity Prayer*: *Accept the things I cannot change.* I've got my own life to save.

Taking in those wonderful eyes again, I come up with something. I put my foot on the picnic table bench next to where she's sitting and lean over close to her. "Tanya, I just want to say one thing," I tell her. "You have the most beautiful green eyes I think I've ever seen. You look *so* much better without all that wild makeup. I'm not trying to hit on you, but I just want to tell you that I think you are very beautiful."

I realize instantly this was the right way to go. She looks up at me and gives me a sweet smile. Tanya says, "Thanks, Eddie. You play the piano pretty good, too. Maybe you can, like, look up that Weezer, like I told you. They're flat-out *sick*!"

Just before 8:00 that night, there's a few of us gathered around the nurse's station. Mike and I have handed Donna our vitals sheets, and Eva and Stanley are waiting directly behind us. Ebby is chatting with Kara and Maxine about ten feet away. The seven of us have created somewhat of a bottle-neck in the hallway, and that was our intent. Matt the En-forcer, standing behind the counter with Donna sees this, and comes out from behind to shoo people along and allow a clearer path for other patients. This also goes according to our plan.

Just as Matt passes Mike and me, he starts saying some-thing to Ebby and the two girls. This is when Mike pounces. He turns away from Donna, and grabs Matt in a bear-hug from behind. "What the hell is this?" Matt says calmly, frown-ing. It appears as though he half-expected this to happen, and doesn't resist. In fact, I learned later that the blabber-mouth Kara had tipped him off—the fink!

After Mike grabs him, I instantly approach and start tickling. I'm immediately joined by our five other confeder-ates. I hit up his mid-section, as Eva, Maxine and Kara attack his flanks. Ebby and Stanley aim higher, and work their fingers around Matt's ears and head. For a few seconds we desperately try to get Matt to laugh, but, as it turns out, the attackers are the only ones howling with hysterics.

The tough guy does chortle a bit, and seems to mildly enjoy all this impromptu attention, but when Nurse Donna booms, "Come on! Knock that shit off!" Matt effortlessly breaks Mike's grasp. In one motion, he spins him around by the arm, and then swiftly applies a firm headlock. We all back away, as the tables have quickly turned. Matt must have been a high-school wrestler, because this is all accomplished with quick precision and with style.

Mike lets out a choked, "Ahh!" and starts flailing his arms. Even Donna's laughing now, and when Mike gags, "My hair!" Matt finally starts showing his amusement.

"Ha Ha HAA!" Matt laughs out with sinister pleasure. "Give me the money, Maury! I want the fucking money!" he screams at the helpless Mike. "Anybody have a phone cord?" He asks no one in particular.

Mike's face is beat-red, and he barely manages, "Okay, okay! I'll give it to ya! I'll give it to ya!" Matt releases his grip, and lets out a hearty guffaw. He raises both hands high in triumph, and struts down the hall to Darcy, leaving the rest of us doubled over in agony.

When Mike Cass finally regains his equilibrium, he staggers back to the nurse's station. "Well," he says, collapsing on the counter. His breathing is ragged, and his face is flushed, but, every hair is still in place. "We showed him, didn't we, Buddy Boy?"

Ebby and I walk into Darcy for the AA meeting. Kara, Maxine, Sal and a few others also filter into the hall. As Ebby and I take our seats, I check out the two guys with bright yellow visitor tags seated in front of the line of chairs. I do a double-take. I whisper to Ebby, "I can't believe this!"

"Believe what?" he whispers back, a puzzled look on his face.

"I know these two guys. They're from the 24 Club in Princeton. The thin guy is Regis, and the chubby one is Payne. They tried to help me when I was doing my brief tour a couple years ago. This is unbelievable!"

"Huh!" says Ebby in my ear. "You know, things like this don't happen by accident. At least that's what it says in the Big Book."

I nod vigorously. So many of these meaningful coincidences have been happening to me these past few days, I half expect Rod Serling to walk through the door.

"This is a meeting of Alcoholics Anonymous," Payne announces. All 10 of us are now seated in from of him. "My name is Payne, and I'm an Alcoholic."

"Hi, Payne," we all reply in unison.

"This reprobate next to me, Regis and I are from the 24 Club in Princeton; and we come out here every month to bring our message of experience, strength and hope."

Payne is an overweight fellow of about 50. He's got well-groomed salt and pepper hair, and is wearing a Rutgers football sweatshirt. Regis, on his left, is about the same age, and has thinning, blond hair. His face is long and thin, and his arms are folded in front of him. The half-serious smirk on his face I remember well. I always enjoyed hearing him share at meetings. He typically spoke in no-nonsense terms, getting right to the heart of the matter of alcoholism in his street-wise and colorful vernacular. I'm at the edge of my seat.

After the Serenity Prayer, and the lengthy reading of "How it Works" from the Big Book, Payne delves into his drunken past. He story is much like mine. For years drinking was his daily companion, and causing little trouble with his work and family life. Then, gradually, progressively, the disease took hold and he searched in vain for a solution. "Every day I'd make another resolution, and every day I'd find myself drunk," he states flatly.

Just like me, he avoided run-ins with the law even though he was constantly drinking and driving. In the end, with marital and work problems coming to a head, he sought help. "I checked myself into the Princeton House—four times—and that finally led me to the rooms of Alcoholics Anonymous," he tells us. "These past two years have been the greatest days of my life," Payne says. "And, it just keeps getting better. I can't believe it."

He talks about having a sponsor and a home-group. "I now have to be accountable to someone, where before, I was trying to deal with my drinking and my other problems all by myself. This was a huge acceptance thing, and it's made all the difference in the world for me," he says.

Payne talks about how going through the 12 steps with his sponsor have given him a "spiritual awakening," as he puts it. "I'm now at a point in my life where I'm in constant contact with my higher power as a result of going through the steps. For me, the promises listed in the Big Book are all coming to fruition, and it's been nothing short of miraculous."

Kara Alcoholic's hand shoots up.

"Yes," says Payne.

Kara takes a big breath and the words come pouring out. "Hi, I'm Kara, alcoholic, and I've heard about these promises before. Don't they refer to step nine, or making amends? I know that I've got lots of amends to make when I get out. My husband won't even speak to me at this point, and then there are all my other family members, friends, and co-workers who I've used so terribly because of my drinking. I'd like to know more about these promises, please."

"Well," says Payne, after pausing to absorb the onslaught of words, "I'm glad you asked that. Hopefully you'll do what I did when I got out of rehab, and find a sponsor who will take you through the steps. As you said, Kara, the promises refer to step-nine to a degree, but can be interpreted as rewards of the program as a whole, I think." He opens up his copy of *Alcoholics Anonymous.* "They're often read at meetings, so I'm going to do that now."

Payne reads, "If we are painstaking about this phase of our development, we will be amazed before we are half-way through. We are going to know a new freedom and a new happiness. We will not regret the past nor wish to shut the door on it. We will comprehend the word serenity and we will know peace. No matter how far down the scale we have gone, we will see how our experience can benefit others. That feeling of uselessness and self-pity will disappear. We will lose interest in selfish things and gain interest in our fellows. Self-seeking will slip away. Our whole attitude and outlook upon life will change. Fear of people and of economic insecurity will leave us. We will intuitively know how to handle situations that used to baffle us. We will suddenly realize that God is doing for us what we could not do for ourselves."

Payne looks up at all of us. "Bill Wilson, our co-founder then asks the question in the book, 'Are these extravagant promises?'"

Regis, in his nasally twang, says forcefully, "We think not!"

Payne says, "The section then concludes with, 'They are being fulfilled among us—sometimes quickly, sometimes slowly. They will always materialize if we work for them.'"

He closes the book. "Those are the promises. They're materializing in me; I can tell you that with confidence. And, with the grace of God, they can materialize in you, too."

Payne pauses for a moment, and then continues. "Before I hand it over to Regis, I just want to talk about grace for a second. A friend in the program recently gave this rather simplistic and crude definition of the word. He said, 'Grace is when you're sitting in a fox-hole with a buddy in the middle of a battle, and there's an explosion. You're buddy gets his head blown off, and you're completely untouched. That's grace." Payne looks around as us. "Every day, many of our 'buddies' are getting their heads blown off—in a matter of speaking—by this incurable and fatal disease known as alcoholism. We, although not at all unscathed, having sought treatment, can find a solution. We have been given the grace to accept help and start to recover. When I got out of rehab, I found that grace in the simple program of Alcoholics Anonymous, and it saved my life. I suggest you do the same."

Payne concludes with this thought: "There are three types of alcoholics: dead, dying and recovering. Keep that in mind when you get out of here. For me, the latter type is much more preferable. That's all I got."

After the applause settles down, Payne, with a degree of pomp, says "Now, I give you Mr. AA—Regis."

Regis shoots Payne a mild look of contempt, sits upright and launches into us with that no-nonsense approach that I remember so well. "I'm Regis and I'm *still* an alcoholic!"

"Hi Regis!" the reply resounds. I glance down at Sal at the end of the line of chairs. Even he's paying close attention.

"I'm not 'Mr. AA,' as my fellow compatriot says. I'm just a drunk. Yeah, I do a lot of commitments and I sponsor more than a few, but I'm no better or worse than anyone else. I'm not here to shake you down or blow smoke up your ass, but only here to tell you how AA has worked for me."

He sits back, and folds his arms again. "Ya see, I knew how it worked years ago. I came into the program at the age of 30, all beaten down and completely fucked up. I was a black-out drinker right from the get-go; and by the time I was 30, I was homeless, helpless and dying. I found these rooms, and AA saved my life."

He pauses and looks up at the ceiling. "We read 'How it Works' at the beginning, but the first word, 'how' is what I needed to understand most—and I did. My sponsor told me that if I wanted to get sober and stay sober, I needed to be honest, open and willing—how." I make note of this fitting acronym.

Regis goes on. "And so, for 10 years, that's how I got my life back together. I did the steps, listened to all the suggestions, and everything was hunky-dory. Then, I took on a new job and got involved in a new relationship. My sponsor died, and I started taking AA for granted. I stopped going to meetings, and started to take my will back. I simply lost sight of how it works. I put all these other things ahead of my sobriety.

"Before you know it, the relationship went bad, and I was having trouble at work. I started feeling sorry for myself and resented the hell out of my ex. So then, one day about eight years ago, I picked up again, and it was off to the races."

Regis talks at length of all the misery that ensued. He emphasizes the intense feeling of isolation and uselessness that engulfed him during this time. "It was poor me, poor me. Pour me another drink!" he says, and continues, "I kept thinking, 'Life's not fair, life's not fair.'" He mimics a whining child. "In retrospect, I thank God that life's not fair. Because if it was, I'd definitely be dead or in prison because of all the terrible things I did. *That* would've been fair!" Ebby and I laugh at this and nod.

He tells us that at the end of all this, had it not been for the men and women of AA, he surely would've died. "It took four years of hell, but I made it back," he tells us. "They didn't pass judgment on me, and thank God for that. I was literally on my hands and knees with despair, but, I made it back, and AA welcomed me with open arms.

"I was pathetic, though," Regis continues. "I was dripping with this awful self-pity and loathing. But my new sponsor wanted to hear none of my bullshit. He told me, 'I'm from Trenton, and down there we don't put up with that kind of shit. We say, "Get down off the cross! We need the wood!"'" We all laugh.

Regis concludes by saying, "That was over four years ago, and I don't plan on putting anything ahead of my sobriety again. At least—not today! I know many of you are having troubles at home," he says. "But, take it from me: in my experience, a relationship or a job—or anything at all—can't keep you sober. I put a relationship and a job ahead of my program, and that shit failed miserably. I needed to be honest, open and willing, but I also needed to accept the fact that I was an alcoholic for the rest of my days. When I lost sight of that fact, and put other things ahead of my sobriety, I was doomed to drink again. Like Payne said, when I went back out, it was only by the grace of God that I didn't get my head blown off." He looks at Payne and chuckles. "I like that analogy, Amigo!"

He looks back at all of us. "Anyway, good luck to all of you. We have a nice way of closing."

As we join hands and recite the *Lord's Prayer*, I start to take in the importance of what Regis just said. I realize that, although it is important that I get back into my home and attempt to get my family back, it's not the *most* important thing. My life itself depends on me not taking another drink. It's as simple as that.

I can accomplish this is by learning "how": I must be *honest* and *open* with myself for once in my life; and I must be *willing* to jump into this life-changing program of AA as Regis and Payne have, and change the way I think. I amazed at the revelation that, with or without Carol in my life, my own sobriety must always come first. My marriage may be coming to an end, but that doesn't mean my life has to. I know that all this change will take time, but it can be done.

This I must earn, I remember. It reinforces what I picked up on in Kevin's group yesterday, but there's more to it than that. Recovery comes first, but I can't ever lose sight of the fact that relapse is only one drink away. I can only look at what happened to Regis when he painfully forgot what was of paramount importance. Now, I think I can clearly see my way forward. I know that if they can do it, then I can, too.

Afterward, I approach Regis. I can see the recognition in his eyes as I shake his hand. "I remember you," he says. "Is it Eddie?"

I laugh out loud. "You're the second person today to call me that. It's Eric, and thank you for that message," I say.

"Yeah, Eric, that's right," Regis says, grinning. "I knew you were only screwing around when you came in, what, a couple years ago?"

"Yeah," I say. "Remember you gave me the Big Book? It's still collecting dust at home. You told me to read the *Doctor's Opinion*, and that would get me off the hook. I took that as a green light to keep drinking."

Regis laughs. "Well, get that mother off the shelf! Are you ready to get serious this time?"

"I have to. I was dying. Man, what you said about putting sobriety first means so much to me right now. Thank you."

"Listen," he tells me, "Don't make the same mistake I did. When do you get out of here?"

"Monday," I tell him.

"Come on by the 24 Club for the 5:30 meeting, and we'll get you hooked up with a temporary sponsor. Just keep it simple, sit back, and enjoy the ride. Just don't drink!" he implores me.

"I'll be there!" I assure him. "I need to learn 'how'—and now!"

"Good enough," he says, and pats me on the back. "Maybe now we can finally help you off that proverbial hook."

It's close to 11:00, and I'm standing once again at the nurse's station. I'm waiting for Donna to return with my nose-strip and sleeping pill. All the excitement of the day has finally caught up with me, and my entire body seems ready to collapse. Night after night of five and six hours of sleep, as well as dealing with my nutty roommate, has taken their toll, as well. I'm plum tuckered out.

Nurse Donna comes out from behind the back door holding the nose-strip and two small paper cups in one hand, and a sheet of paper in the other. "By the look of you, you really don't need this pill, but take it anyway, Eric," she orders me, handing me the pill and the water. After a mighty yawn, I do so.

"I want to show you something," she says, and hands me the paper.

"Oh, my God," I say after looking at it for a second. "I can't even remember them taking this. Shit! What a mess!"

It's my black and white Carrier admission sheet with photo taken an hour or two before I collapsed in my bed for the first time. In the mug-shot, I'm wearing my black, Phillies cap, and my eyes are barely open. Actually, one eye is almost totally shut, but the other is half-open. My face is a puffy, darkened mask of unmistakable alcoholism. The expression on my face can only be described as pitiable.

Donna asks, "What word comes to mind when you see this?"

"Boozehound!" I state emphatically. "Look up the word in the dictionary, and this picture should appear with it."

Donna doesn't even smile. "Eric," she says seriously. "I lost my husband to alcoholism. He was only 52, and he died a horrible death. He never even tried to get help. Even when the jaundice set in, he just sat there in his chair, all yellow and shrunken—and drank and drank" Donna lowers her head and moves it back and forth. Her beautiful Mount St. Helens necklace and earrings rattle as she does so. She appears close to tears when she asks me, "You know what word comes to my mind when I see this photo?"

I put my hand on hers. "What?" I venture.

"Eddie," she says. "That was my husband. You remind me of him," she says quickly. I need to go to bed—now. This is the third time for Eddie, and I need to lie down and go to sleep before a fourth one pops out of a broom closet and chops me down with an ax. Will and Bill, my guardian angels, must be drinking what I've forsaken, the devilish little pranksters.

Donna gets back some level of control and looks up at me. "Are you okay?" She asks me. I nod and try not to let all this Eddie business show; but it really does give me a creepy feeling. She says, "Just promise me you won't end up like Eddie, okay?"

"I promise, Donna!" I say, with total conviction. "I'm doing better, and I don't want ANYTHING to do with Eddie."

"Take this," she hands me the sheet with the photo. "It's a copy. Keep this close by at all times to remember. When you're out there and feeling better, just take a look at this, and remember."

I take the paper, fold it and put it in my notebook. "I will, Donna. That should be even more incentive for me never to pick up again. Thank you."

Donna comes out from behind the counter. "I won't be here again until after you're gone, so take care of yourself. I'm gonna miss you." She gives me a big hug.

"Thank you so much for everything," I say, and mean it. "I'll never forget all that you and Sharon, and everyone here have done for me."

Donna points down the hall past me. "You're roommate's on the phone. I'll tell him to keep it down tonight. Your neighbors were complaining last night."

I laugh. "Haven't they been complaining every night? Good luck trying to control him on his last night here. Goodbye, Donna," I say finally, turning and walking toward the room.

"Good luck, Eric."

I pass Mike Cass on the phone, and he holds up a finger motioning me to wait. "Okay," he says. "Yes, please. I cleared it with them. Yes! Do it before I change my mind. Okay. Great! I'll see you around four. Bye."

He hangs up the phone and takes a long breath. "In through the nose…out through the mouth," he recites, dreamily.

I smile.

He stands up and comes up close to me. His calm but serious expression is much different than the usual devil-may-care one. He says, "That was my brother, Buddy Boy."

We slowly start walking down toward our room. "What news?" I ask.

"I'm out of here tomorrow. He's picking me up around four."

A twinge strikes my stomach. I know I'm going to lose it when he leaves. It's difficult to describe, but I don't think I've ever felt closer to anyone in my life than I have towards Mike these last five days. "I'm gonna miss you, Mike," I say.

He puts his arm around me as we walk. "You too, Buddy Boy." He stops and looks at me. "Get this, I told him to pick up my Xanax at the drug store tomorrow, and get rid of it before he gets here. That stuff is out—Tom!" He laughs a little, as do I.

I say, "That's great, Mike. You're mother is gonna be so happy to have you back—sober."

"Yeah," he replies, and we continue toward our room. "She'll have the pasta and meatballs piled high when we get there for Sunday dinner. I can finally break this fucking diet I've been on."

I laugh out loud. Exhausted as I am, sleep suddenly doesn't appeal to me. Right now, I just want to stay up and talk with Mike. We'll discuss movies and laugh about all the people we've met here. Yeah, sleep can wait. I want every last minute I can get out of my friend.

"Mike?" I ask, as we approach our door. "Can I ask you a question?"

"What?"

"Do I remind you of anybody named Eddie?"

Chapter Sixteen

"Here is the fellow who has been puzzling you, especially in his lack of control. He does absurd, incredible, tragic things when drinking...He is often perfectly sensible and well-balanced concerning everything except liquor; but in that respect he is incredibly dishonest and selfish. He often possesses special abilities, skills, and aptitudes, and has a promising career ahead of him. He uses his gifts to build up a bright outlook for his family and himself, and then pulls the structure down on his head by a senseless series of sprees. He is the fellow who goes to bed so intoxicated he ought to sleep the clock around. Yet early next morning he searches madly for the bottle he misplaced the night before...As matters grow worse, he begins to use a combination of high-powered sedative and liquor to quiet his nerves so he can get to work..."

—Pages 21 and 22, *Alcoholics Anonymous*

It was all Carol's fault. How could she kick you out of your own house, for God's sake? And now, because of her unwillingness to accept you for who you are, the marriage is now in ruins.

Why can't she appreciate how important you are to this family? Instead of rewarding you for all you do around the house—laundry, shopping, bill-paying, help with the kids, everything—she throws you out instead? Where did all the love go with that girl, anyway? She has changed, you haven't. The kind-hearted, loving party girl you married is now an unreasonable, nagging shrew!

*Sure, you've been blowing up a lot more lately, but most of that stems from the fact that Carol won't cut you a break on anything. Yes, you've been hitting the bottle hard, but, you can pin that on Carol, too. Your drinking might be a problem, but Carol has been downright unmanageable. Yeah, that's it. It's step one, with modifications. You're powerless over alcohol **because** your **wife**—not your life—is unmanageable!*

Also, look on the bright side. She still doesn't know anything about the current drinking or drugging. Didn't I tell you that you'd be able to keep all that hidden? Just stick with me, kid, and be extra careful. You do need to take Trevor's advice and keep the coke and Xanax more under control. Money doesn't grow on trees, you know.

Just don't beat yourself up about the Carol situation. You need to take this time away from her and enjoy yourself. You deserve it. After a week or two, she'll see the error of her ways and come around to your way of thinking. Keep showing up every day and get Matt and Natalie off to school as always. Do the laundry and the food shopping, but give Carol some space. Trust me, in no time at all she'll be asking you back. Let her experience the loneliness of all those late nights alone in her bed. Before long, she'll be missing you and begging you to come home. I guarantee it!

If, in the unlikely event that she doesn't get it this time, you might have to be ready to consider the unthinkable. That's right, Eric. If she can't change and come around to your way of thinking, it might be time to go break away for good. Yes, divorce! Don't feel that way! At some point, you might have to face it. Listen, you've got so much going for you. There are so many other women out there waiting for a guy like you. Carol has cut you off completely. Are you to stay celibate forever? Just keep it in the back of your mind, and try to take it easy.

Yes, that's right. Pour yourself a strong one. Send Trevor a text. Good man.

More and more, this was the voice I was hearing and believing during the long, cold, dark winter of 2010. Of course, it was all rubbish. Putting any part of the blame of my situation at the feet of Carol was beyond laughable. Yes, she was getting on my case, but that was because she was trying to talk sense into me. She was trying to reach the old Eric—the understanding, happy-go-lucky soul she had married 21 years before. He had long since checked out, and was now replaced with a living, breathing time-bomb, set to blow after any perceived slight or sideways look.

Just before I moved out, the situation was at a point where Carol would retreat and isolate rather than confront me and risk the terrible outbursts that were occurring right before our children's eyes. More and more, in the interest of peace, she wouldn't say anything to me when I came home, and rather retreat to our room or bed just to avoid any form of confrontation. This would piss me off to no end, and I'd storm around the kitchen, banging pots and pans, cursing under my breath.

During brief periods of lucidity, when there would be a momentary pause in the drinking, I'd be able to see the damage I was causing. This would cause intense guilt, and I'd fall headlong into a pit of wretched self-pity and loathing. Only another spree would take me out of that. It was a daily excursion into hell, but I was completely unable to stop it. I was helpless and afraid, but the booze and drugs kept those emotions at bay.

Much later, after Carrier, dozens of IOP sessions, weeks of one-on-one therapy, and hundreds of AA meetings, was I able to fully grasp the real reason behind my terrible anger directed almost exclusively at Carol.

I had attempted for years to control my drinking, and had failed every single time. The cunning, baffling and powerful nature that is alcoholism traps its victims in an impossible situation. The alcoholic, by picking up that first drink, is simply unable to shake the obsession that enslaves him. He can often see through the haze what is happening; and he tries again and again to stop, or, in my case, control the drinking. As was the case for me, there are often periods of success; but in the end, the inexorable progression wins out. All attempts end in utter failure.

Disgusted with myself for not being able to deal with my progressing alcoholism, I began to lash out. For 20 years, I was able to drink with few adverse consequences, and I kept thinking that *this time* it would be possible to slow things down and return to more normal consumption. Instead, every attempt failed miserably. I could do nothing about it. Filled with frustration and self-loathing, I vented my anger at the person closest to me—Carol.

Toward the end, the disease tore at me. But, it wasn't my flesh the disease was tearing, it was my soul. Not until I was sober for many months, having discussed the subject in depth with a sponsor and other experts on the matter, was I able to come to grips with all of this. It was now possible for me to connect the soul-tearing frustration and tremendous self-loathing with the unstoppable anger directed at Carol.

However, in the midst of all this insanity, I was completely unaware of this inner turmoil ripping me apart. Being deep in my "cups" 90% of the time, I was completely numb and unable to comprehend any part of what was *really* going on in my life. So, I attempted to put on the best face I could and move forward. Despite believing those alcoholic voices that told me that Carol was the primary problem for everything going wrong in my life, I did try to stifle them. For the first few days and weeks living at George's, I feebly attempted to make things right at home.

I would arrive home every weekday morning, already primed with a morning eye-opener, and get Matt and Natalie off to school. I'd often make lunch for Carol, and have a brief chat with her as she prepared for work. I tried to be as pleasant and upbeat as I could in the face of my banishment; and hoped that with a bit of good behavior, I might be permitted to return home soon on something akin to permanent probation.

When she would leave for work, I'd plan my day. I always wanted to do something positive around the house. It might be food shopping or laundry, perhaps vacuum or dust; but I wanted to show Carol that I was serious about making amends. I truly wanted to come home, and always went about my household duties with an eye on my imminent return.

Of course, the *very* first thing I would do after Carol left was steer my mobile bar to the nearest liquor store. There I would be greeted warmly by Dave or Hank, Joe or Nick. Being the supremely people-pleasing alcoholic I was, I never thought it strange that almost every liquor store clerk in Mercer County knew me by name. They'd have my pint of Smirnoff waiting for me, and then I'd be off to seize the day. After a long, relaxing drive around the county, and a few useful chores done at home, I'd eat, nap, and then head off to teach in Princeton.

Later in the evening, refueling at HQ, I'd wait for a call or text from Carol thanking me for all the good things I had done. After all, even in the midst of my exile, I should be recognized as the faithful father/provider I was. Anyone else in my situation would have thrown in the towel long ago, I reckoned, but not me. I was going make it back into my house soon. I would be stalwart, and persevere despite it all.

When the call or text from Carol inevitably didn't materialize, I would stew, and then blow. Sitting there drunk with George and Andy, perhaps Trevor, I'd launch vicious, sarcastic text messages at Carol. After a few weeks, sensing the texts were not having enough of an impact, I would call her to bitterly complain about her latest slight of me, or simply to vent my spleen for no other reason than I was miserable about the direction my life was heading—thanks to her!

George and Andy—even Trevor—would just shake their heads in bafflement at my nightly eruptions. They counseled me on how I might get a better handle on the situation with Carol, but it would always turn into the typical "alcoholic's refrain." That is when one drinker is trying to tell the other that *he* is drinking too much. *That other guy, after all, has a much worse problem than me. Just look at him!* A frequent line might be, "So, let's all have another drink, and discuss how *you* can better handle your drinking problem."

By early March my actions toward Carol had become so bad that I wouldn't even bother trying to apologize in the mornings, and I went out of my way to avoid her. I then retreated to the only safe haven available to me. In the bottle I could escape, while the voices screamed in my head. *The ungrateful bitch! So, now she's now doing the laundry and food shopping. She's looking after the house all by herself now, huh? She's actually enjoying not having you around. Well, then fine! Have another drink. To hell with her!*

Because I was rapidly spinning out of control, work inevitably suffered. I was missing more and more lessons, and I got called into the director's office to explain myself. For weeks I had been coming up with creative excuses for not coming to work, but it was all wearing thin. I had been "sick" with numerous ailments, my car was having all kinds of imaginative mechanical troubles, and cousins or close friends were "passing away" at an alarming rate.

Of course, I told Sean, the director, the "real" reason for my lack of attendance: Carol had kicked me out of the house, we were separated, and it was affecting every aspect of my life. He was supportive, but told me in no uncertain terms that I could expect fewer students in the future if my lack of production continued. I listened, and nodded thoughtfully. Then, I went off and drank and drugged some more.

Half in the bag one day, I stalked around my house, peeved that it was immaculately clean. Enraged, I took our marriage photo and turned it upside down. Then, knowing that Carol would *finally* realize the seriousness of the situation, I took off my wedding ring for the first time in 21 years, and placed it on the dresser in front of the photo. *If that doesn't get her attention*, said the voice, *nothing will!*

Filled with remorse, I returned the next day to retrieve my ring. It was still there in the exact spot where I left it, directly in front of the still inverted photo. Shit! She hadn't even bothered to turn the photo right-side-up. I grabbed the ring and fumed some more.

Could all this madness ever end? Of course, the final, insane "lost weekend" would arrive soon enough. However, no one, especially myself, could possibly have anticipated the events that led to the bizarre ending of my addiction. In the end, my bottom would arrive by way of India, of all places.

In late 2009 my cell-phone rang. I didn't recognize the number but answered it anyway. "Hello, Eric? This is Rose from your Online Pharmacy," came the woman's bright and pleasant voice with a thick, Indian accent.

"Yes? Who? What?" I responded dumbly. She went on to explain that she knew I had been on anxiety medications in the past, and that her company could supply me with almost any type of generic meds to help me with my problem. "We have one milligram generic Xanax available to you," she told me. "Just for today, we have a special: 150 pills for only $250. This offer is only good for today," she assured me.

I couldn't believe my ears. How could she have known this about me? Perhaps I might have been online investigating different medications, but I had never purchased any. The only explanation that made any sense was that Indian hackers had somehow penetrated my pharmacy or doctor's computer files.

I knew the enterprise had to be completely illegal, but that didn't concern me. I had been having close brushes with the law for years, and always came away completely unscathed. This was nothing compared to having cops push my car out of ditches with my pockets stuffed with cocaine, for God's sake. Aside from the outside chance of this being a sting operation, the risk would be minimal, I thought.

The strangest part was that I desperately needed the Xanax right about now. The late-night "blizzards" with Trevor were occurring with greater frequency, and he often didn't have the calming Xanax to help me get some sleep. Without something to help ease me off that cocaine cliff, all-nighters were becoming commonplace. The debilitating effect of those was immense. After an all-nighter, the entire next day would be agonizing; and I eventually ended up missing more work for that reason than any other.

I went ahead and rolled the dice. I made the purchase with my credit card, and Rose promised delivery within two weeks. The price was definitely right. Trevor, when he had them, often charged me $5 for a half-mil tablet. The Indian Xanax mock-up would be less than two bucks a piece for twice the dosage. I could do nothing but wait and see what came in the mail—if anything.

I nearly got busted when the goods arrived. No, it wasn't the cops or mail-inspectors, but Carol herself. I was still living at home, and she intercepted the oddly wrapped package from India. She was quite curious about it, but, miraculously did not open it. She did grill me about it when I returned home that night, and I had to think fast. "Blood-pressure medication," I lied, adding, "I got a better deal on my Lisinopril from the Indians." She bought it, and I started taking them.

By the time the next shipment arrived safely in early February, George, Andy, Trevor and even a few other friends that came around HQ were helping themselves to the sleep-friendly narcotic. Rose was as good as her word. The drug provided the gentle slide toward sleep that I was after. By now, Trevor was coming by almost daily, and after a big night of lines and drinks, I'd pass around the Xanax like candy.

I was also the one buying the lion's share of the coke; and I enjoyed playing the role of the big-shot, handing the straw to anyone present after a round was cut. The cost was monumental, but I didn't care. I could see well enough to comprehend that all this could never last, but that was for another day. It gave my sagging spirit great pleasure to be with friends, and to be able to assist them with any of their partying needs.

By being the catalyst behind these mind-bending orgies, in some twisted way I was able leave behind for the moment the terrible self-loathing and turmoil churning somewhere deep within me. For the time being, with Carol now out of the picture, I was able to shelve any feeling of disgust regarding my failure at dealing with my 30 year obsession with alcohol. I know my alcoholic side-kick was doing jumping-jacks: *That's right, Eric, have a blast. Carol kicked you out, so party it up! Who cares about all the money? You'll make that up eventually. Remember, it's all her fault anyway.*

By now it was a handle of Smirnoff every two days, and the drug use at HQ was reaching epic proportions. For the most part, it was Trevor and I who really dove into the pile of powder. George and Andy, and anyone else who might happen by HQ around this time, were not terribly interested in the stuff. They would partake, to be sure, but their principle interest lay in the booze, and perhaps a bit of weed. Ironically, pot never held an attraction for me, and I can at least check that drug off in the "no" column forever.

As for the coke—my Lord! With Trevor constantly supplied, and cash flying out of my pocket at an alarming rate, the "blizzard" went on with furious abandon. Trevor and I sometimes joked about enduring yet another night's "triathlon," as we called it. That was when we would consume roughly 20 drinks, 20 lines and 20 cigarettes in one, long sitting.

After a triathlon, I was thankful for all those hours of work put in at the gym in the past. They were long gone by now, but I'm pretty sure the vestiges of all those cardio-workouts were helpful in keeping me alive now. I was 47, overweight and out of shape. And now, with every blood-vessel in my body saturated with coke and ready to burst; I probably should have keeled over any number of times. But, somehow my stubborn heart kept pumping.

Playing pool into the wee-hours, blasting Sinatra classics over the internet—line after line, drink after drink—Trevor and I inhabited that rarified air that only a cocaine high can produce. We'd wax-eloquent, philosophizing and debating the geo-political world view. Pontificating on everything from the trade imbalance with China to the pros and cons of Obama's healthcare overhaul bill, each of us gave passionate and heart-felt judgments.

In the end, of course, nothing was ever resolved, and no real points were made. Sitting at the counter in George's kitchen after the lines were all gone, the reality of the agonizing morning staring us in the face, we were but nothing. We were pathetic, drunken, shaky messes. At least I was.

Occasionally, a friend brought by Oxycodone for some added *fun*. We'd crush them up and snort them, as well. It would add a rubbery, numbing grace-note to the high-octane blur. For me, each successive morning greeted me with more and more pain; so increasing the dosage of my "medication" was required. My world was spinning fast now, and I tried to hold on tight. All this went on unabated through March, until the ill-fated third shipment of Indian Xanax put in motion the end to everything.

Rose, that mysterious drug-dealer from Asia, changed the terms on me. Perhaps the Indians were starting to feel the heat, but I'll never know. For whatever reason, this time a simple credit card number wouldn't do, and a money order was needed for the Xanax. I went to the post office, and did as I was instructed—wiring the $250 money order, and putting it all on my credit card.

This unorthodox transaction sent up red flags at Master-Card central, and they phoned us to inquire about it. Actually, they phoned Carol to inquire about it. Completely in the dark, she then asked me about it. I denied any knowledge of a money order, but instead made up some nonsense about Indian hackers stealing our credit information. Carol, knowing something was definitely going on somewhere, had them cancel our existing cards, and told them to provide us with new ones.

By now, Carol was completely disgusted with me, and this credit card fiasco was one of the last straws. She was seeing my erratic behavior escalate, and my physical appearance must have been shocking indeed. The next time she had a chance, she gave me both barrels. "You buy high blood pressure medication from these people, and you think it's all above board? What the fuck is wrong with you? Your mind is going, Eric. And—look at you! You're a mess. I don't want you around our children looking like this. By the way, have you been drinking over there?"

"A little bit," I heard myself mumble.

"Yeah, right, a little bit, huh?" She let out a huge, hollow laugh, and then raged, "You need help! Get the fuck out of here!"

I spouted some choice words, and then retreated to my bottle and my bag. The only thing that mattered to me now was the next drink or drug. In my befuddlement, with those two things, I could escape—at least for the moment—my rapidly disintegrating marriage.

I did take some solace in the fact that Carol hadn't yet found out about the Xanax, *and* that she now knew I was drinking. That sliver of honesty lifted my spirits somewhat, and I drank even more. The madness reached new levels, and the alcoholic voices howled, drowning out any voice of reason. *Yeah, who wouldn't be drinking in your shoes? She treats you like that, and expects you to not drink? She throws you out like so much garbage, and expects you not to drink? She's insane, not you! It's time to plan your next move. It's time to think about life without Carol. Who needs all that bullshit, anyway?*

The final shipment arrived just before Easter Sunday, in early April. Carol and the kids went up to her sister's apartment in New York for the day. For some reason, I wasn't invited. So, I decided to go to my sister's house down the shore and cry on her shoulder for the day. After playing the services in church in Elizabeth, I drove the 90 miles down to Manahawkin—drinking all the way.

Throughout the day, Holly and Tim, my brother-in-law, listened as I rambled and railed at Carol for all her terrible treatment of me. Red-faced and bloated, I indignantly made my demented case against my wife. With both pants pockets bulging with multiple mini-Smirnoffs, I took numerous smoke-breaks out on the porch—to drink. By the time the turkey came out of the oven, I was starting arguments about politics, and carrying on like a fool.

Holly, my wonderful big-sister, always looked out for her brother. She is a seasoned healthcare professional, and also has extensive personal experience in dealing with drunks. She knows the signs. Her first husband, a horrible alcoholic who had recently died from the disease, often displayed some of the same traits that I was now exhibiting.

She never said anything to me that day about my appearance or the way I was acting, but instead, took action in another way. After dinner, I went out back for another "smoke" break, and Holly went out front to my car. She knew where to look. In the glove compartment, she found my stash of 150 Xanax pills, neatly packed in 15 plastic containers.

Again, she said nothing to me, and, as I left, she simply prayed that I get back to Morrisville safely. Of course, I drove perfectly, drinking all the way back to HQ and happy to greet Trevor, George and Andy and a fresh pile of powder.

Holly called Carol.

Now, the pieces of the puzzle were assembled for my wife. She knew I was drinking, but that wasn't the main issue. She *now* knew, by way of Holly, that the blood-pressure medicine story was another ruse, and drugs were now a major factor. Carol still cared enough for me to know that if I didn't get help—and fast—death could be around the corner. Holly, also greatly alarmed, counseled Carol about an intervention. They agreed on a time and place. The following Sunday at our house in Ewing there would be a reckoning.

The final piece of the puzzle lay in the money-trail. That week, Carol researched online bank records, and was stunned to see one ATM withdrawal after another—$200 here, $200 there. Then, even more appalling, were all the transfers from the home-equity line. Over the past two years, Carol discovered that over $20,000 had been moved from the line into our joint-checking account—and then out. Despite being horrified by this revelation, Carol held her fire on that front. Until I agreed to get help, Carol would say nothing to me. Soon she would take steps toward shutting down the credit cards and bank accounts.

I was ignorant of all these events; but, stumbling and staggering along in the drug and alcoholic stupor that was now my life, I did have a strange feeling that the end was near. Like a wild animal looking for shelter upon sensing an approaching storm, I just knew something was going to happen to me. I knew that this non-stop binge had to end somewhere, but I had no idea how this was going to happen.

I simply went ahead—careening toward oblivion.

Chapter Seventeen

"Our stories disclose in a general way what we used to be like, what happened, and what we are like now. If you have decided that you want what we have and are willing to go to any length to get it—then you are ready to take certain steps.

At some of these we balked. We thought we could find an easier, softer way. But we could not. With all the earnestness at our command, we beg of you to be fearless and thorough from the very start. Some of us have tried to hold on to our old ideas and the result was nil until we let go absolutely.

Remember that we deal with alcohol—cunning, baffling and powerful! Without help it is too much for us. But there is one who has all power—that one is God. May you find him now!"

—Pages 58 and 59, *Alcoholics Anonymous*

Sunday morning's weather is damp and dreary, but I feel clear and dry. It's just past 8:00 and I've already had my vitals checked and my morning meds. Angie took care of me with the drugs and vitamins. She's the large African-American nurse filling in for Sharon behind the counter. I remembered her from her thankless task of taking late-night vitals earlier in the week. After receiving my meds I asked her if my blood-test results were in yet, but she told me they wouldn't be until first thing tomorrow morning.

I'm sitting in Darcy making notes when Mike Cass and Ebby amble in. "Wazzup!?" Mike yells at me. Everyone in Darcy turns their heads. Mike is all "denimed up" in cowboy-blue, and his dyed-black, creamed and sprayed hair is cemented in place for the day. He's got that devilishly happy expression on his face. Ebby is smiling, too. They come over to my table, but don't take a seat.

"No groups this morning," Ebby announces brightly. "Sunday chapel is at 9:00. Are you interested?"

"Definitely," I say. "I've got plenty to be grateful for."

"Yeah," says Mike. "Your wife just called. She's grateful, too."

"And why's that?" I ask, waiting for the kicker.

"She's grateful for one more day of peace and fucking quiet without you around."

"I like that," I tell him. "That means I will be home tomorrow. Good thinking, Maury!"

Mike snickers. "I'm always looking out for ya, Buddy Boy."

"Let's get breakfast," Ebby says. I stand up, and the three of us start walking.

Mike says, "Why don't we go see that supposed peacock first, okay? I'd like to see that fucking bird once before I get out of here."

This surprises me. For the first time since I've met him, something else has taken precedence over food.

Ebby laughs and says, "Yeah, maybe we can pluck a few feathers for your head-dress, Chief Awopaho!"

Mike grins, "That's right! I need a new head-dress to show my squaw and goom-bahs up in Manheim."

We all head out the front door of Blake and make a left toward the open fields.

The day is misty and overcast, but our light jackets are sufficient as the temperature is mild. After walking only a few minutes, we hear the high-pitched, piercing call, "Ah-EH! Ah-EH! Ah-EH!"

The three of us freeze in our tracks. "That's it!" Mike announces excitedly. "That's the sound Steve McQueen heard in the jungle in *Papillion*."

We stop and look toward the sound. Mike says solemnly, "I accuse you of a wasted life!"

"Guilty," I mutter, remembering the scene well. "Guilty."

"There he is," Ebby says, pointing toward the tree-line about 100 yards away, just past the end of the last parking lot. "Let's get closer."

We walk to within 20 or 30 yards of the proud bird. He's indifferent to our appearance, and is stepping along the tree-line, pecking at the ground. His huge plumage is bundled up behind him as he walks.

"Ah-eh! Ah-eh!" I mimic the bird. He doesn't even acknowledge the lame attempt at communication.

"Let's see your fucking feathers!" Mike yells at him. "That's the way we communicate up in Manheim," he tells us.

At Mike's command, the peacock actually stops, turns his head and stares at us. He sticks his long neck out toward us and calls again. "Ah-EH! Ah-EH! Ah-EH!"

"Wow!" says Ebby, impressed. "I didn't know you spoke peacock."

Mike laughs. "Nah, it's just my animal magnetism." We all laugh.

"Well, let's see it! Don't be shy!" Mike yells, opening his arms wide. This entreaty the great bird ignores, and puts his head back down and starts pecking again.

After a minute or two, he wanders off into the woods. The entire time, he keeps his plumage to himself.

"I guess that's the show," Ebby says, as we turn and start back.

"Oh, well, let's go get breakfast," Mike says. "All this exploring shit has me famished."

We circle around back toward the admissions building. "Look, my guinea hens!" I say, pointing toward north entrance. "Let's go in that way."

We walk over to where the 20 or 30 guinea hens are pecking profusely around the main entrance of admissions. We generally use the back door of the building when going to the cafeteria, but it's no problem using this one. We stop just before entering to observe the frenetic birds.

Mike says, "Industrious little fuckers, aren't they? They look like me going after the Xanax—one after another." He shakes his head.

"You did take care of that prescription, didn't you Mike?" Ebby asks him.

Mike sighs. "Yeah, I took care of it." He doesn't sound convincing. "I hope to God I can *keep* taking care of it."

I put my hand on Mike's shoulder. "Get to meetings, Mike. Get a sponsor."

"I know, I know. I plan on it," Mike replies, nodding and smiling slightly. He looks at the two of us. "I'm gonna miss you guys, I can tell you that."

We leave the pecking birds and go inside.

After breakfast, Ebby and I walk into the small chapel room, just down the hall from the cafeteria. Mike told us that he might meet us there in a bit, but he had to call his brother first to pin-down his expected pickup time. He seemed quite subdued during breakfast, consuming only two heaping plates of pancakes and bacon, not his customary three or four. Moreover, he didn't talk very much. With Mike there were uncommon periods of prolonged silence, broken only by brief one-liners and jabs directed at me or someone sitting at a nearby table. At one point just before leaving, Mike looked at his empty plate and simply said, "I hate fucking goodbyes."

We're greeted warmly at the door by a woman wearing a bright-yellow visitor name-tag that reads "Deacon." She hands us a single sheet of paper with the words to *Amazing Grace* typed on it, and we find a seat.

There are about 20 people sitting in the pews of the chapel. The converted room resembles a micro-church, with rows of chairs, an altar—even a small stained-glass window beyond the altar. Also, I see a tiny, electronic organ sitting forlornly in the corner of the room behind the altar.

A second woman with a deacon tag is milling about the tiny altar. I ask her quietly, "Do you want me to play that organ for this hymn? I can do it."

She says, "No, I don't think so. I don't even know how to turn it on. Are you a musician?"

"Yes," I say. "Actually, right now, I should be at my church playing the organ, but I'm not."

Ebby leans up and whispers loudly, "Yeah, he got a little side-tracked."

The deacon lady gives me a sad smile and then says, "You can lead us, though, okay?"

"No problem," I reply. "Just tell me when."

She gives me a nod.

There are patients from Blake and other wings at Carrier present—a few in wheelchairs. Also, I see a few staff members in the room. Carley, looking stunning as usual, comes in and take a seat to our right. She gives me a pretty smile and looks down at her sheet.

The service begins when the greeting deacon walks up to the front and takes a seat next to the one standing at the altar.

Deacon Joan, as she calls herself, greets us warmly. She tells us that she and Connie are from a nearby Catholic church, and they come in two Sundays every month to perform this simple service. The liturgical readings of the week are first.

While Joan begins the first reading, I look at my sheet. How many hundreds of times have I performed this hymn, I wonder? I must have played it at two or three hundred funerals alone, not to mention the dozens of times I've used it as an opening hymn at regular services. At this moment, however, I look at the words as if for the first time.

I hear Joan say, "The word of the Lord," and I consider the first line of the classic hymn:

> *Amazing Grace, how sweet the sound*
> *that saved a wretch like me.*

My stomach twitches and I swallow hard. Payne's foxhole definition of "grace" comes to mind: "Your buddy gets his head blown off and you're untouched—that's grace."

We rise for the gospel. In the reading, Joan tells about Jesus reappearing. He goes out fishing with his pals in waters already searched. The disciples are dubious, but soon the boat is miraculously overflowing with fish. I consider John Newton, the author of the first four verses of *Amazing Grace*. He knew the seas well, but in a different way. Here was a wretched seaman indeed. Everybody knows the time-honored hymn, of course, but few know about Newton.

In the late-1700's John Newton was captain of a number of slave ships. Being a minister, his role in the slave trade took on even more horrific ramifications. This "man of God" had to live forever with the memories of transporting chained and suffering human cargo from Africa to the West Indies. What terrible demons must have haunted him as he considered the consequences of his life? Perhaps by writing these words he was able to find a measure of that "amazing grace."

> *I once was lost, but now am found,*
> *was blind but now I see.*

"The gospel of the Lord," Joan intones, and we sit. Connie walks over to the small altar and begins a short homily. I hear her speak, but I don't listen. I can only think about John Newton, grace, and my life. As I read the second verse on my sheet, I feel my insides churning.

> *Twas grace that taught my heart to fear,*
> *and grace my fears relieved.*

How precious did that grace appear
the hour I first believed.

My eyes start filling with tears, and my nose begins to run. *How wretched I had been. All those terrible lies I told for so long. I stole all that money from my family to feed my habit.* I'm looking down at the paper, as tears fall freely. *How could Carol ever forgive me for all those terrible things I said to her for so long? It was all such an awful mess. My dear children, Katie, Matt and Natalie, had to endure my insane outbursts. Would they be damaged forever by my actions?*

I'm inconsolable now. My entire body trembles as I blubber like a six-year-old. I feel a hand on my back. I go on like this for a couple minutes. I finally regard the third verse:

Through many dangers, toils, and snares
I have already come,
'tis grace has brought me safe thus far,
and grace will lead me home.

After I read this, I begin to pull it together. If John Newton could find that grace, than surely I can too. *Please forgive me, Lord*, I say to myself. *Please forgive me.* I take a few deep breaths and feel better.

Carley hands me a box of tissues. I nod and glance her way. She's standing, as is everybody else, I notice. Carley points forward and I stand up and look. Joan is beckoning me to begin. I blow my nose, clear my throat and breathe deeply.

My voice is strong and steady throughout the famous hymn. A few more tears come, but I do my job well. Others in the room join in the singing with varying degrees of success at pitch control. I save a little extra for the fifth verse—added anonymously years after Newton died in 1807:

> *When we've been there ten-thousand years,*
> *bright shining as the sun,*
> *we've no less days to sing God's praise*
> *than when we'd first begun.*

Later, after lunch, I'm sitting out back behind Blake having a smoke with Eva and Stanley. The second afternoon group is about to begin. I've tried calling home a couple of times, but only got the machine. Up until now, Mike has also been unable to reach his brother, and all his things are packed and sitting by the front doors. He and Ebby come out through the group lounge doors and walk over to us.

"I finally talked to my brother," he announces, after striding up to us. "Give me a smoke, Buddy Boy, will ya?"

I hand him one. "What's the word?" I ask.

"He says he'll be here around six," Mike says. I see Ebby frown and look away, as if he knows something else.

"Really?" I ask my friend.

"Yeah, but I have to be ready. I'm not going to sit in on group. Ebby says he'll take notes and send them to me later." Ebby snorts and the rest of us laugh.

Just then, Matt sticks his head out the door and booms, "Put out your smokes! Group starts now!"

As we walk back, Mike puts his arm around me and hands me a slip of paper. "Here's my number. Give me a call sometime."

I stop and face him. Everyone else continues inside. "Mike, I can't tell you enough how much you've meant to me in here. I, I just want you to know…"

"Don't start, Buddy Boy," he interrupts me. "I'm gonna lose it like you did in church, so for Christ's sake, don't start!" He gives me a pained expression, and I can see his eyes moistening. "I hate fucking goodbyes," he says. We start walking again. "Anyway, I'll still be here after group. We can talk then."

"Okay, Mike," I say, and we walk together back inside. I hate goodbyes, too.

Matt hands out a few sheets of paper to the patients gathered in the group lounge. Glancing at the papers, I see that this group discussion will be centered on household items and foods containing alcohol, and other seemingly innocuous components that can be combined with other typical household items to create illegal drugs.

I notice quite a few empty chairs, and a few others filled by newcomers. The revolving door at Carrier Clinic never stops. "Old-timers" like Ebby, Eva and Stanley, Kara and Maxine, Sal and a few others are still here; but at least half of the 30 or so chairs are now filled with newly arrived unfortunates.

I see Tanya secreted in a corner chair, all Gothed-out yet again in black leather, purple hair and all that ghastly makeup. She's holding up her pocket mirror and making constant dabs at her face. It seems as though she purposely wants to hide those wondrous, green eyes. I look away and sigh.

Matt directs us to the first page listing the components of methamphetamines. "Many of the ingredients listed here are readily available for those who want to start a lab at home," Matt says. I see a couple of the newcomers nodding. Perhaps their experience in such a lab has brought them here.

"You'll notice the over-the-counter cold pills listed containing ephedrine and pseudoephedrine," Matt continues. "In the past few years, they have been moved out of public reach in drugstores because meth-producers were going in and buying up the entire stock for their labs."

Matt continues, talking about other items such as rubbing alcohol, mouthwash, cologne—even shoe polish. "All these items contain alcohol," he tells us. "And I've seen first-hand how far an alcoholic will go to get their drink. I've seen the terrible consequences of people who drink these things."

I stick up my hand. Matt points at me. "Yeah, Nurse Sharon wouldn't give Mike his Aqua Velva because she was afraid that I would drink it," I say. Everybody laughs, except the always serious "enforcer."

He says, "I was with you when you came in, remember?"

"Not really," I say.

"Hell, you might have drunk it," Matt says. "You were bad."

I nod knowingly. I look to my right through the windows facing the hallway. I see Mike gesticulating wildly in front of Angie at the station. She's just standing there unfazed and smiling, while he carries on as no one else can. I bump Ebby sitting next to me, and point my head that way. He starts chuckling.

Matt continues, turning the page, and begins to tackle the widely misunderstood subject of cooking with alcohol. "You'll notice the recipes listed on the third page," he tells us. I see Beef Bourguignon and Beef Burgundy, clams with white-wine sauce and a few others. Matt says, "All these recipes call for alcohol. Most people think it totally burns off during cooking, but that simply is not the case. You'll see at the bottom of the page that seven to ten percent of the alcohol remains after cooking."

I notice Eva and Maxine frowning. Out of the corner of my eye, I see Mike pacing back and forth in the hallway near the front door.

Matt continues. "Although your motive is not to get drunk on food, the alcohol can become a trigger, and should be completely omitted from the recipes. Perhaps you'll begin to serve yourself a bit of the wine with the dinner. Then, maybe an extra glass," he tells us. "The next thing you know, you're back on that merry-go-round, and drinking just like you were before. Avoid all alcohol in cooking," he admonishes us.

Kara Alcoholic's hand shoots up. Matt nods in her direction. "Yes, Kara, alcoholic, I just love poppy-seed bagels in the morning. You know, fresh from the Jewish deli down the street? Anyway, someone told me that the poppy-seeds can be a trigger of sorts, and can skew a blood-test or something like that. I don't want to have to give up my poppy-seed bagels. After all, when they're so warm and fresh, and spread with cream cheese and, maybe, lox or something…"

I see Mike picking up his two bags in the hallway, and handing them to another man—his brother, I presume. I poke Ebby and he looks, too. Mike quickly comes to the glass, bends over and gives the two of us a quick wave. I see for an instant his goofy smile displaying his shiny, false teeth. He then turns and walks quickly out the front door.

I start to get up, but Ebby puts an arm on mine to stop me. He leans over. "Don't, Eric. Mike wants it this way. He hates fucking goodbyes."

I look down at my feet. As Kara rattles on, I feel the tears coming again.

"…Anyway, I can see not having them *all* the time, but what's the harm in eating one on special occasions? I mean, I don't get high off of them, for goodness sake. People eat them all the time, don't they? I mean, if it's Sunday morning—today is Sunday, yes? I mean…"

Not unlike one of those intense but brief, summer flings of my youth down on Long Beach Island, so it has been with Mike Cass, I sadly realize. Then it was a 14 or 15 year-old girl who had broken my heart. I recall a few Labor Days of long ago being painfully separated from my quixotic puppy-loves only by the end of another summer. The relationships were always sweet and simple, but destined to end nonetheless. But, here in this place, under these circumstances, it happened with Mike, and it all overwhelms me. Sitting there with tears falling about my feet, I feel the loss of a friend. Mike Cass is gone from my life.

Ebby hands me a box of tissues. He whispers and gestures at the unstoppable Kara. "We're all gonna be in tears soon if she doesn't shut the fuck up."

I blow my nose and wipe my eyes. What a wreck I am. I haven't had such an emotionally-charged day in 40 years, I realize. *What about calling home?* I think. I haven't been able to reach them yet today, and talking to Carol might set me off again. *Ah!* An idea comes to me. *I know how to handle that. I'll call home, all right.*

Matt finally cuts off Kara in mid-sentence. "Listen, Kara. Eat your poppy-seed bagels, already! You'd have to eat 50 of them to even come close to failing a drug test. Just relax, and take a few deep breaths." He looks at his watch. "That's enough for today. We'll end a little early."

Most of the patients get up and walk out of the room. Ebby stays with me, and Matt walks over. He looks at me sitting slumped in my chair and says, "Are you okay, Eric? Carley told me you lost it in chapel, too."

I look up at him. "Yeah, Mike just left. It's been a rough day."

"Oh," he says, looking out toward the main doors. "I understand. You can get really close to some people in here, I know—I've been right where you are."

I'm caught off guard. So, Matt is a graduate of Carrier, too? I never knew that. I've got enough on my mind right about now so I don't ask him about it. I simply say, "I'm gonna miss him."

Matt sighs and looks down at us. "Well, I have some more bad news for you guys."

"What's that?" Ebby asks.

"The group from Flemington canceled tonight's commitment. You two are running the AA meeting."

"You got to be kidding me!" I moan. I see Ebby put his head in his hands. I say, "We don't know how to run an AA meeting."

Ebby looks at him, pleading, "Can't you find anybody else?"

"Like who?" replies Matt, "That asshole, Sal or that nut, Kara? If she ran it, Christ, you'd be stuck in Darcy until midnight!"

I laugh out loud, despite myself. Ebby concedes Matt's thought, adding, "A couple hours listening to that and even the staunchest of AA's would be *begging* for a drink!"

Matt laughs and says, "I'd prefer water-boarding myself." He continues, "No, it's you two. I'll put out the literature later.

Just do the Serenity Prayer, How it Works—whatever. Then, tell your stories. It'll be a piece of cake. Shit, Ebby, you had to do much worse yesterday."

Ebby nods. "Yeah, you're right."

"Okay, we'll do it," I say.

"Good, thanks!" says Matt, turning to leave. "I'm doing vitals now, so get in line guys. Thanks again."

After Matt leaves, Ebby puts his hand on my shoulder. "Are you sure you're okay? We're running out of fucking tissues!"

I smile. "Yeah, oh, I have to call home." Ebby gives me pained look. I say, "Don't worry; I need to talk with one of my kids, that's all. It will work out." We get up and start toward the door. Rushing ahead of him, I say, "Let's go for a walk before dinner, okay?"

"Okay," he says.

I hurry to the phone.

"Hello?"

"Hi, Carol, How are you?"

"I'm okay. We just got back from shopping. How are you?"

She sounds a bit more upbeat than the last time.

"I'm better. So much has been going on here. They just told me that I have to run the AA meeting tonight. Can you believe that?"

"You? Not really. Are you still getting out tomorrow?"

"Yes. I told Carley—she's doing the counseling session— that you'll be up here at about 10. Is that okay?"

"I guess that will work. I'll do a Google search for directions."

"That's great! Carol, I've had a really emotional day. My roommate just left and I lost it."

"Yeah, well, join the club."

That didn't go over well. Get to the reason for the call.

"I really need to talk with Matt or Natalie—or Katie if she's there. I need to hear their voices."

"Matt is at a friend's house, and Katie's not here. 'Natalie!' She's upstairs getting in the tub."

She must be walking with the phone. I hear the water running.

"Eric, I sold the Honda to a junk-yard owner. He gave me $500, so I finally have a little money."

"That's good. Did those checks clear?"

"Yeah, finally; the bank isn't after the house yet."

Be nice, Eric.

"Carol, I'm guilty of many things, but not paying the bills isn't one of them."

"Yeah, well, you paid our bills by increasing our debt. I can't get over this anger I feel."

The reason…

"Is Natalie there?"

"Natalie, your father wants to talk to you."

"DADDY? Yeah, I wanna talk to daddy!"

I can see her standing there naked in front of the tub, bouncing up and down on her toes. Here come the tears again.

"Daddy? Hello?"

"Hi, sweetheart, how are you?"

"I'm good. Daddy, when are you coming home?"

"I'm getting out tomorrow. *A sudden thought: Use the intermediary. Thank you, God.*

"Ask mommy if I'm coming home tomorrow."

"Mommy, is daddy coming home tomorrow?"

Long pause...

"Well, I guess so."

I heard it! It was nowhere near enthusiastic, but I got the nod, regardless. YES! Tears are flowing again. I like these tears! Where's that fucking Ebby with the tissues?

"Mommy said yes, Daddy! Mommy said yes!"

"That's wonderful, sweetie. Can you and I sleep together in Katie's bed tomorrow?"

"Yes, Daddy! I want lots of stories—lots of stories!"

"It's a promise. See you tomorrow after school. Put Mommy back on the phone, please."

"Okay, bye Daddy. I love you!"

"I love you, too, sweetheart."

Long pause again...

"Well, I guess that was your plan, huh, use Natalie?"

"Honestly, no. I just wanted to hear her voice, but I must admit it did work out..."

"Yeah, well, it's not going to be pleasant, I can tell you that. You can start off here, but I know now that I can make it without you. I'm making no promises."

She's not happy about accepting me back, that's for sure.

"Carol, I'll be making amends to you forever, I know that. But, the most important thing for me is to get going on my recovery—period. Regis and Payne were up here yesterday. You remember Regis?"

"Yeah, isn't that the guy you were friendly with the last time you lied about AA?"

"Yes, and I *was* lying. I'm going to the 24 Club tomorrow, and he's hooking me up with a temporary sponsor. This time, I have to get it right."

"I'm not gonna put up with any bullshit, I can tell you that. One slip and you're out. I mean it!"

"Carol, if I don't get it this time, I'll be out alright—dead! Thank you for giving me this last chance. You won't regret it."

"Yeah, whatever, I'll see you tomorrow."

"Bye, Honey."

I hang up and wipe my weary eyes with my already soiled sleeve, turn and walk toward the vitals line. I see Ebby, Eva and Stanley looking at me. A huge grin comes bubbling up from my toes, radiating outward and upward throughout my entire body. They all smile back at me. I raise my hands high and whoop, "Yeah, Baby! I'm going home!"

Eva comes at me and gives me a big hug. "I knew you would make it back home. I just *knew* it!"

Ebby gives me a slap on the back. "How did you, I mean, what did she say?"

"I used my 9-year-old as a buffer," I tell them. "It just popped into my mind. I had *her* ask Carol if I could get back home."

"You sly dog," Ebby says.

"You went for the heart-strings, huh? Good thinking," Stanley says, impressed.

"Maury would've been proud of that move," Eva says, finally releasing me. "That was a move right out of his play-book."

"You know," I say, "The thought of talking to one of my kids came to me almost the instant Mike left. It was as if it *was* his idea. It's very strange."

Ebby says, "Well, we can change his famous *Godfather* line a little bit. Now it's 'you're *in*, Tom!'"

"At least for tomorrow," I say, a bit of reality settling in.

Eva smiles again at me. Her penetrating look and positive outlook has been such a support to me ever since she was able to pull her head out of the toilet. Her face still bears the scars of addiction, as do all of ours I'm sure, but in her sweet smile I've always seen hope. She says quietly, "It's the same for all of us—one day at a time."

At 8:00, Ebby and I are sitting next to one another in two chairs against the far wall in Darcy. These are the chairs usually occupied at this time by visiting AA group members, but tonight, it's only the two of us. The dozen or so chairs in front of us are now filled with patients from Blake. I see Maxine and Kara, Sal and a couple others who have been around for a while. There are also a few alcoholic newcomers to Blake present. The other 20 or so patients on the floor are attending the NA meeting.

Ebby begins the meeting by introducing himself. He then asks for a moment of silence followed by the *Serenity Prayer*. After the prayer I see Matt standing at the entrance door, his arms folded, his stern countenance fixed in place as usual. He wants to ensure a smoothly run meeting, regardless of the obvious ineptitude of at least one of the leaders.

Ebby, much more familiar with how things work at AA meetings, has gladly taken charge; and, after reading the AA Preamble, asks everyone to introduce themselves. One by one, down the row of chairs people pronounce themselves as either "alcoholic" or "alcoholic/addict."

Sal, recalcitrant as always, has changed his status. What used to be "I'm Sal," and then "I'm Sal, and I have a problem with alcohol," has now become, "I'm Sal, and I'm a *potential* alcoholic." I suppose that's progress, but who am I to judge. The only person in this room that I'm certain to be a true alcoholic is Eric H. However, I can say with a fair degree of certainty that Sal *is* an asshole.

Ebby launches into his story. It is a 25-minute, detailed account of his sad history with alcohol. Many of the things he talks about are a re-hashing of what we heard yesterday during his trying fifth-step in group. Again we hear about the rages at his wife and children, and the isolation that his alcoholism caused. Like me, there was the inevitable turn to drugs for added "relief" when booze just wasn't enough by itself.

He ends his talk with a ray of hope for his future. This part takes him only a minute or two, but I realize that is the way it is with all of us. We all have years of drinking and drugging behind us, and only a few precious days of sobriety. Sitting there nervous as I am, I know that my story will be 99% drunk and 1% sober as well.

Ebby says, "I know that I can never drink again," he tells us. "I know that I am an alcoholic, and I will be until the day I die." With this line I see him glance at Sal, who is studying his feet as usual. Ebby continues. "I can see that AA is the only way for me, and when I get out of here, I'm going to jump into this program big-time." He pauses, looks down at his feet, and then back up at the group. His handsome face shines a little. "There is hope," he says. "I can see that now. I couldn't before, but now I can. For the first time in my life I can see hope in my future. And that feels good. Thanks for listening."

After the applause dies down, Ebby taps me on the knee. "I now give you—Eric."

I take a deep breath and say, "I'm Eric, and I'm an alcoholic."

"Hi, Eric," they all respond.

I begin at the beginning. "I grew up in a happy, loving family down the shore on Long Beach Island," I tell them. I explain about how the first seeds of my eventual illness were sown. "I would sneak up on my father in the living room after he returned home from work," I say. "I was only six or seven, and I'd crawl behind the furniture, surprising my dad—at least he always pretended to be surprised. And then I'd get my reward: a sip of his beer."

I explain that growing up in a tourist location meant that for nine months of the year, the island was basically deserted; so I found comfort and security being alone with myself. "This self-seeking and comfort with myself suited me well when drinking became a part of my life," I say.

I tell them that I discovered an affinity for the piano, and music came to me naturally. "I started late—13—and I practiced hard every day after school," I say. "In the piano I was able to escape within myself even more, and I liked that."

I explain that when I started driving I found the "vehicle" for my boozing. "I loved to get a six-pack and drive alone up and down the deserted island. For the next 30 years, my car was my bar," I tell them. "It was my one, true escape mechanism from the reality of life."

"I was the youngest of four—the baby," I say. "I was a good student, a faithful son to my parents, and did everything they asked of me." I explain that by the time I went off to college to be trained as a concert pianist, my parents didn't mind me drinking with them during cocktail hour or at parties. "Even though I often drank to excess, I was well-behaved and in control. I knew not to cross that line into obvious drunkenness."

I continue this thought by saying that for my entire life I despised seeing people lose control when they drank. "I always prided myself on being able to handle my liquor, and I never once remember deliberately setting out with the sole purpose of getting drunk. Of course," I say, "Eventually, that's exactly where I ended up."

I touch on my undergraduate college days, where it was one party after another. "I drank every day to excess," I tell them. "But, I went to class every day, too. I had developed a finely-tuned drinking regimen that worked for me. I was simply a heavy-hitter. I knew how to drink properly."

I tell them of the life-changing experience I had hunting with my first love's father down in the mountains of Virginia. "I'll never forget that taste," I tell them, recalling my first experience with bourbon. "It was almost magical, up there in the snowy Blue-Ridge Mountains. And, for the next 20 years—until Mr. Smirnoff took its place—Jack Daniels and Jim Beam were my constant companions." I see a few heads nodding in recognition. I must be making at least a little sense, because I see that even Sal is paying attention.

Next on the "drunkalog" is graduate school in the Big Apple. "I was still hopeful of a performing career, but that changed in a hurry," I say. "I was having too much fun drinking! I was enjoying the high-life, and getting a fine education to boot," I tell them.

I explain how I settled into a comfortable life after New York. "I met my true love after undergrad school in Princeton; and then nearly blew it by fooling around up in New York," I say. I tell them how thankful I was that Carol took me back when I was nearing the end of grad school; and that we then settled down and got married in 1988.

I talk about the first warning signs of excess drinking I endured within the first few years of my marriage, and how I brushed them off. "I had some panic attacks and went to see my doctor," I tell them. I explain that he ordered a blood-test and the results showed elevated liver enzymes. "This was over 20 years ago!" I say. "The doctor told me to 'not drink on a regular basis,' so I took that to heart." I snicker at this. "So, every time I went to see the doctor or had a blood-test, I wouldn't drink on a 'regular basis' for a few days." This draws a few laughs from the group.

I delve into the next 10 years, relating our move to Ewing and the arrival of our three children. I tell them of the constancy of my work life. "I've held the same two jobs since 1985: teaching piano at a music school in Princeton, and being music director at a Catholic church in Elizabeth." I say, "Change has been a problem for me throughout my life. I guess I'm fearful of change. So, the status-quo—the stability of work, family and especially drink—kept me going me through all those years."

I explain that, ever-so-slowly, I could see the progression of my drinking, and tried time and again to keep it in check. "I had an older friend, Tom, who I used to bike with," I tell them. "Tom knew how to drink, and, more importantly, how to control it. He would counsel me wisely, and I attempted over and over again through these years to slow down a bit. I never could, and it frustrated me greatly."

I tell them that, as a direct result of my drinking, my bad behavior toward my wife was starting to strain our marriage.

"I was now picking fights with my wife over everything, and she was getting disgusted."

I explain to them that the progression led to morning drinking. "To help me cope with the pain of hangovers," I say, "I started drinking in the mornings, and I just knew this was truly alcoholic behavior, but I went ahead and did it anyway—every weekday."

I relate that finally in early 2004, I decided to stop. I tell them that things were going badly at home, and I had gained 30 pounds. I pat my ample belly. "Not quite as much as you see here," I say to a few laughs, "but pretty darn close!" I tell them that I had made up my mind, and I was going to do it.

I proudly explain that I did indeed stop drinking on my own for close to 18 months. "Things were going well at home, and I had joined a gym and lost all this weight," I say. "My work was moving ahead nicely, and the money was rolling in. I had three wonderful children, and life was good. I wanted it all!" I tell them.

And so, no one is surprised when I tell them about that fateful night in late 2005 in Hopewell when I stopped at the bar and ordered that first drink. "I had three at the bar, and they tasted *so* good," I tell them. "But, afterward on the way home, I just knew it was a terrible decision. I just knew I would be back at it full-time before long. But, I told no one."

I carefully explain to them how this was a key point in my alcoholism. This was the point where the lying and the deceit began in earnest. "For the next three years," I tell them, "I concealed my drinking, and it became a total obsession. There was the morning drunk, and the evening drunk. And there was cocaine, too," I tell them.

I explain how I isolated more and more because of my inability to come to terms with my illness. "I escaped to the drink or the drug, and I was starting to believe all these alcoholic voices speaking to me," I say.

I explain that by the time I gave myself up in late 2008, my wife was at her wit's end trying to figure out what was wrong with me. "She still didn't know that I was drinking. I was an expert at concealment," I tell them. "But she was completely unhappy. She just thought I had become an asshole!"

"Finally," I tell them, "on Labor Day weekend in 2008, a friend down the shore took my car keys away from me at a party, and I just gave up. I called Carol and confessed to everything." I shake my head. "Well, not everything, I'm not stupid! Of course there was no mention of morning drinking or drugs, but I did agree to seek help," I say. "We had a long walk on the beach, and I told her that I would start going to AA, and my behavior would improve. Carol said she would give me one more chance."

I take a breath and sigh heavily. "The voices told me other things, though, and I believed them," I say. I tell them that I believed that since I hadn't been caught—that I technically had given myself up—I could keep up the charade if only I was more careful. "I quit alright—for one fucking day," I say. "Sure, I went to meetings, and brought home stories and phone numbers, but then I just kept on drinking and drugging. It was a joke."

I explain how I started to believe the voices telling me that Carol was now the problem. "This was total insanity," I say. "Just like my drinking, I found it impossible to control my temper, and soon it was terrible at home again," I say. "As my marriage continued to deteriorate, I lashed out at the one closest to me. I believed that she had changed, not me. I believed she was going through the change of life, and suggested she see a hormone specialist," I shake my head, disbelieving even now that I could have suggested such things. "When I'd mention that, I had to watch out for the flying pots and pans, I can tell you!" Everyone laughs.

I tell them that I had a friend with a spare room, and in January, I mentioned to Carol that I might be going to live with him for a while. "When I told her this," I explain, "I expected her to say, 'Oh, no, please, dear, not that! Don't move out!' Instead, the look I got was like, 'Don't let the door hit you on the way out!'"

I explain that I stormed out of the house, and those final two months were nothing less than a non-stop death-spiral of 24/7 boozing and drugging. "I didn't have to hide it anymore," I tell them. "It was drinking, cocaine, and then Xanax to help me get a little sleep. There were the all-nighters, the lost work, the missed appointments with my kids—you name it. Nothing else mattered but the next drink or drug. But I didn't see it that way. I was just having fun!" I tell them. "But, I did have to pay for it all. And the money-trail is what finally led to the crash—and here."

I tell them about Rose from India and the Xanax shipments that eventually led to Carol's discovery of all those thousands I pilfered from the home-equity line. "I knew it had all come to the end. Something finally got through to me, so here I am," I say.

"Last Monday was the worst day of my life," I tell them. "I had two run-ins with the law, two trips to the ER, and two accidents. And, I was now to quit drinking? Impossible! The fear of me waking up dead in this place was real," I say. "I had no idea how I was going to stop, or whether I would live or die. Sitting in that ER for six hours tied to that gurney, I was at the absolute bottom. I felt helpless, alone and terrified of what might happen."

I look at them and smile slightly. "Then, I woke up—and I was alive. I felt as if I was dead, but I was alive. The nurse's and doctor Shariff helped me get through detox; and I can't believe how good I feel in only six days. At least for today, the obsession to drink has been lifted, and I just found out that I'll be going home. I can't believe Carol is letting me back into my home," I say, rubbing my head.

"I was so afraid of who my roommates might be, but instead I was blessed with two of the most amazing people I've ever known. Mike and Ebby here have helped me beyond words." I look over at him. "Thank you." He nods, and touches his watch, and raises his eyebrows. "Oh, shit! Sorry, I have to wrap up here," I say.

"It's been one miracle after another in this place," I say. "But the biggest one was discovering that I can start to live again without alcohol and drugs in my life. I now know how to go on with my life. I've learned the importance of 'how.' That is, honesty, openness and willingness. If I'm truly honest with myself, then I can be honest about everything else in my life and move forward without fear," I say.

I tell them that I'm not some kind of "uber-drunk," some kind of special case, as it were, but only your every-day, run-of-the-mill alcoholic. "I'm no better or worse than anybody else," I say. "This disease can hit anybody. I've learned that alcoholism is an equal-opportunity ass-kicker! I like that description," I say, to more laughter and nods. Maxine lets out a hearty, "Amen!"

"It took me a long time to get to here," I say. "And I know it will take me a long time to get well. I know it's going to be long and hard. But I think I can start to see my way forward. I think I'm finally ready to try to change the way I think, and listen to people who have been where I am. I'm not afraid anymore."

I pause and look down. "There have been so many miracles," I tell them. "Yesterday's AA meeting was hosted by two guys I met when I was pretending with AA a couple years ago. It's like God put them here yesterday just for me! When I leave tomorrow I'm going to a meeting where they're going to hook me up with a temporary sponsor, and I can really begin to immerse myself in the program. I call that a miracle. You can't make this shit up!" I say.

"I love the street-wise spiritualism I see in these recovering alcoholics," I tell them. "They speak like me, and I know they won't put up with my bullshit. That's what I need. They're happy and peaceful, and I want that, too. I want to live again. There's only death for me if I start up again, and that's no way to live."

I finish up with this, "Today in chapel I lost it. I was looking at the words to *Amazing Grace,* and I started blubbering like a child. The third verse ends with, ''tis grace has brought me safe thus far, and grace will lead me home.'

"God's grace has saved me so many times from arrest and accidents. Shit, I've been walking around for 20 years with a bad liver, drinking every single day! And somehow God's grace has kept me alive. It brought me safe thus far," I say. "And now, with God's grace, I'm going home. Thank you."

"Ya know," Ebby says to me later, as we lie in the darkness of our room, "A guy running a meeting the other night told me that the one thing that sparks resentment more than anything else among drunks at AA meetings is when some blow-hard takes the meeting past time."

I laugh. "I said I was sorry! It was only 10 minutes. I was on a roll!"

"You did good, Eric, really good."

"It felt good, that's for sure," I say.

"Someone else told me a good story about that," continues Ebby. "Some lady was speaking at a meeting. She was going on and on—kind of like you—and one by one people started getting up and leaving. Finally, she finished and looked up. Only one person was left sitting in the chairs. She looks at the lady and says, 'Oh, I'm sorry. I didn't realize how long I spoke. Why didn't you leave like everybody else?'"

The woman says, "Because I'm the next speaker!"

We both laugh.

"Was that Kara speaking?" I ask.

"Yeah, right!" Ebby laughs.

We lie there in silence for a time. Finally, I say, "I wonder what Mike is doing?"

Ebby says, "I know what he'd say if he were laying there and you had left today."

"What's that?"

"I hope tonight they don't bring in a fat, snoring, drunken fucking asshole like the one we got the last time!"

After I stop laughing, I say quietly, "Mike's out, Tom!"

"Yeah," Ebby says tiredly, "I miss him."

"Me too," I say.

After a time I say, "Do you think he'll stay clean?"

Ebby says, "Do you think any of us will?"

I don't answer. Ebby continues, "Think about it, Eric. At the end of the day, after all the meetings and counseling, and talks with your sponsor—whatever; at the end of the day, it's still just you and your thoughts. Can we overcome that?"

"They talk about avoiding the people, places and things," I say, "But the biggest problem I face is myself."

"That goes for Mike and me, and the rest of us," he says.

We retreat to our thoughts. I think about tomorrow.

Chapter Eighteen

"Rarely have we seen a person fail who has thoroughly followed our path. Those who do not recover are people who cannot or will not completely give themselves to this simple program, usually men and women who are constitutionally incapable of being honest with themselves. There are such unfortunates. They are not at fault; they seem to have been born that way. They are naturally incapable of grasping and developing a manner of living which requires vigorous honesty. Their chances are less than average."

—Page 58, *Alcoholics Anonymous*

"Thwonk" goes the rattling pipes behind the urinal, exactly three seconds after I pull the handle. I smile. I wonder if they will *ever* get around to fixing this. It is 6:30 in the morning on my last day here at Carrier, and I wash, grab my notebook and head out the door toward Darcy.

I stop at the nurse's station and see Sharon seated at a desk looking at a chart. "Hi there!" I say.

Sharon looks up and smiles at me. "Good morning!" Her blond, wavy hair is pulled back behind her ears, and her glasses are sitting on the end of her nose, as usual. "Are you ready to get out of here?" she asks me in her gravelly voice.

"I guess so," I say, leaning on the open door frame. "I really could use a few more days, but…" I shrug.

"I know, I know—insurance." Sharon gets up and comes over to me. "I hear it every day. How are you getting along without Mike?"

I shrug. "Yesterday was tough," I say. "But things certainly are a bit calmer."

Sharon shakes her head and laughs a little. "My God, he was something else. He was like some kind of cartoon character."

I smile. "Yeah, Walt Disney would've loved Mike Cass."

We both laugh. "Are my test results in yet, Sharon?" I ask.

She points down the hall. "Dr. Shariff is already here," she tells me. "You need to see her one last time. She'll talk to you about them. Are you going down to Darcy?"

"Yes."

"I'll come get you when she's ready for you." She grabs a small pile of paperwork and hands it to me. "You need to sign a few items here," she says. "Read it all over and sign where it's highlighted."

I nod and take the papers.

"Also," she says, "There's a questionnaire in there. Please fill that out, too, okay?"

"I will," I tell her, and head down the hall.

I sit at a table with my coffee near the long set of windows facing outside. The weather looks to be picture-perfect, as the early morning grayness is fast giving way to brilliant sunshine. At this early hour Darcy is largely deserted. A few patients wander in and grab a cup of coffee, but I'm left to myself.

I finish signing all the business-related paperwork, and start delving into the questionnaire. I'm asked to comment on many aspects of my experiences at Carrier. I give the staff, nurses, and doctors all rave reviews. I write that the group meetings and AA meetings have been of vital importance in my early recovery. Every couple minutes or so, I look up and glance outside over the open fields toward the distant fencing guarding the solar-panel farm.

I write how important it is that the staff keeps us busy most of the time, assigning us specific jobs to keep Darcy clean and running smoothly. I think of my job. Ebby and I have been in charge of keeping the smoking area and the Darcy Memorial Garden clean.

I smile when I think about the time I asked Matt for a long screwdriver to help us get after the budding dandelions in the garden. He told me that for obvious reasons he couldn't let us have one. "We can't give out such things to patients," he had told me, adding, "And that idiot roommate of yours would go wild with a screwdriver. He'd unscrew every fucking bed frame and toilet seat!"

The last question on the questionnaire asks for the reason or reasons for coming to Carrier Clinic. I think about this. I could write all day about my progressing alcoholism and all the marital and financial difficulties the disease had spawn. I could write about the accelerated drug use and the precarious state of my liver. Instead, I decide to be brief and to the point. I write one word: "Boozehound!"

Just as I'm signing the questionnaire, I hear Nurse Sharon behind me say solemnly, "Eric, the doctor will see you now."

"Hello, Eric. Take a seat," Dr. Shariff says as I enter her small office. She's dressed beautifully as ever, in a crisp, blue pants-suit. Her long, dark hair is pulled behind her head in a pony-tail, and her large, brown eyes are soothing. I smell a faint odor of lilac.

"How are you feeling?" she asks me. "You certainly look much better."

"I feel great, Doctor," I reply, taking a seat on the exam-table with my paperwork. "I can't believe it's been less than a week. It seems like months ago when I was sitting here in all that pain."

She smiles at me and nods. "That's good, Eric," she says. "You received the help you needed." She glances at a sheet of paper. "Your liver numbers continue to improve. The enzyme levels have dropped in half."

I sigh and take a deep breath. "Thank God," I say. "What are the numbers?"

"657," she tells me. "The liver has tremendous recuperative powers, but this turn-around is quite extraordinary, I must say."

"Will they continue to drop?" I ask, smiling to myself that Mike was correct with his prediction of the results.

"I think so. Get them tested again by your doctor in a couple weeks, but I think they should continue to improve." She looks at me seriously. "That is, if you don't start drinking again."

"I've got a program in place, Doctor," I tell her. "When I get out today, I'm going to a meeting, and I'm getting myself a temporary sponsor. I cannot return to that life again."

"I'm glad to hear you say that," she says, nodding approvingly, "Because, there may not be a next time. Those numbers were alarmingly high. They will return in a hurry if you pick up again."

"I'm very lucky, Doctor," I say. "I've been given a second chance, and I can't waste it. For today, I must not drink—I know it!"

"That's the way to go—one day at a time," she tells me. "Those few words are so simple and overused, but that's how it has to work!" She looks at the paper again. "I'm writing you a script for the Buspirone and the increased dose of Lisinopril. Your pressure is now under control, I see." She signs a couple pieces of paper. "Is the Busiprone helping with anxiety?"

"Yes, it's very subtle, but I can tell it helps," I say. "It's kind of like putting on a warm sweater on a chilly day."

"Nice way of putting it; and the best part is that it's non-addictive," she tells me, writing some more. "I'm so glad you've improved to this extent."

"All thanks to you, Doctor."

She smiles at me again, stands and shakes my hand. "Good luck to you, Eric. I'm sorry if this comes out the wrong way, but I hope to never see you again under similar circumstances."

I laugh. "I hope so, too, Doctor."

I drop off my paperwork with Nurse Sharon. I see Carley sitting inside the station and say, "My wife's going to be here at about 10, Carley."

"That's perfect, Eric. Matt's running that group. We'll have that family meeting and then you'll be free to go."

I feel a twinge and grimace. "It's going to be tough, I think. Do you have any pads or a helmet I can wear?"

They both laugh. "Just sit there and take it," Sharon says. "You deserve it, don't you?"

"Oh yeah, I deserve everything and more. I can't believe she's letting me come home." I look down and shake my head.

Carley says, "It's going to be just like your recovery from alcoholism, Eric. Slowly, over time, it will all get better."

"Exactly," Sharon says. "I believe it will all work out."

I see Ebby and Eva walking by me, and I turn and ask if they want to go with me for a walk.

"No, we're going to breakfast," Ebby says. "Meet us there."

"Okay," I respond.

Carley says, "Make sure you make it back for first group, Eric. We all want to say good bye."

"Okay," I say, turning to leave.

"And Eric," Sharon says. I stop and face her. "Can we have one more piece on the piano before you go?"

"Sure."

I take the long-way around the vast grounds. After about 30 minutes, I walk toward the area where Mike, Ebby and I saw the peacock yesterday. He's nowhere to be seen.

I begin walking in the general direction of the admissions building when I hear his now-familiar three-part call. I can tell the sound is emanating from an area near the coupe where the chickens and that pissed-off turkey reside. I turn and quickly walk in that direction.

About 300 yards away, I see him standing just outside the large coupe. The peacock is casually strutting along the perimeter, making perfunctory pecks at the ground. As I approach, I see that the turkey is within a few feet of the peacock, on the other side of the fence; and I can tell right away that he is *not* a happy camper. I walk up even closer, to within about 20 yards.

The peacock swivels his head and looks straight at me. The turkey ignores me completely, and is busy clawing madly at the dirt, hurling his bearded head at the fencing, and gobbling what must be profane insults at the nearby peacock. As I watch in wonder, the peacock, still looking directly at me, produces his piercing call again: "Ah-EH! Ah-EH! Ah-EH!"

Flabbergasted already at the spectacle, I then get treated to an even more wondrous sight. Seconds after calling, the peacock lifts his head and long neck straight up in the air and then, ever so slowly, opens wide his massive plumage. The deep blues and greens and browns of the five-foot-long feathers astound me. He rustles the assemblage with a tiny flick of his rear-end, and the entire array quivers and then stands out even straighter. He takes a couple steps in my direction and then slowly turns—as if a high-fashion model on the end of a runway.

I almost forget about the turkey, but I see his rage quickly escalate as the cocky peacock goes about his nonchalant strut. The white turkey flaps his small wings wildly, trying to somehow fly out of the fenced-in area. His massive bulk, years in the making, prevents him from attaining even a single vertical inch. "White turkey's disease!" I yell at him, laughing. This causes the irate bird to suddenly stop yapping for a split second; and he quickly shifts his head in my direction—his long, red beard quivering. I nearly double over.

Now the turkey is even more livid. He sends out volleys of vehement paroxysms of gobbler-guk both at me and at the arrogant peacock. In what I view as an even more egregious slap at the turkey, the peacock now turns his back on him and haughtily shakes his massive retinue. Watching him scratch and claw and rant, the turkey reminds me of myself. That was me so often in a drunken rage, I think, yelling and screaming at Carol. At the end, I realize, she was able to tune me out just like the peacock is now doing to the turkey.

Finally, as the peacock lowers his feathers and slowly struts into the woods, I consider the scene differently. A moment of clarity strikes me. The peacock represents my life from here on out, I believe. He is free as I am, and separated from that possessed turkey only by a fence. The turkey, in a sense, is my disease. My alcoholism is now caged and I can move ahead—as the peacock does—without fear. But, I must guard against arrogance or overconfidence. The peacock need not worry at all about the caged turkey, but I cannot afford for one minute to take my disease for granted. I recall the words of Frank at that first AA meeting up here: "*Remember the pain that brought you here.*"

Walking back toward the admissions building, I offer up another prayer of gratitude.

It is 9:00, and the morning business meeting run by Carley is about to begin. I glance around for the last time at my fellow patients. I see many "fresh recruits" present, most appearing more or less ragged from their recent exploits out in the field. I shake my head upon viewing Tanya snoozing in a corner chair, still dressed in her loose-fitting pajamas—her wild, purple hair poking out in a hundred directions. Kara and

Maxine are chatting away by the windows, and Eva and Stanley are seated to my left. Sal and Ebby are by the door leading to the hallway.

Carley begins by calling on Kara and Eva to read a passage or two from recovery-oriented inspirational books. That accomplished, she goes through the jobs-list. Carley asks for a fresh volunteer to assist Ebby in outside cleanup duties. To my surprise, Sal raises his hand. I lean over to Eva, "Sal seems to be coming around," I whisper.

"Yeah, he actually said 'good morning' to me today," she responds.

"Eric is leaving us today," Carley announces.

"It's about fucking time," Ebby mumbles, just loud enough for most to hear. Raucous laughter ensues.

"Now, now," says Carley. "He's made tremendous progress with us. Let's just hope he can keep the momentum going away from this controlled environment." She looks at me and smiles. Her stunning good-looks are abundant. "Do you want to say anything to the group, Eric?"

I sit up and clear my throat. "Yes, thank you, Carley," I say. "I'm Eric, and I'm an alcoholic."

"Hi, Eric," the group intones.

"A little less than a week ago, I came in here, nearly dead from alcoholism. My liver was ready to fail and I was afraid I wouldn't survive the detox. I woke up last Tuesday, and I was alive. I felt like death, but I was alive. The nurses, Dr. Shariff and you, Carley—everyone—helped me begin my recovery.

"The next day, I felt better, and you helped me some more; and every single day since I've felt stronger and more alive. The entire time I've been here, the AA meetings and the groups were all perfect. It seemed that everything being discussed was directed solely for my benefit. I couldn't believe it!

"I was so worried about who my roommates would be. Again, I was blessed with Ebby here, and that nut, Mike Cass. Also, so many of the rest of you have been helpful to me. Thank you, Eva. I'm so glad you finally stopped puking, and came to my aid." The group laughs. Eva blushes. "Your wisdom has been such a help. Kara, Maxine, Stanley—you helped me more than you could know.

"Today, thank God, I'm able to return home to my family. This is another miracle, but I know the real miracle will be me not returning to the bottle. I understand this, but it's not going to be easy. One day at a time, I have to do my best to make it all work out. I came in here kicking and screaming, but I can tell you that coming here to Carrier Clinic was the most important thing I've ever done. I thank you all very much."

After the meeting, I catch Nurse Sharon's attention as I pass the station. I nod my head toward Darcy, and make a beeline for the old upright sitting forlornly in the far corner. I know what I am going to play. *The Entertainer*, a Scott Joplin classic made popular by *The Sting* nearly 40 years ago, is known by most people; and I ignore the ping-pong, television and chatting patients and launch right into it.

It was one of the first pieces I ever learned back when I started at age 13, and I begin the introduction in the slow, almost melancholic style Joplin intended. Much of the "King of Ragtime's" music is joyous to be sure, but there is also a heart-tugging sadness omnipresent just under the surface. Joplin deplored hearing his music performed at break-neck speeds, and he constantly wrote at the heading of his pieces: "It is never right to play Ragtime fast!"

Employing this slow tempo, many of his rags take on a reflective, almost fatalistic characteristic. After all, Joplin, successful as he was in his time, was still a black man living in the age of reconstruction and "Jim Crow" laws barring him from many things now taken for granted by blacks. This reality is readily apparent in much of his music when the performer applies a suitable tempo.

No one is dancing as I plod through the familiar strains. I see Nurse Sharon, Carley and Matt watching and listening from the door, as I pick up the speed slightly in the B section. When the A section returns, I reduce the tempo even further. I feel as the music suggests: Happy to a point, yet apprehensive and reflective at the same time. I stand up after finishing the return of the A section, neglecting the trio and D sections altogether. Acknowledging the lukewarm applause, I realize that, not unlike my playing, my life's work is far from finished. This is only the beginning.

I see her coming. Carol's shoulder-length brown hair moves slightly with every stride. I can now make out her distinct facial outline. Somewhere in Carol's lineage there is a drop or two of Cherokee blood. As minute and distant as it is, the entrenched gene provides Carol and her siblings their distinctive facial bone-structure. Behind the sunglasses shielding her from the bright April sunshine, I see that proud ancestral trait moving closer and closer. In her bearing, I also see a determination—a purpose with every step. She's wearing a light jacket and blue jeans, and my stomach does leaps as she approaches the front door.

Today I opt for the St. Louis Cardinals' 2006 World Series Championship tee-shirt that her parents gave me a few years back. After all, Carol grew up in St. Louis, and is a life-long Cardinal fan. She even worked for five years as an usher at Busch Stadium back in the early 80's.

It was one of three shirts that I brought with me. The other two were Phillies shirts; and I was confusing a lot of patients with what they perceived as my back-and-forth allegiances. I figured that by wearing this shirt today Carol might be a bit easier on me. At the very least, I figured the Cardinal garb couldn't hurt my chances of at least a somewhat friendly greeting. I figured wrong.

She walks through the door and looks up at me. There is no smile. Her lips are pursed as I reach out for her with arms wide. "Hi, Carol!" I gush, trying to embrace her.

"Don't—no," she says, turning her face from me. She fends me away by quickly folding her arms in front of her. It hurts me at once, but I quickly realize this is to be expected. I have put this woman through so much pain and misery over the past few years, how can I possibly expect anything else? Quite frankly, I can rightly expect much worse in the days, weeks and months ahead, and this, too, I must accept.

I nod at Carol and say, "Sorry, I, uh, just wanted to give you a hug."

Carol doesn't have time to respond. Carley, poised nearby, deftly hurries to my side. I let out a huge sigh, as she sticks out her hand and introduces herself. Carol shakes it, and gives her a half-smile. "Shall we go to my office?" Carley asks, beckoning us to follow her.

We sit down in the small office. Carley sits behind her desk, and Carol and I sit in two chairs facing her. The two chairs are close enough, I realize, that Carol can easily reach over and slug me, if the spirit moves her. I am ready for any type of assault, and have stoically steeled myself mentally. No matter what, I am resigned to simply "take it."

Carley begins by telling Carol a bit about my stay at Carrier. She tells her about the wide variety of group meetings, AA meetings, and other important aspects of life here that have helped me get to the point where I am now. "The changes—both physical and mental—that I have noticed in Eric since he first arrived last week are truly amazing," she tells Carol. "He was a beaten-down wreck when he came in here, and now he's…"

"Just a wreck!" I say, cutting her off. Carol laughs a little at this.

Carol uses this moment of levity to voice her little pipe-dream. "Don't you have a room up here where we can tie him up, and I can just beat the shit out of him for an hour or so? This is what I really want." Carley laughs. Carol appears dead serious.

"I would be fine with that," I say and truly mean it.

Instead, for the next 45 minutes, Carol is free to attack me in words. Again and again she clobbers me with the truth. With Carley acting as referee, Carol recites a litany of griev-ances against me. She mostly addresses Carley, only occasion-ally glancing at me when on the attack. Carol sits with her legs crossed, bouncing her dangling foot up and down, exposing me time and again as the serial liar I was.

"He looked me directly in the eye, on so many occasions, and just lied," she says. "He stole thousands from our family, using the home-equity line for his drugs and booze. And I was stupid enough to not pick up on any of it," she says at one point, her eyes glistening. "I think that's the worst part," Carol continues. "I'm so angry with *myself* for letting myself be taken in by all those lies. I'm so stupid!"

For the most part, I simply sit there and say nothing. Occasionally, I offer an apology for some specific offense, but mostly I just take it. Carley had told me to expect a "big-time ass-whooping," as she put it, and that's just what it is.

Toward the end of our session, Carol says, "I really don't know why I'm letting him come back home. Everyone I talk to says I shouldn't, but for some stupid reason, I'm willing to give it one last try." I'm buoyed a bit when she looks at me sadly and says, "I guess it's because I know that you really don't have anywhere else to turn."

I nod slowly and take a deep breath. "Carol, I'll never be able to make up for all my lies. I may never be able to restore all the lost trust. But, I promise you, if it takes me the rest of my life, I promise to try to make things right. You were happy once, and I will begin working every day to make you happy again. I am *so sorry* for all the pain I've caused you and the kids. I am so sorry." I feel a few tears coming again.

"I understand that you must now be in charge of all the finances," I say.

"You're damn right I will be!" she storms.

"I get it, Carol. I accept that. I will begin making amends immediately. Put me on a strict budget. I have a lifetime of dishes and laundry to do," I splutter. "I will do all these things without so much as a frown. I will do it all happily. I know that I can."

Carley says, "Carol, this is no excuse, of course, but Eric has learned much about the disease of alcoholism. In a sense, it was the disease causing all this mayhem."

I jump in. "Carol, no, I did all these things. It was me, make no mistake, but I *was* sick. I had to come in here and learn that I *had* to get help to combat my alcoholism. I tried for so long to fight it on my own, and that was obviously a complete failure. I needed help. I *need* help. I see now, that without help—AA starts today for me at 5:30—I am bound to go back out and drink."

"Well, if you do that, you'll be out of the house forever," says Carol forcefully.

"Carol," I say, "If I do that, I'll be dead. DEAD! It won't matter whether I go home or not. I have to learn to live without alcohol, or it's simply over for me. I don't want to die. I want to live with you and the kids, and be happy again. That's all I want."

I stop. Carley checks her watch. "Well, is there anything else?" She asks us.

I think of one more thing. I sit up and look directly at my wife. "Yes. Carol, in one of the groups, Kevin, the leader, talked about earning trust back after all the lies and cheating and stuff. He told us that regaining this trust, if at all possible, will require lots of time. And 'time' stands for 'This I Must Earn.' I know this is going to take a long, long time, but if you're willing to give me this chance, I promise to do everything I can to earn it back."

She doesn't smile, but nods slightly. Carley says, "I think this was very important for both of you. It helped to clear the air, and get things off of your chest. I strongly suggest more counseling sessions down the road."

"Definitely," I say.

"Yes," Carol agrees.

We go out into the hallway. The 10:00 group is now over and patients are milling about. We both thank Carley, and Carol excuses herself to use the facilities. After Carol disappears inside the bathroom down the hall, I go to shake Carley's hand. She hugs me instead. "Good luck to you, Eric," she says to me warmly, and then releases me. "How do you feel after that?"

"Kind of numb, I think," I respond. "But I'm okay. I was prepared for that. She needed to let it out. I just kept thinking about how lucky I am to be going to home."

"That's right, Eric," she says. "And be ready for more steam—lots of it! You'll be in a safe environment, though, and you can concentrate on your recovery."

I nod. "That is key for me. I can't wait to see my kids!" I say.

Sharon comes up to join us. "I'm gonna miss you, Eric," she says, wrapping her arms tightly around me. "Remember, you're coming back to speak, right?"

"That is a promise!" I say. "You guys have been the best. Thank you for everything."

"You can thank us by staying sober," Sharon says. "You got it?"

"I got it!"

I move away down the hall a bit. I see Eva and Stanley talking with Kara, Maxine and Ebby. I give each of them a big hug, and say my goodbyes.

After I hug Eva, she says, "She's beautiful. I always knew you were going to be alright."

Maxine says, "You keep playin' that piano, white boy, you hear? That's some *good shit!*" She rolls out those last two words deliciously.

Ebby says, "Your stuff is still in the room on your bed. You want me to get it?"

"Oh," I say, surprised. "No, I'll go." Just then, Carol walks toward us. She's smiling a little, and I feel good. I introduce her to "the gang," and leave her to go get my things.

Back in the room, I quickly gather up my belongings and stuff them into my small overnight bag. I start to leave and glance back. I see my overstuffed notebooks sitting on the desk by my bed. "I'll need you," I say to the books, and stick them in my bag.

Walking back down the hallway, I see Carol talking with Ebby. The others have disbursed. Carol has her back to me, and Ebby sees me coming. He flashes me a quick thumbs up, and I grin broadly. *He's attempting some repair work on my image*, I think.

"Ready?" I ask Carol, when I get to them.

She nods.

"Let's go," I say. I give Ebby another big hug. "I'll never forget you, Ebby," I say with all the earnestness at my command.

"And I won't forget you, my friend," he says. Ebby releases me, and Carol and I leave Blake Hall.

Heading to the parking lot, we pass the tree where my visit to Carrier Clinic began so inauspiciously one week before. I say, "That's where I fell last week."

Carol doesn't even look where I'm pointing, but keeps her eyes forward. I see her face is rigid with determination again.

I continue, "You should have seen all the people running after I fell. Sirens went off and…"

"Eric, I don't want to hear about it!" she cuts me off, her eyes bearing into me. "I don't really care. Everything in life is not one big story to be told. I just don't want to hear it, okay?"

"Sorry," I mumble, chastened, and we continue in silence.

Most of the trip home is edgy and silent, as well. Carol does the driving, and keeps her intense, brown eyes fixed on the road. Finally, at some point I say, "Are you going back to work today?"

"No, I took the day off."

This gives me an idea. It's not much of one, but I know Carol and what she needs.

"Why don't we stop and get a little lunch?" I ask.

She looks over at me. It's a slightly less angry glance, and that buoys me a bit. I say, "There's a pizza place up here in Pennington. Sound good?"

"Yeah, okay," she says. "I haven't eaten all day," she tells me.

Carol's brother, Ken once told me the importance of keeping her little sister well-fed. "If you want the Smith-girls to be happy," I remember him telling me in no uncertain terms, "then feed them!" I always remembered this line, and what better time than now to try it on for size?

We pull into the strip-mall and walk inside the pizza place. We order two slices of their gourmet pie, and we go outside in the beautiful April sunshine to sit at a table. After only a few bites, Carol's mood improves dramatically. We chat about nothing in particular, and the tone is civil and relaxed.

I am under no illusions about the long journey that lay ahead of me. Where Carol and the kids are concerned, the grief and misery I have caused will be long lasting. Our future as a married couple is not assured by any stretch, and I understand all this. Still, at this particular moment, it is pleasant to simply sit here with the one I love and enjoy a slice of pizza. Still better is the feeling I get knowing that I can do it sober. I can enjoy life without a drink—at least for this moment. And, *that* feels good indeed.

While we lunch, a man passes by and stops. He sticks his head straight up in the air and puts drops in his eyes. This reminds me of Mike Cass and his nose spray. I start giggling.

"What's the matter?" Carol inquires.

I start telling her about the night Mike concocted the elaborate plan that involved me distracting Nurse Donna. "While I caught her attention, admiring all her gaudy jewelry," I tell her, "Mike went after that nose-spray like you can't imagine." I demonstrate his wild movements and grunts. "He must've snorted half of the spray bottle in about 30 seconds," I say.

Carol starts laughing.

"Donna finally picked up on it and went bananas!" I tell her. "*That stuff's addicting*! She kept yelling. *That stuff's addicting!* It was hilarious."

Carol laughs some more. She says, "He must have really been something."

"He was a gift from God, Carol, I'll tell ya."

We both calm down and get back to our slices. Carol takes a bite and looks out into the parking lot. I see something in her attractive brown eyes. It is only a faint glimpse of what once was, but it's there nonetheless. She briefly looks over at me, and then takes another bite. There it is again.

For the longest time now, the only look I've received from Carol has been one of total loathing and disgust. Many times, when I was drunk, it only took one of those looks to send me off in a wild rage. Now, with my head and body free from alcohol, I can see clearly again. I can see that this look is different. I remember it from all those good times in the distant past, and my spirit soars as I see it once more. At this moment in time, I am happy.

Carol turns her head. Now she's giving me that long forgotten look. And now, for the first time in a long time, she gives me a small but genuine smile.

I return it.

Slowly, she reaches over, and gently puts her hand on mine.

...The Beginning

Eric T. Houghton
Writer, Composer, Pianist, Teacher,

Born and raised in the Jersey Shore community of Harvey Cedars, Eric T. Houghton trained to become a concert pianist. In the mid-80's he received two advanced degrees in Piano Performance, and subsequently began a busy performing and teaching career that continues to this day. For 29 years he has been Artist Faculty member of the Westminster Conservatory of Music in Princeton, New Jersey.

During the last 30 years, Houghton has performed both solo and chamber recitals throughout the United States, most notably debuting his own works. In 2012 he presented a deeply personal series of concerts, *Musical Program of Recovery*, where he shared through music his past struggles and current victory over alcoholism. More shows are planned, and a live-CD recording of one of the shows is available.

As writer, Houghton just completed his 12th year writing a weekly summer column for *The Beachcomber* of Long Beach Island, New Jersey. *Clammer's Diary* merrily delves into Houghton's life growing up at the shore, digging clams, working at his dad's boat rental business and general beach-bum activities.

Houghton's tell-all memoir, *Boozehound! Breaking a 30-Year Obsession*, will be released in January 2013 by My Green Publisher, LLC. Book and other related information can be found at @Boozehoundbook on Twitter and http://www.facebook.com/boozehoundthebook. He lives in Ewing, New Jersey with his wife and three beautiful children.

POEM TO DADDY

You just had to have a drink,
And throw your whole life down the sink.
You really hurt me bad,
But it was mom who was really mad.
Teachers that year were saying, "Pick up the slack,"
But I was too afraid that you'd never be back.
You promised a lot of things,
But you had a hard time remembering.
And when you went to rehab,
I felt like I just got stabbed!
Those were the worst days of my life,
'Cause the whole time I was filled with strife.
You and mom would've gotten a divorce,
I cried so much, my throat went hoarse!
You caused me so much pain,
I felt that my whole world rained.
And when you finally quit,
I felt that my world was finally lit!
Everything worked out in the end,
And not only are you my dad, you're my best friend.
You should've said on your second-year meeting,
"If you quit drinking, you'll get a happy greeting."
I'm really proud,
And I'm glad that you're finally around.
I hope that these are things that you rue,
But daddy, I'll always love you.
-Natalie R. Houghton
Age 11

Acknowledgements:

My gratitude is wide-ranging and deep, but I would like to acknowledge people whose help and support have made this *Boozehound!* thing possible.

Michael Kelley, your no-nonsense yet elegant editorial hand was with me every step of the way. I have and will continue to learn a great deal from you. Thank you, my friend. My agent, Faye Swetky--why you took me on continues to mystify me. I chalk it up to another in a long line of small miracles in my life since that fateful day in April 2010. My everlasting gratitude goes out to you. Fiona Thomas, you saw *Boozehound*! first and grabbed it. You would not let it go. Thank you from the bottom of my heart.

And finally I'd like to thank the fine people at Carrier Clinic in Belle Mead, New Jersey, who have been saving lives--including mine--for over 100 years now. The cover of this book shows my admittance sheet and photo from the night I entered Carrier and put my life into their hands.

Visit Us At:

My Green Publisher
P.O. Box 702
Richland, MI 49083

www.mygreenpublisher.com